ROBERT BROWNING
A PORTRAIT

Robert Browning

A PORTRAIT BY

BETTY MILLER

CHARLES SCRIBNER'S SONS

NEW YORK

A—11.72(I)

Printed in Great Britain
Library of Congress Catalog Card Number 72–4127
SBN 684–13131–5 (trade cloth)

We must in every case betake ourselves to the review of a poet's life ere we determine some of the nicer questions concerning his poetry—more especially if the performance we seek to estimate aright, has been obstructed and cut short of completion by circumstances—a disastrous youth or a premature death. We may learn from the biography whether his spirit invariably saw and spoke from the last height to which it had attained . . . Did the poet ever attain to a higher platform than where he rested and exhibited a result? Did he know more than he spoke of?

Robert Browning. Introductory Essay to 25 [spurious] *Letters of Percy Bysshe Shelley.*

TO E.M, TO J.W.M, AND TO S.J.M.
WITH MY LOVE

PREFACE

L ike the water-diviner, the biographer anticipates a moment when the forked twig will leap suddenly between his hands. The best dowsers, according to the *Encyclopædia Britannica*, " have generally been more or less illiterate men, engaged in some humble vocation " ; but the biographer, however humble his vocation, is justly required to support the claims of intuition with such material evidence as he has been able to collect. I am happy to acknowledge the kindness of those who have given me access to ground protected by the laws of copyright or of possession. My greatest debt in this respect is to Sir John Murray ; other material is reproduced by kind permission of Wellesley College Library ; the University of Illinois Library ; the Berg Collection of the New York Public Library ; the British Library of Political and Economic Science ; the British Museum ; and the Victoria and Albert Museum.

I am indebted to Lieut.-Colonel Fordham Flower for his kindness in placing a large collection of family papers at my disposal ; to Sir Vincent Baddeley for information about his kinsman and for the loan of a caricature by Pellegrini ; to Mrs. Phyllis de Kay Wheelock for information, and for the photograph of her aunt, Mrs. Arthur Bronson ; to the Conte Rucellai for permission to reproduce a portrait of his mother ; and to Balliol College for the use of photographs in the Browning collection. To Miss Freya Stark, I owe some very happy memories of Asolo, as well as a photograph taken there fifty years ago by Herbert Young ; and to Miss Valentine Britten, the eerie experience of listening, through the huskiness of an aged wax cylinder, to the still resonant voice of Robert Browning himself.

I also wish to acknowledge, with gratitude, the assistance of Professor A. J. Armstrong ; Professor A. C. Baugh ; Mrs. R. C. Lehmann ; the Marchesa Iris Origo ; Miss Eirene Skilbeck ; Miss Elizabeth Johnson ; and Mr. J. G. Wilson. I am indebted for much useful information to Mr. Kenneth Garside, Deputy Librarian, University College, London ; Mr. W. G. Hiscock, Deputy Librarian, Christ Church, Oxford ; Mr. W. J. A. Hahn, Chief Librarian, Camberwell Public

Libraries ; Mr. H. J. Rengert, Borough Librarian, Deptford ; and Mr. H. W. Moore, Borough Librarian, Hackney ; and have enjoyed at all times the neighbourly co-operation of Mr. S. J. Green and the staff of the St. John's Wood Branch Library.

Finally, an attempt to acknowledge a debt which has accumulated steadily during the past three years. It is easy to assess, less easy to express, how much I feel that I have owed, throughout, to the good will and the good humour of Mr. John Grey Murray.

CONTENTS

xi

ILLUSTRATIONS

1

A Garden in the Environs

Throughout his life, Robert Browning was as turbulent in sickness as in health. A septic throat, and his ravings could be heard in every room in the house : another, and his head had to be shaved : yet again, the whole of one long night, to the distress of his mother, he insisted on reciting aloud what he afterwards described as " a complete version of the Psalms by Donne ". On this occasion, as soon as the fever abated, he sat down at this desk and wrote the opening scene of *Paracelsus*.

> . . . not alone when life flows still do truth
> And power emerge, but also when strange chance
> Affects its current ; in unused conjuncture,
> Where sickness breaks the body—hunger, watching,
> Excess, or languor—oftenest death's approach—
> Peril, deep joy, or woe.

But no strange chance, other than the morbid condition just described, had ruffled the remarkably even current of the poet's life ; and the young man who sat in his room writing those words, the " truth and power " of which the more discriminating of his own generation were soon to acknowledge, had led from childhood into manhood an existence that was to all intents and purposes as sheltered, as enclosed, as dependent even, as that endured during her years in Wimpole Street by the invalid poetess, Miss Barrett herself. On the other hand, whereas the invalid condition of Miss Barrett was recognised by all, the invalid condition of the active young man was apparent to a few, only, of his contemporaries : fostered by the climate of family life, it was re-created rather than resolved in the circumstances of his marriage ; and letters written after the death of his wife show that the same pattern, fainter, now, but with the original outline still intact, persisted beneath the genial façade of Henry James's " accomplished, saturated, sane, sound man of the London world ".

It was early in October, 1834, that Robert Browning, emaciated still by fever and the prolonged addiction to " cresses and cold water ", set to work in his room on the first scene of *Paracelsus*. Beneath his window, the autumn leaves were falling in the long walled garden of his Camberwell home ; across the fields, a setting sun dropped slowly behind the spire of St. George's church. " *Würzburg*," wrote the poet, " *a garden in the environs*." The scene takes shape ; it is an autumn evening in the year 1507 : in the sequestered garden, " pining leaves " drop from the branches ; gradually " the sun sinks broad Behind Saint Saviour's . . . wholly gone, at last ! " A few more lines, and it is plain enough that " Würzburg, with its church and spire, And garden-walls and all that they contain " is in fact pre-Victorian Camberwell ; the garden in the environs, " limited Alone by one old populous green wall ", none other than the suburban garden of Browning's early home in Hanover Cottage. Pursued, the evidence, the scope of enquiry enlarge simultaneously : behind the mask of the Renaissance scientist we discern the features of the nineteenth-century poet : with a shock of intimacy, we meet across the years that which contemporary portraiture has denied us, the direct glance of the young Robert Browning himself. For it is here, in the first scene of *Paracelsus*, with a circumstantial fidelity that complements the wholly subjective " confession " of *Pauline*, that there is to be found a remarkable account of Browning's life and development between the age of fourteen, when he first came to live at Hanover Cottage, and the age of twenty-eight, when the family left Camberwell and settled in another, and more spacious cottage at Hatcham, New Cross.

In this first scene of the poem, which takes place on the eve of his departure for " strange and untried paths ", Paracelsus, a student, is talking in the garden to his two friends, Festus and Michal. Paracelsus, of course, is an historical figure ; Festus and Michal, the creation, both, of the poet. They speak ; and in the accent they adopt it is obvious at once that these two, at least, spring not from the sultry *coulisses* of occult science, but out of the social and domestic environment of Robert Browning himself. For, united as they are in a common solicitude for one governed by so vast and compelling an ambition, they reveal, and with a singular candour on the part of their creator, the attitude of Browning's own father and mother towards their brilliant, if ill-comprehended son. (This inner equation seems to have governed the choice of names : Festus, Father : Michal, Mother.) And if, in the discussion between the sober Festus and the impatient, aspiring Paracelsus, we catch an echo of the family conflict that pre-ceded, at Hanover Cottage, the renunciation of a practical for a poetic career, it is in the gentle Michal that there lies a reflection of that submerged influence whose effect was to magnetise over so many years the main current of Robert Browning's emotional life.

" Little need be said about the poet's mother, Sarah Anne Wiedemann," wrote Mrs. Orr in her authorised biography of Robert Browning. And accordingly, singularly little has been said, either by her, or by any subsequent writer. Mrs. Browning, we are told " had nothing of the artist about her . . . in all her goodness and sweetness she seems to have been somewhat matter-of-fact ". We are in no position to judge. Her son's description of her as " a divine woman ", Carlyle's " true type of a Scottish gentlewoman ", a reference to her piety, a glimpse of her parasol hovering above the strawberry beds of Rainbow Cottage (it was in this house that the poet—poetically enough—was born) these are the sidelights by whose perfunctory gleam we are permitted to observe and assess her. For she is the only member of the family whose portrait has not been preserved, or at least reproduced ; the only one whose bearing is not mirrored for a moment in the glances or the memories of those who knew her. (Forty years later, all that Alfred Domett could recall of his friend's mother was the fact that she had " the *squarest* head and forehead I almost ever saw in a human being, putting me in mind, absurdly enough, no doubt, of a tea-chest or tea caddy ".) [1] Later still, Dr. Furnivall, eager to preserve the slightest reminiscence on the part of the poet, had to confess that he had heard Browning " speak of his father, but never of his mother, probably because he saw but little of her ". She remains, thus, an obscure, if not an enigmatic figure within the family circle ; and it is to Field Talfourd's portrait of her son, to this alone, that we must go now to seek an acknowledged, if necessarily indirect, reflection of those unfamiliar features.

No such restriction obscures our view of the poet's father. Attentively, his ancestry has been traced ; his library analysed ;

[1] April 30, 1878. Alfred Domett's diary. Extract from a copy made by Professor Hall Griffin. British Museum. Add. Mss. 45559–60.

his portrait reproduced ; the assumption being, therein, that his was the decisive influence in the life of his son. Superficially, all the indications lie in this direction. A bank clerk by profession, by inclination Mr. Browning was both a bibliophile and a scholar. The small semi-detached house in Camberwell overflowed with the many thousands of volumes he collected ; and, as Professor Griffin has effectively demonstrated, it was from the study of these books, the " wisest, ancient books " of *Pauline,* that Robert Browning derived not only the main substance of his early education, but a persistent source of literary inspiration, from *Paracelsus* down to the penultimate *Parleyings With Certain People of Importance in their Day.* There is, however, another side to the picture. Early in life, while in charge of slave labour on a sugar plantation at St. Kitt's, the father of the poet had undergone an experience whose effect was permanently to qualify his own ability to deal with the external world. " I have never known more of those circumstances in his youth than I told you," wrote Browning to Elizabeth Barrett, " in consequence of his invincible repugnance to allude to the matter—and I have a fancy, to account for some peculiarities in him, which connects them with some abominable early experience. Thus,—if you question him about it, he shuts his eyes involuntarily and shows exactly the same marks of loathing that may be noticed while a piece of cruelty is mentioned . . and the *word* ' blood ', even, makes him change colour." In other ways, too, there are to be discerned in him the maiming effects of that early experience. This tender-hearted being—" gentle as a gentle woman " is how a friend describes him—was continually drawing in red and black chalk page after page of " grim heads ", of masks and faces that " crowding together with malevolent or agonised or terrific expressions " inspired in the children who saw them a " creeping " sensation of terror and alarm. Most marked of all, however, there was in him an almost total dependence upon the will of others. In his own household, the father of the family took his place like a second and more docile son ; the vital decisions of life being delegated to the women of the family, in whom lay vested all that practical ability suspended, so curiously, in father and son alike. To the end of his life, Mr. Browning retained, undiminished, the " perpetual juvenility of a blessed child ". Meeting, five years after her marriage, an elderly gentleman who submitted to having his face washed and his hair brushed for him by a briskly impatient daughter, Elizabeth Barrett Browning was moved to remark that " the relations of life seem reversed in their case, and the father appears the child of the child ".

It is clear, then, that whatever may have been the state of affairs amongst the Barretts of Hope End, it was neither the personality nor the authority of a dominant father that regulated the tempo of domestic life at Camberwell. The regime here, as benign in operation as it was enduring in its effect, was pre-eminently a matriarchal one. From its influence, no member of the family was exempt : even Sarianna, we learn, " was a most devoted daughter ; giving up all society (for which her accomplishments peculiarly fit her) and refusing to marry . . all, that her invalid mother might not miss a comfort she could offer. Her mother was the beginning and end of life to her." [1] Sarah Anna Wiedemann was of mixed German and Scottish descent. Inheriting, in the combination, a certain formality and inelasticity of temperament, she appears to have found in religion the main inspiration of her emotional life. Already in girlhood she had attached herself to the Congregational Church in Walworth ; and nine years after his marriage we see in the records that her husband, too, became a member there. There is no reason to believe that the man who appreciated the wit of Voltaire and the subversive sting of Bernard de Mandeville found in the chapel at York Street the most congenial form of public worship. The regular attendance there of the Browning family is to be attributed wholly to the maternal influence ; and even that, it seems, had its limitations, since on one occasion the preacher, George Clayton, found it necessary publicly to reprove " for restlessness and inattention Master Robert Browning ".

This restlessness was perhaps the most characteristic feature of the poet's early years. From babyhood, the destructive nature of his activity had been a source of anxiety, if not of

[1] Florence 2–3–4–5 [March, 1849]. Passage deleted from original typescript, later edited by Leonard Huxley, of E. B. B.'s *Letters to her Sister, 1846–1859* ; afterwards referred to as Huxley typescript. As in all E. B. B. letters, the use of two dots represents her own punctuation and not an omission from the text.

exhaustion, to the adults about him. With the growth of intellectual power, the boisterous child became the self-opinionated youth, ready openly to deride the ideas and the opinions of others. " In my early boyhood," he later confided to Miss Barrett, " I had a habit of calling people ' fools ' with as little reverence as could be." The habit does not seem to have perturbed his father : it was his mother, then, who, he says, " solemnly represented to me after such offences that ' whoso calleth his brother " fool " is in danger &c. for he hath committed murder in his heart already ' &c. in short —there was no help for it—I stood there a convicted *murderer* . . to which I was forced penitently to agree. . . ." There must have been many such scenes between the growing boy and the mother who was also a Sunday school teacher : through them we can gauge something of the force and the simplicity of Mrs. Browning's piety ; as we can, perhaps, from the fact that amongst the six thousand books upon the shelves at Hanover Cottage, one only bore her signature, and that was Elisha Coles's *A Practical Discourse of Effectual Calling and of Perseverance.* It is possible also to see in the circumstance something of the divided atmosphere in which Robert Browning was brought up. On the one hand, he was given the freedom of a liberal and erudite library : on the other, he found himself, like Hazlitt, who accounted it a misfortune, " bred up among dissenters, who look with too jaundiced an eye at others, and set too high a value on their own peculiar pretensions. From being proscribed themselves, they learn to proscribe others ; and come in the end to reduce all integrity of principle and soundness of opinion within the pale of their own little communion." Coles's book can have held at the time as little appeal for the young Robert Browning as his mother's gift to him of Cruden's *Complete Concordance to the Holy Scriptures.* For in 1826, when Browning was fourteen, there was published by William Benbow, of High Holborn, a pirated edition of the *Miscellaneous Poems* of Percy Bysshe Shelley. This book was presented to the future poet, " probably as soon as published ", by his cousin James Silverthorne : and to find an adequate parallel for the effect created upon Browning, one must go to the two-volume edition of the *Poems* of Elizabeth Barrett Barrett, which, eighteen years later, was to form the basis of his introduction to his future wife. It is not too much to say that the whole of Browning's life was fundamentally affected by " the impression made on a boy by this first specimen of Shelley's poetry " ; and that the least significant, as well as the least durable, result of this passionate preoccupation was the adolescent atheism and vegetarianism which for a time accompanied it. " Poets—the best of them," wrote Shelley, " are a very cameleonic race ; they take the colour not only of what they feed on, but of the very leaves under which they pass." Although it is possible to trace and isolate the influence of Shelley's poetry upon the early work of Robert Browning, it was not in his poetry but in his life that the full impact of the encounter was to be experienced. For, as Shelley himself had desired, four years after his death his words, sparks from an " unextinguish'd hearth ", had ignited a kindred conflagration in the soul of another poet. This conflagration was to die down ; it was to be smothered ; it was to be forcibly quenched : but one thing remained : Browning had recognised in the fearless spiritual independence of Shelley a principle of conduct whereby to measure, in the years to come, not only the sum of his own poetic achievement, but the very nature of human integrity itself.

By the time that *Pauline* came to be written, that integrity had already been compromised ; and it is the history of this early fall from grace which forms the subject of Browning's first published poem. Between the year 1826, when Browning became acquainted with the work of Shelley, and 1832, when *Pauline* was written, there took place in the life of the poet a crisis so radical that everything that followed upon it, including his marriage with Elizabeth Barrett, was qualified in one way or another by the effects of that initial experience. In *Queen Mab*, in *Prometheus Unbound*, in *The Revolt of Islam*, the youthful Browning had found what seemed to him " the key to a new world ".

I threw myself
To meet it. I was vowed to liberty,
Men were to be as gods, and earth as heaven.
And I—ah ! what a life was mine to be.
My whole soul rose to meet it. Now, Pauline,
I shall go mad, if I recall that time.

9

Robert Browning, of course, did not go mad : but it is a measure, both of the quality of his admiration for Shelley and the strength of his love for his mother, that this sanity was based on a consistent suppression of everything connected with " that time ". (When the death of his mother forced him to contemplate anew the events concerned, the necessity brought on a prolonged state of total depression.) The copy of *Queen Mab*, which inspired so much of his early atheism, Professor Pottle believes that he destroyed altogether : to efface from the public eye the " foolish scribblings " with which, in his exaltation, he covered his .copy of the *Miscellaneous Poems*, he went to quite extraordinary lengths : he blotted out : he scribbled over with a heavy pen ; he scrubbed with a moistened forefinger ; he scratched so vehemently with his knife that the point went right through the paper : finally, where nothing else would serve, he cut whole pieces bodily out of the page itself. What was the reason for this uneasiness ; for the elaborate precautions he elsewhere took to obliterate all record of his early life ? The answer seems to be simple enough. That which Robert Browning wished to conceal, not only from the public view but from his own conscience, was the occasion on which, as he afterwards put it, I " flung All honour from my soul ". The ideals of Shelley and those of Sarah Anna Browning could not continue to exist under the same roof : the moment had come in which he must either deny his " wild dreams of beauty and of good ", or irreparably wound and alienate his mother, " the one being ", we are told, " whom he entirely loved ". Faced with this deadlock between head and heart, Browning found his own solution. Reason divided him from the one being he could love : reason, therefore, must be sacrificed. With a truly Herculean effort, which seems to have absorbed all his youth's strength, Browning performed upon himself an act of re-grafting : reversing, deliberately, the laws of his own growth. The agony of that effort is reflected in *Paracelsus* : inspiring both the cry

> God ! Thou art Mind ! Unto the Master-Mind
> Mind should be precious. Spare my mind alone !
> All else I will endure . . .

and its antithesis

> mind is nothing but disease,
> And natural health is ignorance.

Forcibly, in the course of this struggle, reason was dethroned and degraded : that " power Repressed ", as he had it, " to LOVE " became, thenceforward, more important than " to KNOW." How this remarkable transformation affected, in the years to come not only his relationship with other human beings but the whole structure of his philosophic outlook, one may judge by a statement that the poet himself made on the subject nearly fifty years later. In 1876, in a letter to his friend Mrs. Fitzgerald, he wrote : " What strikes me so much in that life of Schopenhauer which you gave me was the doctrine which he considered his grand discovery, and which *I* had been persuaded of from my boyhood—and have based my whole life upon—that the soul is above and *behind* the intellect, which is merely its servant. . . . The consequences of this doctrine were so momentous to me, so destructive of vanity on the one hand, or undue depression at failure on the other, that I am sure there must be references to and deductions from it throughout the whole of my works." [1] There are indeed : and only one of these (from *A Pillar at Sebzevar*) need be quoted in order to reveal the curious intellectual position in which the man born with a " wolfish hunger after knowledge " found himself in the last years of his life.

> Wholly distrust thy knowledge, then, and trust
> As wholly love allied to ignorance !
> There lies thy truth and safety.

In his early years, Browning held a profoundly serious view of the nature of poetic responsibility. " I desire," he told Elizabeth Barrett, " to write out certain things which are in me, and so save my soul." He believed that the poet was chosen by God to receive His " great commission " : that a sacred duty was laid upon him to speak the truth as, from his station, he alone could see it. This truth, this " imprisoned

---

[1] Catalogue extract : Hornstein sale : 56 letters of Robert Browning to Mrs. Fitzgerald of Shalstone, [*sic*] written between 1876–89.

splendour ", Browning had at a moment of crisis chosen to obscure : and it was the consciousness of having done so, of delivering falsely or imperfectly the message with which he had been entrusted, that was the primary inspiration of the poet's life-long obsession with the psychology of the charlatan, the quack, the second-rater and the " apparent failure ". *Paracelsus* is the first portrait in this great gallery of brilliant tainted characters : and here (where the sundered halves of Browning's personality confront each other as Paracelsus who " aspired to KNOW " and Aprile who " would LOVE infinitely and be loved "), the poet's.own failure is lamented in a passage that anticipates the mood and setting of *Childe Roland.*

Alas !

> I have address'd a frock of heavy mail,
> Yet may not join the troop of sacred knights ;
> And now the forest creatures fly from me,
> The grass-banks cool, the sunbeams warm no more !
> Best follow, dreaming that ere night arrive
> I shall o'ertake the company, and ride
> Glittering as they !

Paracelsus was published in 1835. Ten years later, Robert Browning wrote to Elizabeth Barrett : " *My* poetry is far from ' the completest expression of my being '—I hate to refer to it, or I could tell you why, wherefore . . ." And again : " You speak out, *you,*—I only make men and women speak —give you the truth broken into prismatic hues, and fear the pure white light . . ."

> (For a new thought sprung up—that it were well
> To leave all shadowy hopes, and weave· such lays
> As would encircle me with praise and love;
> So, I should not die utterly—I should bring
> One branch from the gold forest, like the knight
> Of old tales, witnessing I had been there.) [1]

[1]Compare revised edition of 1888 :

> For a new thought sprang up how well it were,
> Discarding shadowy hope, to weave such lays
> As straight encircle men with praise and love—

and note the effect of the insertion of a single letter, *n,* in the fourth word of the third line.

It is difficult not to sympathise with Robert Browning in his predicament. In no century save our own have the extravagances of maternal love been regarded with other than an unqualified approval ; and it is as well to remind ourselves here that until the end of the nineteenth century, at least, filial piety, in all its extremes, still had behind it the full weight of social approval. Alfred Tennyson's *Supposed Confessions of a Second-Rate Sensitive Mind not in Unity with Itself*, published three years before *Pauline*, is inspired by an analogous situation : passionate love for and veneration of his mother (" a thing enskied and sainted " as he elsewhere describes her) and a tormenting regret that intellectual pride—" the sin of devils " —has intervened between them : " Thrice happy state again to be, The trustful infant on the knee ! " This happy state Robert Browning was no less unwilling to relinquish : thirteen years after the publication of *Pauline*, he was to describe to Elizabeth Barrett the " great delight " he took in the " pro- longed relation of childhood " in which, voluntarily, he still continued to live. In his thirty-fourth year—a young man who had " been ' spoiled ' in this world "—he was still dependent for every necessity of life upon his father : he still looked to his mother to buy his personal belongings for him, to pack his carpet-bag when he went on a journey, to relieve him of all responsibility for his own material welfare. He loved his mother so much, he was once heard to say, " that even as a grown man he could not sit by her otherwise than with an arm round her waist ". As a grown man, he would not go to bed without receiving from her the good-night kiss of his childhood : delayed in town, whatever the hour of his return, he went at once to her bedroom in order to seek it. Even at night, the separation between mother and son was only partial. " My room ", wrote Browning, " is next to hers and the door is left ajar." Physiologically, too, the intimacy between them was a remarkably close one. So finely did the rhythms of their lives intertwine, that no sooner was the mother indisposed than the son, too, suffered : as promptly, when the mother recovered, the son, in turn, regained his health. It is not perhaps sufficiently recognised that despite the unembarrassed vigour of his maturity, Robert Browning was " pale, thin and rather delicate-looking " in youth, enjoying what he himself described as " very indifferent health and very uncertain spirits ". Both persisted as long as he continued to live in the same house as his mother. Elizabeth Barrett remarked continually on his thinness and pallor : he gave her the impression, she said, of one requiring " support, and something to stimulate ". And in fact, during the many months of their correspondence, it is almost as much a question of his health as of hers : to such a degree that, apologetically, at one moment, he refers to the " eternal account of aches and pains " which he has inflicted upon her. The recurrent complaint is always headache : his own, and that of his mother. " I will write more to-morrow—the stupid head will not be quiet to-day—my mother's is sadly affected too " . . . " I am quite well to-day, and my mother is quite well " . . . " I am not too well this morning, and write with an aching head. My mother's suffering continues too " . . . " I am much better to-day ; and my mother is better " . . . Finally, Elizabeth Barrett taxed him with the " superstition ", as she called it, of " being ill or well " with his mother. He replied : " The connection between our ailings is no fanciful one. A few weeks ago when my medical advisor was speaking about the pain and its cause . . my mother sitting by me . . he exclaimed, ' Why, has anybody to search far for a cause of whatever nervous disorder you suffer from, when *there* sits your mother . . whom you so absolutely resemble . . I can trace every feature &c. &c.' To which I did *not* answer, ' And will anybody wonder that the said disorder flies away, when there sits my Ba, whom I so thoroughly adore.' "

Robert Browning did not attend either a public school or a university. If access to Oxford or Cambridge was barred to a dissenter, there is no doubt that any desire on his part to attend a public school would have been granted by parents who, as he said, " if I could bring myself to ask them to give up everything in the world . . . would do it and cheerfully ". Upon examination, it appears that it is to the same insistent need of the maternal presence that one must attribute the sporadic nature of the poet's education. When first he was separated from his mother by his early attendance at Miss Ready's school, his conviction was, he told Mrs. Orr, that " he would not survive " the ordeal. Precisely the same situation arose when at the age of sixteen he was entered by his father for classes in Greek, Latin and German at the newly created London University in Gower Street. At the beginning of the term, convenient lodgings were taken for him with a Mr. Hughes of Bedford Square. Barely a week had passed however before, impulsively, he had packed up his belongings and returned to Hanover Cottage. Nor did daily attendance offer a better solution. The distance between Gower Street and Camberwell put too great a strain upon the heart-strings : after little more than a term of University life—(" I was lonely . . . And amid dullest sights ")—he gave up the struggle, and at his mother's side once more resumed that " careless ' sweet habitude of living ' " of which her presence was for him both the symbol and the guarantee.

The return to Hanover Cottage at so critical a period is symptomatic. Faced with independence, the young Robert Browning shrank from it as from a menace. Deliberately, in that gesture, he withdrew from the centres of contemporary life : he withdrew from the city in order to establish himself once more at its peripheries, its environs. Thus viewed, London presented itself neither as a challenge to be accepted nor a discipline to be endured, but as a glow on the night sky whose reflection enhanced the poetic isolation of a suburban hill-top. Daily, in the crowded streets beneath, his former classmates hurried to attend the sessions at Gower Street ; but Browning—" I can abjure so well the secret arts These pedants strive to learn "—stretched himself at ease under the elm trees and watched the shape and shadow of the passing clouds.

> Shall I still sit beside
> Their dry wells, with white lips and filmed eye,
> While in the distance heaven is blue above
> Mountains where sleep the unsunn'd tarns ?

A hint, perhaps, of sour grapes in all this ? It is illuminating, in this context, to consult the letter of April 22, 1828, in which " as a parent anxious for the welfare of an only Son " Robert Browning senior applied for that son's admission to London University. Putting forward as a " Test of his Moral char-

acter " the fact that " I never knew him from his earliest
infancy, guilty of the slightest deviation from Truth ", he goes
on to say that " he so earnestly desires I would interest myself
in procuring his admittance, that I should feel myself wanting
as a Parent, were I to neglect any step to procure what he deems
so essential to his future happiness ".[1]   There is a faithful echo
of the situation in *Paracelsus* itself.   The Swiss student has
denounced, with scorn, the prospect of plodding after truth
in " one of Learning's many palaces ".   Reproachfully, Festus
reminds him of the time, not so long distant, when

> to crown your dearest wish,
> With a tumultuous heart, you left with me
> Our childhood's home to join the favour'd few
> Whom famed Trithemius condescends to teach
> A portion of his lore—and not the dullest [2]
> Of those so favour'd, whom you now despise,
> Was earnest as you were ; resolved, like you,
> To grasp all, and retain all, and deserve
> By patient toil a wide renown like his.

Why, then, did this " dearest wish ", these creditable intentions, miscarry ?   We have seen in the situation Browning's
inability to separate himself from his family : we must now
also see in it the reluctance of an over-valued son to face the
competition of his fellow students.   The necessity aroused in him
an immediate conflict :   " restless, nothing satisfied, Distrustful,
most perplex'd ", he sat in " that dim chamber where the
noon-streaks peer," and only " rare outbreaks, fierce and brief,
Reveal'd the hidden scorn " he felt for " the meanest plodder
Tritheim deems A marvel ".   His reaction to the whole situation was a curious one ; for rather than accept, as others, the
common challenge, he felt he must take extreme measures to
avoid or transcend it.

> And from the tumult in my breast, this only
> Could I collect—that I must thenceforth die,
> Or elevate myself far, far above
> The gorgeous spectacle.

[1] Corres. No. 655.   University College Library.
[2] 1863 edition, more tactfully : " . . . and not one youth."

The alternative is, of course, a rhetorical one : no man was less in love with easeful death ; no poet, perhaps, more fortified against its lure. Nevertheless, as we have seen, a decision was made ; and the record of it remains in the oddly phrased letter which once more, at the earnest request of his son, Mr. Browning addressed to Leonard Horner, Esqre., of London University.

> *Southampton S^t. Camberwell.*
> 4th May, 1829.

DEAR SIR,

I am very sorry to communicate my son's determination to withdraw from the London University, (an event as painful as it was unexpected) but I must at the same time assure you that I am entirely satisfied with everything that has been done on your part, and make my grateful acknowledgements for the kind and affectionate treatment with which you have always behaved to him.

> I am,
> Dear Sir,
> Your obliged & humble Servt
> R. BROWNING Junr.[1]

As vehemently, then, as he had rebelled against the " undiluted misery " of what he later acknowledged to be a wholly benign school, Robert Browning rejected, too, the discipline of University life. His mind was made up. He would prepare himself for no career, he decided, that subjected him to the competition or the authority of others.

> I ran over the grassy fields
> Startling the flocks of nameless birds, to tell
> Poor Festus, leaping all the while for joy,
> To leave all trouble for my future plans,
> For I had just determin'd to become
> The greatest and most glorious being on earth.

There was one solution only, he told his father : he was to be a Poet : perhaps even " *the* Poet ". " Song," he wrote, " not Deeds . . . was chosen." There is a tradition, sponsored by

[1] Corres. No. 1252. University College Library.

Edmund Gosse, that this choice received the unqualified approval of Browning's parents. " He appealed to his father whether it would not be better for him to see life in the best sense, and cultivate the powers of his mind, than to shackle himself in the very outset of his career by a laborious training, foreign to that aim. . . . So great was the confidence of the father in the genius of the son that the former at once acquiesced in the proposal." But there is evidence that the acquiescence was by no means as prompt or as willing as Gosse suggests, or even as Browning himself, in later life, chose to believe. It is true that the versatile Mr. Browning had once " had the intention of devoting himself to art " ; and that his son, therefore, would have been justified in exclaiming, like Paracelsus to Festus, " blame me not, Because I dare to act on your own views ". The views of Festus, however, did not include " scorn or neglect of ordinary means of success " : and this scorn, it is plain, was a marked feature of the adolescence and early manhood of Robert Browning. " For my own future way in the world I have always refused to care " said the poet blithely. His parents, however, were forced to take a more realistic view of the prospect of supporting, indefinitely, an able-bodied son. For the Brownings were poor, as Robert himself confessed to Elizabeth Barrett. His mother, always referred to in the poet's lifetime as the daughter of a " ship-owner ", was in fact the daughter of a " mariner in Dundee ".[1] His father was a clerk in the Bank of England ; and one may judge of his status by the fact that his salary, at the conclusion of " upwards of forty-nine years " of " faithful service ", was £275 a year.[2] Robert's closest friends, Alfred Domett and Joseph Arnould, were both barristers ; it was Mr. Browning's wish, Mrs. Orr tells us, that his son, too, " should qualify himself for the Bar ". Robert, however, preferred to " groom a horse " all day long, rather than " succeed Mr. Fitzroy Kelly in the Solicitor-General-

[1] William Wiedeman [*sic*] is thus described in the *Register of Sasines*, Dundee, June 21, 1787. His name does not appear in the lists of ship-owners of the period.

[2] Although Mr. Browning had inherited money from his " Uncle Tittle and Aunt Mill ", the amount cannot have been substantial. The Tittles were of humble origin ; old Edward Tittle being described in the records as a " cordwainer of Port Royal." Jeanette Marks asserts that in the West Indies " the Tittles made boots and shoes for some of the members of the Family of the Barrett ".

ship ". Repeated efforts were made to persuade him to change his mind, for others besides the acidulated Mrs. Procter were shocked by the situation of a man who lacked " seven or eight hours a day of occupation " ; and as late as 1845 " dear foolish old Basil Montagu " was still bothering the poet to read " Law gratis " under his patronage. That the situation had become a subject of gossip in literary circles is proved by a letter written early in the same year by Miss Mitford to her friend Miss Barrett. The letter itself has been destroyed : but in Elizabeth's answer to it, it is possible to read clearly enough a reflection of Miss Mitford's words. In this, repudiating indignantly the charge that Robert Browning lacked either money or the inclination to work, Elizabeth went on to assert that, on the contrary, " he reproaches other poets for that very thing of which his friend accuses him—a want of masculine resolve to work like common men, when they want money like them. ' How can work do dishonour to any man ? ' he has said—' and what is there in poetry to disqualify one from ordinary duties ? ' So I *quite* quite disbelieve. You know my dearest candid friend, it is quite possible to be a ' visitor and family friend ' without knowing very accurately, and without *talking* very accurately. His family may regret perhaps that he does not, by means of his talents, climb the woolsack rather than Parnassus Hill—that sort of regret is possible enough !—but I feel quite confident that if his position had required him to work, he is the last man under the sun to shrink from it." [1] Possibly. But what assurance have we that Robert Browning's position did not require him to work ? It is the poet himself who has told us of the necessity which forced his father to relinquish an artistic career and " go at once and consume his life after a fashion he always detested " : and if we want conclusive proof that the son's mode of life evoked some very real opposition in the family circle, it is to be found in his own statement that " many good battles " had to be fought—(" for that has happened too ")—before he could convince " the people *here* what was my ' true honourable position in society ', &c. &c." The point gained, it did not seem to distress him unduly that " this light rational life I lead, and know so well I lead " was purchased wholly at another's

[1] Thursday ' [July, 1845]. Wellesley College Library.

expense.[1] Browning's explanation of the fact is a curious one.
" I had the less repugnance to my father's generosity," he
wrote, " that I knew that an effort at some time or other
might furnish me with a few hundred pounds which would
soon cover my very simple expenses." But the effort was not
made ; nor, in this sense, was it ever to be made : from the
day he left Gower Street until the hour of his death in a
Venetian Palazzo, Robert Browning never knew " what it was
to have to do a certain thing to-day and not to-morrow ".
Meanwhile, during the years that he continued to live under
his father's roof, his " simple expenses " included two long
journeys to Italy and the Continent and, (*Strafford* excluded),
the cost of publication of all his poems from *Paracelsus* down to
the eighth and last pamphlet of the *Bells and Pomegranates* series.

" But, in spite of all the babble," wrote Browning to Elizabeth Barrett, " I feel sure that whenever I make up my mind
to that, I can be rich enough and to spare—because along
with what you have thought *genius* in me, is certainly talent,
what the world recognizes as such ; and I have tried it in
various ways, just to be sure that I *was* a little magnanimous
in never intending to use it. Thus, in more than one of the
reviews and newspapers that laughed my ' Paracelsus ' to
scorn ten years ago—in the same column, often, of these
reviews, would follow a most laudatory notice of an Elementary
French book, on a new plan, which I ' *did* ' for my old French
master, and he published—' *that* was really an useful work ' ! "
A search of the relevant periodicals reveals that a week after
Paracelsus was reviewed in their columns, the *Atlas* and the
Spectator both noticed, briefly, a book called *Le Gil Blas de la
Jeunesse. A L'Usage des Ecoles. Par Charles Le Roy, Professeur
de Langue Française au College de Camberwell, et A. Loradoux,
Professeur de Langues, Walworth.* It is of course impossible to
assess the extent of Browning's collaboration in this " abridge-
ment and purification of Gil Blas ", an exercise which, as he
says, he " did " for his old French master, Monsieur Loradoux.
It is, however, possible to detect a mild, unremarkable echo

[1] My father and my mother died of want,
Well, had I riches of my own ? . . .
                    Some good son
Paint my two hundred pictures—let him try !
                    (*Andrea del Sarto.*)

of Lesage's picaresque novel in one of Browning's later poems. In *Gil Blas*, in the chapter called " Histoire de dona Mencia de Mosquera ", it is more than once a question of the " corrégidor de Valladolid " : as of the licencié Sédillo, also of Valladolid, whose housekeeper is called Jacinte. Twenty years after the publication of *Le Gil Blas de La Jeunesse*, Browning published a poem called *How it Strikes a Contemporary*. His poet—" The town's true master if the town but knew ! " —lives in Valladolid : he is referred to as the Corregidor. He plays cribbage in the evening with his maid. The name of the maid is Jacynth.

> Calmly, then,
> About this secret lodge of Adelaide's
> Glided his youth away ; beyond the glades
> On the fir-forest border, and the rim
> Of the low range of mountain, was for him
> No other world : but this appeared his own
> To wander through at pleasure and alone.

The notorious, the " wholly unintelligible " *Sordello* took seven years to complete. It was destined by its author to correct the imperfections of *Pauline* and compensate for the humiliation inflicted by its failure. This failure was epitomised, for Browning, in the comments of John Stuart Mill, pencilled in the margins of a review copy of *Pauline*, and summarised at length, and with severity, on one of the blank pages at the end of the volume. How the young Robert Browning writhed under the sting of this merciless analysis is revealed in his next published work, in the attitude of Paracelsus to his critics.

> How they talk calmly of my throes—my fierce
> Aspirings, terrible watchings—each one claiming
> Its price of blood and brain ; how they dissect
> And sneeringly disparage the few truths
> Got at a life's cost . . . Wretched crew !

More disconcerting still, however, was not only Mill's dislike of the " intense and morbid self-consciousness " of the young poet, but his recognition of the fact that in *Pauline* Robert Browning had offered to the world a " psychological history of himself ". The realisation that in this " Fragment of a Confession " he betrayed the secret of his own guilt seems to have come as a profound shock to Browning. The recoil was a violent one. More than fifty years later, he was to tell an acquaintance that " his early poems were so transparent in their meaning as to draw down upon him the ridicule of the critics, and that, boy as he was, this ridicule and censure stung him into quite another style of writing ".

> You know they made me
> A laughing-stock : I was a fool ; you know
> The when and the how : hardly those means again.

And indeed the means were instantaneously abandoned : never again, after *Pauline*, was Robert Browning to attempt, as he had there done, to " strip my mind bare ". On the contrary. He was to adopt a series of disguises : to insist, as, repetitively, he did throughout his life, that his poetry was " dramatic in principle, and so many utterances of so many imaginary persons, not mine ". In *Sordello* (begun before *Paracelsus*, but not published until five years afterwards) he donned the first of these disguises : but not before he had acknowledged his own descent from grace, and addressed in valedictory terms his youthful god Shelley.

> —thou, spirit, come not near
> Now—not this time desert thy cloudy place
> To scare me, thus employed, with that pure face !
> I need not fear this audience, I make free
> With them, but then this is no place for thee !

The spirit of Shelley, however, is by no means absent from *Sordello*, which, beneath a weight of historical trappings, dwells with so bemused an absorption upon the variegated sensibilities of a poetic nature. Once more, elaborately disguised this time, we are offered a glimpse of the early life and development of Robert Browning. For Goito, the mountain fastness in which the young Sordello grows up " fenced about From most that nurtures judgement, care and pain ", is to all intents and purposes another " garden in the environs " :

22

the environs, this time, being those of Mantua. A retreat, hill-encircled, secluded wholly from the " world's business and embroiled ado ", Goito is to that city what Camberwell was to London. So, too, " built amid a few low mountains ", the " secret lodge " of Adelaide is to the young Troubadour what Hanover Cottage was to Browning : a " drowsy Paradise ", in which, while " springs summers and winters quietly came and went ", peacefully, all the while, " amid his wildwood sights he lived alone ". And it is here, in the second book of *Sordello*, in the incident which " Opened, like any flash that cures the blind, The veritable business of mankind " that there lies an allusion to a capital experience in the early life of the poet himself.

The young Sordello, venturing forth for the first time from Goito, walking through the woods and marshy plains, finds himself suddenly at Mantua. Before him he sees " a crowd Indeed—real men and women—gay and loud Round a pavilion ". He waits. " What next ? The curtains, see, dividing ! " : before the audience, " a showy man " appears : Eglamor, celebrated Troubadour of the Court of Love. It was on the 22nd of October, 1832, that Robert Browning walked ten miles from Camberwell to the village of Richmond, where, in the little theatre on the Green, he joined the crowd assembling to see Edmund Kean in *Richard III*. And October 22 was the date, too, not only of the conception of *Pauline*, but, accompanying it, of a gigantic resurgence of energy, pride and ambition in which, galvanised by the performance of Kean, the twenty-year old poet conceived a grandiose scheme of creative activity that embraced all branches of the arts—" I don't know whether I had not made up my mind to *act* as well as to make verses, music, and God knows what,—que de *châteaux en Espagne* ! "

What was there, then, about the performance of Kean which could release, in a spectator, this sudden passion of creative energy ? Certainly not the perfection of a great actor in his prime ; for by 1832 Kean, who " did not take an ounce of solid food for weeks together ", was living on brandy, and the embers of his own vitality. Like Eglamor, in fact, Kean " had seen his day : Old worshippers were something shamed, old friends Nigh Weary . . ." Dr. Doran also saw

23

him in *Richard III* in 1832. " The sight was pitiable," he
wrote. " Genius was not traceable in that bloated face ;
intellect was all but quenched in those once matchless eyes ;
and the power seemed gone, despite the will that would recall
it." Dr. Doran added, nevertheless, that " by bursts he was
as grand as he had ever been ". However grand he may have
been by bursts, he cannot have exhibited that power which,
seventeen years earlier, had caused the pit to rise at him,
women to faint, and Lord Byron to fall over in a convulsion.
And yet a convulsion of sorts was undoubtedly provoked in
the soul of the young Robert Browning. Sitting with others,
·obscure, in the obscurity of a theatre, he saw an actor, a single
man in the exercise of his art dominate and control the emotions
of a whole audience. With a " prick and tingle " of recognition, Browning felt this same power within himself : here,
he knew, was something that he might one day not only
emulate but surpass. This conviction was confirmed, mysteriously, by a fact which cannot have failed to make its effect :
namely, that there existed an actual physical resemblance
between Edmund Kean and Robert Browning.[1]

> and though I must abide
> With dreams, now, I may find a thorough vent
> For all myself, acquire an instrument
> For acting what these people act ; my soul
> Hunting a body out may gain its whole
> Desire some day !

In the body and personality of Kean, that evening, Browning's
soul obtained vicariously its whole desire : and when at
length the momentous performance came to an end, it was,
like Sordello, in a " luscious trance " that the future poet
stumbled out of the theatre and, " in his brain . . . a light
that turned glare ", set out to walk through the night back to
Camberwell and Hanover Cottage.

> And when he woke 'twas many a furlong thence,
> At home : the sun shining his ruddy wont ;

---

[1] A man of small stature, Kean, like Browning, was sometimes described as
looking like an Italian, and sometimes like a Jew. Nor was the rôle of actor
wholly unfamiliar to Browning, " who at school revived ' The Royal Convert ',
and acted ' Aribert ' therein ".

The customary bird's chirp ; but his front
Was crowned—was crowned ! [1]

The glory still upon him, he sat down at his desk and began
to write his " Fragment of a Confession ". Three months
later the poem was finished :—" completed last to Eglamor's
discomfiture and death." For Eglamor dies at Mantua in
the hour of Sordello's triumph. *Pauline* was published in
March, 1833. Two months later, Robert Browning stood by
the grave of Edmund Kean at Richmond.

> So much for Eglamor. My own month came ;
> 'Twas a sunrise of blossoming and May.
> Beneath a flowering laurel thicket lay
> Sordello. . . . [2]

For, " yielding himself up as to an embrace ", Sordello had
returned to Goito. " Back rushed the dream and enwrapt
him wholly." Once more, the secluded castle " confined
Him with his hopes and fears ". The confinement, a volun-
tary one, was less a discipline than a prolonged indulgence.
The garden in the environs remained a sanctuary, a defence
against the outer world. " Well," muses Sordello, " there's
Goito to retire upon if the worst happen " . . . " Well,"
Robert Browning wrote, " when they won't pay me for my
cabbages, nor praise me for my poems, I may, if I please,
say ' more's the shame ' . . . and *yet* go very light-hearted
back to a garden-full of rose-trees, and a soul-full of comforts."
Nevertheless, and despite this withdrawal, the time was not so
distant when the inner process and exigencies of growth were
of their own accord to " undo the trance Lapping Sordello ".
" The fame as a singer, which comes suddenly to him," wrote
Dowden, " draws Sordello out of his Goito solitude, to the
worldly society of Mantua " : and, after the publication of
Paracelsus, this, for a brief but rewarding moment, was the
experience of Browning himself. For the first time, the city
and not its environs became a centre of attraction : the more

---

[1] In a letter to Miss Barrett, Browning talks of " polking all night and walking home by broad daylight to the surprise of the thrushes in the bush here ".
[2] And there he still lay in May, 1844, where *Sibrandus Schafnaburgensis* finds him
reading in the garden, at ease " under the arbute and laurustine ".

strongly so in that, as Sarianna Browning remarked to Mrs. Orr, her brother had already " outgrown his social surroundings ". Those surroundings, she hastened to add, " were absolutely good, but they were narrow ; it could not be otherwise ; he chafed under them ". The situation is characteristically described by Browning himself in a letter to Julia Wedgwood. Referring to a remark he had previously made—" about one's family not ' growing ' proportionately to one's own growth "—the poet continued : " I meant *symmetrically*, rather : for they may grow just as you grow, only—here's the fault—you none of you profit by each other's growth, it is not in your direction, but for somebody else to profit by—much as with a cluster of fruits on a common twig : each may bulge out round and red enough in the sun's eye, but the place where all the clustered knobs touch, where each continues to be known to the other, *that* is as hard and green, and insipid as ever. . . ." The moment had come, in other words, in which to turn outwards ; to seek beyond the walls of Hanover Cottage and the close juncture of family affections, the resources of a new and untried relationship. But with the impulse, no less resolute, came the accompanying check :

> for if you gave me
> Leave to take or to refuse,
> In earnest, do you think I'd choose
> That sort of new love to enslave me ?
> Mine should have lapped me round from the beginning ;
> As little fear of losing it as winning :
> Lovers grow cold, men learn to hate their wives,
> And only parents' love can last our lives.

2

" I seem to have foretold, *foreknown* you in other likings of mine," wrote Robert Browning to Elizabeth Barrett. The term " other likings " has about it a ring of cautious under-statement : not inappropriate, perhaps, in a man who openly declared that he " could not believe in ' love ' nor understand it—nor be subject to it consequently ". In spite of which, in

the years before he began to call at Wimpole Street, the names
of two women, at least, were associated with his : those of
Eliza Flower and Fanny Haworth. Is it possible, then, as
Browning alleged, to discern in her predecessors a recognisable
outline of Elizabeth Barrett herself? Examined in this light,
a common factor emerges at once : Elizabeth Barrett was six
years older than the man she married : Eliza Flower, the
records tell us, was nine years older than the poet ; and
Fanny Haworth (always unhappily conscious of the fact) was
his senior by as much as eleven years. Robert Browning
consistently avoided, with " a kind of male prudery " which
laid him open at times to ridicule, the company of " young
ladies ". He could never, he said in a disparaging voice, see
" any attractiveness in the class."

The house occupied by Benjamin Flower and his daughters
was situated amongst the green lanes and nursery gardens of
Dalston near Hackney ; a district celebrated for its high-
waymen and its dissenters ; as for its successful cultivation, in
earlier centuries, of the orange and the pine. There was
something wholly individual, not only in the atmosphere of the
small tree-shaded house, but in the circumstances and associations of those who lived in it. Benjamin Flower, who was in
France in 1791, " the most innocent part of the revolution ",
later became editor of *The Cambridge Intelligencer* ; a journal
which gave six of Coleridge's early poems to the world, and by
its outspoken comment earned for its editor a term of six
months' imprisonment at Newgate. During the same period,
a Miss Eliza Gould, schoolmistress, of South Molton, was
ordered by reactionary opinion to relinquish either her pupils
or her allegiance to the *Cambridge Intelligencer* : visiting Benjamin Flower in his cell, she transferred her allegiance from
the journal to its editor ; and upon his release, Flower and
the attractive young schoolmistress were married. They lived
at Harlow, in Essex, where Flower edited the *Political Register*,
and where their two daughters, Eliza and Sarah, were born.
Mrs. Flower died in 1810, leaving the little girls in the care
of their father. Their upbringing, comments Mrs. Bridell-
Fox, was " original and erratic ". Eliza—at two and a half,

27

it seems, a musical prodigy—took occasional lessons from the village organist ; but otherwise the sisters were thrown very much upon their own resources : and Harriet Martineau, in *Five Years of Youth, or Sense and Sentiment*, has left us a picture of the motherless girls, " ignorant of many of the important proprieties of life ", who, given the one a silk, the other a straw bonnet, used the first as a cradle for the kitten, and the second as a basket in which to gather strawberries.[1]

At the time of her first meeting with Robert Browning, Eliza Flower was twenty-three or twenty-four years old. Fragile and ardent, with sensibilities heightened, already, by the disease which was later to claim her, she was known to her intimate friends as " Ariel ". A drawing by Mrs. Bridell-Fox that hangs today in the library of Conway Hall shows us a gentle smiling young woman with shoulder-length ringlets and upraised, luminous eyes : and although, necessarily, we must distrust the sentimental radiance of a portrait made from memory, we need not doubt the evidence of contemporaries : the effect produced by the Flower sisters on minds more critical or more detached. Amongst these, in the " number, very small " of his personal friends, John Stuart Mill classed Eliza Flower as " a person of genius " ; while so hardened a theatre man as Macready wrote of Sarah that " she displayed more poetical conception, more imagination, and more genius than Malibran, Grisi and Pasta combined ". Another observer, W. J. Linton, describes the daughters of Benjamin Flower as " two of the most beautiful women of their day " : and goes on to say : " With their love and feeling for music and pictorial art, their high poetic thought, they were such women in their purity, intelligence and high-souled enthusiasm, as Shelley might have sung as fitted to redeem a world by their very presence." [2]

Easy enough, then, to imagine the effect upon an adolescent

---

[1] That Harriet Martineau's book was inspired by the Flower family is confirmed by Mrs. Bridell-Fox. " The little comic incident of the child's cutting off the tips of the visitor's gloves, I can remember hearing Mrs. Adams [Sarah Flower] relate of herself—and the tiny sitting room with the big balcony, I can faintly remember in my childhood at Dalston." MS. letter. To Mrs. Flower : April 13, 1896. Fordham Flower papers.

[2] It is only fair to add that Carlyle describes the author of this statement as " a well enough meaning, but, I fear, extremely windy creature ".

and a poet : a poet, moreover, who presented himself upon their doorstep with the fever of his infatuation for Shelley still smouldering in his veins, and " with a crowd of loves to give to *something* and so get rid of their pain and burden ". In the young Robert Browning the pain and burden were of recent origin ; the result of a sharp emotional constriction. No longer, at Hanover Cottage, could love be given or received in unmarred reciprocity : between mother and son, the barrier of doctrine had driven a hard unyielding wedge. The point of that wedge, separating brain and heart, had divided the foundations of Browning's nature. At a critical stage in his development, he found that one part of his nature forced him to reject the very being whom the other part held in the greatest esteem. To the poet and to the tender-hearted son alike, the situation was an intolerable one : and it was in intervening at such a time that Eliza Flower offered him in her own person a temporary release from his predicament. Half consciously, already, his quest was for a woman whose attributes would enable him not only to love and respect in the same person—(what happiness could I find in " allying myself with a woman to whose intellect, as well as goodness, I could *not* look up ? ")—but who would restore to him the paradise of trust, of submissiveness, from which prematurely he had found himself severed. No woman who did not offer such a solution could gain his affection ; and no man, surely, can have been more explicit in the expression of his demands.

Twenty years later : there must, he insisted to Elizabeth Barrett (she protested continually at being nailed up " into a false position with your gold-headed nails of chivalry "), there must be " this disproportionateness in a beloved object —before I knew you, women seemed not so much better than myself—therefore no love for them ! There is no love but from beneath, far beneath. . . ." In another letter, the poet dwells on " the exquisiteness of being *transcended* " by the woman he loves ; a sentiment which echoes closely a passage in one of his own plays. In this, *The Return of the Druses*—(the history of an impostor, in which once more the basic schism of his own nature is explored : " My Frank brain, thwarted by my Arab heart ")—Djabal confesses that he could not love

the beauteous Anael until now, the moment of his exposure
and degradation, for—

> How could I love while thou adoredst me ?
> Now thou despisest, art above me so
> Immeasurably ! . . .
> Oh, luxury to worship, to submit,
> To be transcended, doomed to death by thee ! [1]

That luxury, in the early days at least of their relationship,
Eliza Flower could offer him ; for the frail and spiritual young
woman, dark-eyed and dark-ringleted, must indeed have
seemed immeasurably superior to the immature schoolboy
who sat and watched her, as " with heart, soul, voice, finger,
frame, seeming all but borne upward by the strain, as on
wings to heaven ", she played or sang for him the hymns and
anthems of her own composition.[2] She cannot, even then,
have been unaware of the emotion she aroused in one trembling
so palpably upon the brink of " strange powers, and feelings,
and desires " : but whatever the nature of her own response,
her reticence was such that at no time would she proffer more,
in return, than the semblance of a gentle and solicitous affection. Nevertheless, when Robert Browning wrote, years
later, to Elizabeth Barrett that before her " no human being
ever ministered " to the wants of his soul, he was doing less
than justice to one whose unfailing sympathy helped to ease
him through a very troubled phase in his own career. For
the turbulent stream of ideas and emotions damned, unhappily, at Hanover Cottage, was diverted now to Dalston :
and Eliza Flower, untouched herself by such distemper, was
called upon to receive the whole burden of adolescent *sturm
und drang*. An echo of the situation finds its way into *Pauline*.

> These are wild fancies, but I feel, sweet friend,
> As one breathing his weakness to the ear
> Of pitying angel—dear as a winter flower ;

---

[1] When, conversely, it is revealed in the poem of that name that Porphyria
" worshipped " her lover, the latter can find no alternative but to strangle her.

[2] An objective description of Eliza Flower is difficult to find. In an unnamed
newspaper clipping of February 20, 1896, a writer signing himself " Christopher
Crayon " recalls seeing Eliza at an anti-Corn Law meeting in Drury Lane
theatre, and describes her " dark eyes and hair ". Fordham Flower papers.

A slight flower growing alone, and offering
Its frail cup of three leaves to the cold sun . . .

And to the pitying angel, from the small room at Camberwell,
went poem after poem, letter after letter ; poems and letters
that, secretly, Eliza pasted into an album, and cherished for
the rest of her life. She would have been disagreeably surprised, one feels, if she had known Browning's attitude in
later years to what he savagely called her " vice of keeping
every such contemptible thing " ; and the lengths to which
the poet went, after her death, in order to recover and suppress
those same letters and poems : those " stupid scrawlings " as
he called them, which, he feared, in some " horrible raking
up of the correspondence in general " might turn up " to
bother one's survivors and make them ashamed of one—and
all for what ?—for having played at verses and letters, instead
of cricket and trap-ball ! "

H. L. Hovelaque, in his book *La Jeunesse de Robert Browning*,
has suggested that *Pauline* is a composite picture of both Eliza
and Sarah Flower : that it was with both women that the
young Robert Browning was simultaneously in love. In
effect, the sisters were so closely associated in all the circumstances of their lives that it is difficult at times to distinguish the
attributes of one from those of the other. Nevertheless, it was
in virtue of certain distinct and contrasted qualities that Eliza
and Sarah Flower played their respective rôles in the emotional
life of the poet. And here again Harriet Martineau, at one
time an intimate friend of the family, has given us the clue
to a fundamental difference of temperament when, still under
the guise of fiction, she describes the elder sister as capable of
a " silent, perpetual self-denial " : while the younger, in the
ominous phraseology of the time, is in danger of " losing all
energy of character, all vigour of body as well as of mind,
through an unbounded indulgence of the imagination ". This
imagination, whose effect Miss Martineau so cordially distrusted, produced in Sarah Flower an obsessive hankering
after the limelight : for many years, and through constant
vicissitudes of health, it was her fixed determination to become
an actress. If we may accept the opinion of Macready, she was
in fact an exceptionally talented young woman : her voice

31

alone, " as regards expression, pathos and power ", he proclaimed " unsurpassed (I question if equalled) by any singer
I ever heard ". Nevertheless, and despite this spectacular
array of talents (she wrote fiction and poetry with equal
facility) it is certain that she was the less mature of the two
sisters ; being dependent to a quite abnormal degree upon
the presence and the authority of Eliza, for whom, motherless
since infancy, she cherished a passionate admiration. (" In
thy content, I win a wreath more bright, Than Earth's wide
garden ·ever could supply.") Characteristically, too, it was
Sarah and not Eliza who, in religious discussion with Robert
Browning, was seduced by the argumentative fervour of the
" bright handsome youth with long black hair falling over
his shoulders ". She was swayed, one suspects, as much by
the ardour of his personality as by the force of his opinions ;
and it was, perhaps, in order to remove herself, temporarily
at least, from a subversive influence, that she returned in the
autumn of 1827 to Harlow : for it was from the safe retreat
of that village that the future author of the hymn *Nearer My
God to Thee* wrote a long letter appealing for the sympathy,
and guidance of that old-established friend of the family,
the Reverend W. J. Fox. " I would fain go to my Bible as I
used to, but I cannot," she wrote. " The cloud has come
over me gradually, and I did not discover the darkness in
which my soul was shrouded until, in seeking to give light to
others, my own gloomy state became too settled to admit of
doubt. It was in answering Robert Browning that my mind
refused to bring forward argument, turned recreant, and sided
with the enemy. . . ." The confession continues : " I dare
not apply to Papa. I dare not let him have a glimpse at the
infatuation that possesses me. . . ." It is necessary to add
that Sarah Flower was a highly susceptible young woman ;
and that, a month or so before this letter was written, the
sight of a " lad of eighteen " preaching his first sermon, led
to her " being so excited ", as she put it, " that I dare not
think of sleep though it is past twelve o'clock ".

Every student of Browning is aware of the impact upon the
poet of Shelley's atheism, as of his propaganda in favour of
" vegetables and pure water ". What has received less attention is the effect produced upon an excitable adolescent by the

assertion that " Chastity is a monkish and evangelical superstition ", and the emphatic denunciation of those " mistakes
cherished by society respecting the connection of the sexes,
whence the misery and diseases of unsatisfied celibacy, un-
enjoying prostitution, and the premature arrival of puberty
necessarily spring ".   There is, here, a singular blank in the
evidence, filled, very sketchily, by Mrs. Orr's assertion that
at no time did Mr. Browning consort with " gipsies and
tramps ", or seek for " low-life pleasures ".   This being so,
in what spirit, one wonders, did the poet approach those
" modest and accomplished women " from whose favours,
according to Shelley, he was debarred only by an erroneous
and wholly " fanatical idea of chastity " ?   There is no means
of knowing.   Nevertheless, it is reasonable to suggest that
Browning was, for a time at least, susceptible to the beauty of
this young woman in whom, in return, he awoke so docile a
response ; and such few—very few—passages in the poem in
which *Pauline* takes on a fleshly shape, may well have been
inspired by a moment, however incomplete, of intimacy.

> How the blood lies upon her cheek, all spread
> As thinned by kisses ; only in her lips
> It wells and pulses like a living thing,
> And her neck looks, like marble misted o'er
> With love-breath, a dear thing to kiss and love,
> Standing beneath me—looking out to me
> As I might kill her and be loved for it.[1]

There may even be an echo of the situation in Browning's
tortuous play, *A Blot in the 'Scutcheon,* in which the early death
of the heroine's mother is the excuse offered for her offence in
admitting a lover to her bedchamber.   (" I know nothing ",
wrote Dickens, " that is so affecting, nothing in any book I
have ever read, as Mildred's recurrence, to that ' I was so
young—I had no mother '.")   If, nevertheless, it is possible
to claim with confidence that it was not Sarah but Eliza
whom the young Robert Browning loved, it is because Browning himself has left us in no doubt on the matter.   " There
is no love but from beneath, far beneath . . . "   This, Browning once admitted, was a law of his own nature.   Between

[1] Cf. *Porphyria's Lover.*

33

him and Sarah Flower, the prescribed, the essential distance did not exist. Too easily infected with his own doubts and desires—" whoso sucks a poisoned wound Envenoms his own veins "—she appeared to him " not so much better than myself " ; and as such, as he has made it plain, a woman for whom he could experience friendship, admiration, even desire, but " no love ".[1]

In February 1829, Benjamin Flower died, and the house at Dalston was given up. This event marks the end of the early relationship of the " poet boy " with the Flower sisters. Four years were to elapse before they met again ; and when they did, new circumstances and new preoccupations had claimed them all. Eliza and Sarah now lived at Stamford Grove West, in the house of their guardian, William Johnson Fox. Minister of the South Place chapel, Fox was a married man, with two sons (one a deaf-mute) and a daughter, the future Mrs. Bridell-Fox, then a small alert child known in the family circle as Tottie. It was no secret to his congregation that Fox and his wife were not happy together. The young minister had married unwillingly, and his wife repaid this unwillingness very promptly after the ceremony by an inertia that combined indifference to her husband's material well-being with hostility to his intellectual pretensions. What, under the circumstances, she found peculiarly trying was to see another offering him the devotion she withheld : and this, from the moment of Eliza Flower's arrival in the house, was a spectacle she was forced constantly to endure. The sight of the gentle and industrious Eliza tirelessly looking up references, correcting proof sheets, transcribing sermons and articles, became more intolerable to her, perhaps, than the deep romantic attachment which, insidiously, all the while, was growing up between Fox and his devoted friend. Seventeen years older than Eliza, Fox was described in 1834 as a " little thick-set bushy-locked man of five and forty, with

---

[1] This is confirmed by a tradition in the Flower family itself. In a letter of October 23, 1901, Alfred Flower refers to certain writers who are, he says, " sadly mistaken about Sarah Flower having been Browning's first love. If I remember correctly it was her sister Eliza who was his special ideal." Fordham Flower papers.

bright sympathetic-thoughtful eyes " and a face " compressed, and well-buttressed out into broadness ". The description is Carlyle's, who also imputes to the " Socinian Philosophist ", as he contemptuously calls him, " a tendency to pot-belly, and *snuffiness* ". Another writer discerned " a furtive look about the eyes and mouth, an appearance as if he were playing a part that did not become him. He seemed as if he had done something which made him feel unquietly, like a monk of La Trappe addicted to eating beefsteak in the dark." Eliza Flower, however, saw in him nothing but the orator, the out-spoken journalist, the man with a mission ; and it was at this level that she was ready to dedicate to his service all the reserves of a sensitive and finely-strung nature. A dangerous tension grew up in the small household. " O you—no not even you can imagine what the wretchedness of this state is —I mean when one *must* bear—and so quietly too !—and one's whole existence is condensed into the mere effort of enduring. You say you wouldn't stand it—sometimes I believe [t'will ?] sink me dead." [1] This letter was addressed to a young woman who, through the peculiarity of her own position, was able fully to sympathise with the distress of Eliza, and who for the same reason, as will be seen, was to exert an indirect influence upon the life of Robert Browning himself. It was in the summer or early autumn of 1830 that Fox introduced John Stuart Mill to the dark-eyed wife of John Taylor : and it was Eliza Flower, the only woman, as Mill said, with " capacities of feeling or intellect kindred with her own ", who became thereafter the intimate friend and confidante of Mrs. Taylor. The confidences were mutual : so, it seems, was a certain romantic attachment between the two women. " What an awful night—wind and rain and such high winds together—but the sunset yesterday—*Did* you see it, it was worth living for. I wondered how you got home. If it were not for fear of accidents and making Mr. Taylor jealous, I could say now ' I would I *were* a man ' to have laid my heart at your feet—while you were talking yesterday—" [2] Harriet

---

[1] Friday night. [1831 ?] Eliza Flower to Harriet Taylor. MS. letter. Mill-Taylor collection : British Library of Political and Economic Science. Volumes XXVII and XXIX
[2] Undated. Eliza Flower to Harriet Taylor. Ibid.

was a passionate admirer of Shelley ; and poetry written under his influence appeared in Fox's journal, the *Monthly Repository*, during 1832 ; one poem, *To the Summer Wind*, anticipating somewhat in manner a poem which Browning also published in that journal, *Still ailing wind? Wilt be appeased or no?* Before his meeting with Harriet, John Stuart Mill had considered himself a man wholly devoid of poetical sentiment. Harriet, however, subjected him to an intensive course of " poetic culture " ; the first-fruit of which was the article " What is Poetry? " which appeared in the *Monthly Repository* in January, 1833. It is at this point that Robert Browning re-enters upon the scene, preceded by a letter to W. J. Fox in which, describing himself as the " oddish sort of boy who had the honour of being introduced to you at Hackney some years back ", he submitted for inspection a copy of *Pauline* with the suggestion, artlessly conveyed, that Fox might care to review it in the *Westminster*. This letter was followed in quick succession by a dozen copies of *Pauline* ; by some eager assiduous letters ; and by a volume of *Rosalind and Helen*, " the getting back of which ", Robert Browning wrote, if you do not " think me too encroaching ", will be " an excuse for calling on you some evening ". The excuse, it seems, was judged adequate ; and thus it came about that on a spring evening when the early fruit trees were in blossom, with an eager step—(" when I have anything to occupy my mind I all but run ")—Robert Browning crossed the city from south to north on his way, once more, from Camberwell to Hackney and Upper Clapton.

But the young man who turned, finally, into Stamford Grove West, who pushed open a small garden gate and mounted the narrow flight of steps to the front door, was very different, to all outward appearance, from the impetuous schoolboy who had once preceded him on this mission to a potential patron. Robert Browning stood now on the porch of Mr. Fox's house, elegantly gloved and cravated, a cloak with a velvet collar slung negligently about his shoulders. Dark hair, parted at the side, lay in opulent curves over a wide brow : beneath heavy lids, grey-blue eyes looked eagerly forth out of a sallow, Italianate face that was framed, from cheekbone to chin, in dark crisply-curling whiskers. This graceful stranger it was, then, and no longer the "poet boy" of early acquaintance, who entered on that evening the sitting-room of W. J. Fox : and it was only gradually, as the evening wore on, that his former friends perceived that this elegant young man who fenced and waltzed and wore lemon-yellow kid gloves, who had written a confession so candid that, prefaced with the words of Cornelius Agrippa ("it is harmful, poisonous ; the gate of Hell is in this book") it could only be published anonymously—this intimidating young man, they found, had learnt neither to smoke tobacco nor to drink wine and, forbearing equally to assert the rights of his own manhood, lived peaceably all the while beneath the authority of his parents in his childhood's home at Hanover Cottage, in Camberwell.

Fox gave a copy of *Pauline* to John Stuart Mill, in the hope that he would review it either for the *Examiner* or for Tait's *Edinburgh Magazine*. Like Carlyle's ill-fated manuscript, this copy had "not only the *one* reader you mention but a second just as good" : a critical collaboration recorded in the comments pencilled in the margins of the book, more than one of which, Professor Hayek believes, is in the handwriting not of Mill but of Harriet Taylor. (One is driven to speculate as to the effect on Browning's poetry if this copy had suffered the same fate as befell the first volume of Carlyle's *French Revolution*.) No mishap took place, however, other than the inability of Mill to secure publication for his review : and on October 10, Mill returned it to Fox, "having done all I could, which was to annotate copiously in the margin and sum up on the flyleaf. On the whole the observations are not flattering to the author—perhaps too strong in the expression to be shown to him." They were shown to him, however ; for a few weeks later, on October 30, 1833, the copy was once more in Browning's possession : and passionately, in his turn, he scribbled in the margins his answers to Mill's queries and charges. Since Mill wrote at times as if he were addressing Browning personally—"What does this mean? His opinion of yourself?" . . . "explain better what this means" . . . "do you mean is to *you* as a voice?"—and Browning, no less spontaneously and emphatically replied to each of these queries, the effect is that of a dialogue between the two young men, and as such the book may be regarded as one of the curiosities of literature. On the same occasion, it seems, Browning availed himself of the opportunity of doing some proof-correcting : punctuation was tightened up ; an occasional word altered ; a whole phrase deleted by a stroke of the pen : corrections which do not tally with the amended versions of 1868 or 1888. By that time, it is true, the book was no longer in Browning's possession. It had passed into the keeping of John Forster (" you know whom I mean," wrote Lamb slyly, " —the Pym-praiser—not Pimp-raiser "). The assumption has been, heretofore, that this transfer took place in 1837, on the occasion of Forster's help over the production of *Strafford*. But the book was still in Browning's possession on December 14, 1838, when he was able to refer to it while inscribing, for another friend, a copy of the " foolish plan " note. It is difficult to ascertain when the annotated copy was given to " my true friend John Forster " ; for the course of this true friendship did not run smooth, and from 1837 onwards the two men were continually falling out, and continually making it up. (On one such occasion, Browning gave Forster a 1612 quarto of *Richard III* reputed to have belonged to Edmund Kean[1]: while Forster gave Browning a green silk purse found in the actor's pocket " without a sixpence therein "). Browning, however, quickly repented of the impulse which had caused him to surrender *Pauline*. That he made an attempt to get the book back we know from a letter of Eliza Flower to Harriet Taylor. " It was so gracious of you to write—and so kindly too ! It came just as we were setting off to . . . dine with Mr. Forster—for a most extraordinary event—he read us Athelwold—we thought it capital of course . . . and then he said who sent it him. The first time I ever set foot in Mr. Forster's tenement was a morning of a note of yours—I had it upon me, and the first thing we heard and saw was ' I have just received a note from R. Browning begging me to send him his Pauline—which contains *his* Mr. *Mill's*—criticisms in pencil mark (and how

---

[1] Forster Collection. Victoria and Albert Museum. Given to Browning by his father in 1837. Bound up with it is a copy of *The Atheist's Tragedy* : a publication which at this time Browning was very anxious to consult, " as it would be of essential service to him in a work he is about to begin ".

true and just they were)—and how odd the coincidence. . . .
But it did happen so again yesterday." [1]

This was not the only attempt that Browning was to make
to recover his copy of *Pauline*. How many applications he
made in the lifetime of Forster is not known : what is
known is that when Forster died, Browning applied " to
the Executor, Mr. Chitty, that the book might be returned to
me,—which he promised to attend to, but of which I heard
no more ". He " heard no more ", no doubt, because the book
had been all the while on prolonged loan to Mr. Justice Chitty
himself ; and it was not until after his death, in 1899, that it
was restored to the Forster library at South Kensington, where
it now reposes, and where the biographer who consults it can
only be grateful for a series of events that conspired so fortui-
tously to preserve from destruction a document so essential
to his own purposes.

Meanwhile (to return once more to Dalston) the long-
simmering dissatisfaction between Fox and his wife had come,
abruptly, to a head. In 1834, a year after the resumption of
friendship with Robert Browning, the embittered woman
lodged a complaint against her husband with certain members
of the South Place congregation. There followed upon this
accusation levelled at their minister months of communal
scandal and controversy, in which the resignation of Fox
was alternately demanded and rejected ; and in which Eliza
Flower, whose heart, Fox wrote, " is as brave as it is pure and
true ", was on all sides " fiercely and falsely attacked ". At
the end of it all, Fox and his wife decided formally to separate.
The household was divided up accordingly : Franklin Fox, the
younger son, remained with his mother ; while Florance and
Tottie, devoted, both, to Eliza, elected to accompany their
father. Courageously, Eliza Flower accepted the rôle that
was offered to her ; and, platonic lovers, she and Fox sought
for a house in which to begin the new life that was to be for
them but an extension of the old. It was at this juncture
that Sarah Flower saw the necessity of resigning herself, in
turn, to marriage ; and, characteristically, her choice fell

---

[1] Undated. Mill-Taylor Collection. *Athelwold*, a tragedy by William Henry
Smith of the Middle Temple was published by Blackwood in 1842, and produced
by Macready at Drury Lane on May 18, 1843.

upon William Bridges Adams who, a widower and the former
son-in-law of Francis Place, might be trusted to fulfil in some
respects a rôle analogous to that of Fox in the life of her sister.
The marriage of Sarah Flower to Adams took place at the
end of September ; and not long after, a second couple,
Eliza Flower and William Johnson Fox, moved into their
new home at Number 5, Craven Hill, Bayswater.

Since this house was to play for the next five years so important a part in the life of Robert Browning, it is permissible
to dwell upon the circumstances, pleasingly picturesque, many
of them, that he encountered there ; and of these the retentive
memory of Tottie (Mrs. Bridell-Fox) has afforded us an
oblique but authoritative reflection.   Facing Kensington Gardens (at the gates of which, a few years earlier, it was possible
to buy halfpenny mugs of curds-and-whey), the cottage was
situated amongst meadows, in which, during the summer
months, white cows grazed under the flowering lime-trees.
Pushing open, with difficulty, a gate overgrown with ivy, the
poet would often come upon the whole family seated inside
the porch, reading or talking together under the drooping
fronds of honeysuckle and sweetbriar.   Or, if Fox were absent,
still, at his office (he had accepted the post of leader-writer on
Daniel Whittle Harvey's paper, *The True Sun*), Browning
would find the devoted Eliza playing at trap-ball in the long
untidy back-garden with her deaf and dumb charge, Florance,
while in the branch of a tree Tottie crouched absorbedly
reading *Sandford and Merton*.   (On the trunk of this tree, in
protest against a neighbour who shot such poachers, Fox had
pinned a placard which read " Blackbirds May Eat the
Cherries Here ".)   The house itself—" that open cage hung
in the tree boughs "—was filled with music at all hours of the
day ; and when Eliza was not singing or composing, from the
house next door, the " parent-nest " of Vincent Novello and
his family, came the soprano trills of Victoria and Sabilla
who conducted, twice weekly, a singing class for young ladies.
Separated from the Fox household by a low ivy-covered wall,
if not also, perhaps, by their own distrust of a suspected
irregularity, the Novellos could not fail to find in Eliza a most
" graceful-minded " neighbour ; and if she was not always
present at Novello parties where crab-apples were roasted

and spiced elder-wine drunk out of taper glasses, there were, on the other hand, many tranquil afternoons in which, sewing or reading under the apple-tree in her garden, Eliza was partnered by the industrious Mrs. Novello who, beneath the branches of a massive acacia, was busy embroidering a wreath of ivy-leaves and red berries on the black satin waistcoat she designed for her son-in-law, Charles Cowden Clarke. There is no doubt that the peaceful and productive hours spent in these surroundings, her " snug out-of-the-world corner " as she called it, were amongst the happiest in Eliza's life : and as for Fox—" I am ", he wrote to his mother, " several years younger this last birthday than I was the one before." So idyllic, indeed, was the whole atmosphere, that nearly fifty years later, writing of " old, old times that seem to belong to another life . . . when the Misses Flower were living, and Mr. Fox was in the bloom of his early fame " the aged Mary Howitt was impelled to exclaim, " How beautiful it all was ! " ; adding with evident emotion—" there was a poetry, a grace, a beauty, and a life about it, that remained its own to the last."

To such a concentration of qualities, Robert Browning cannot have been insensible. But the motives which led him, from 1835 onwards, to frequent so assiduously the household in Craven Hill were very different from those which, nearly ten years earlier, had driven him week after week to Dalston. No longer did he seek, in the presence of Eliza Flower or her sister, a lightning-conductor for the flame of his own emotional life : the requirements of that life lay deeply buried, to all intents and purposes extinct ; and what he discerned now at Craven Hill was simply a field—the only one accessible to him—for the timely cultivation of literary success. For W. J. Fox, who had abandoned the editorship of the *Monthly Repository*, was launched already upon the broader slopes of literary and dramatic criticism, where many of the most influential critics of the day, (Forster, of the *Examiner*, amongst them) were his personal friends. Browning was naturally aware of this fact : as he was aware, too, on his visits to Craven Hill, of the presence next door of a family who, more than once, had seen not only Shelley plain, but also John Keats, Leigh Hunt, and Charles and Mary Lamb. That he

41

perceived with equal clarity the potentialities of cheerful ruddy-faced Charley Cowden Clarke, school-fellow of Keats, friend of Moxon the publisher, is a fact borne out by the substance of a letter that the poet sat down to write on April 2nd 1835—barely a fortnight, that is to say, after the completion of *Paracelsus*. The letter is addressed to Fox, with whom Browning had been discussing the subject of a publisher for his poem. " You will oblige me indeed by forwarding the introduction to Moxon," he wrote. And, casually, he added, " I merely suggested him in particular, on account of his good name and fame among author-folk. . . ." Fox accordingly tackled his next-door neighbour ; and a fortnight later, when Browning set off to visit Moxon with the MS. of *Paracelsus* under his arm, it was a letter of commendation from " Mr. Clarke " that he presented to the poet-publisher of Dover Street. Moxon, however, declined the poem, and Browning returned, unabashed, to Craven Hill. " I am not much afraid of the issue," he wrote to Fox, " and I would give something to be allowed to read it some morning to you—for every rap o' the knuckles I should get a clap o' the back, I know." There follows upon this outburst of youthful " swagger " a passage in which, boldly, once more, the identification with Edmund Kean rises to the surface, as Browning goes on to demand that, henceforward, John Mill, his former critic, " must be benignant or supercilious as he shall choose, but in no case an idle spectator of my first appearance on any stage (having previously only dabbled in private theatricals) and bawl ' Hats off ! ' ' Down in front ! ' &c. as soon as I get to the proscenium ; and he may depend that tho' my ' Now is the winter of our discontent ' be rather awkward, yet there shall be occasional outbreaks of good stuff—that I shall warm as I get on, and finally wish ' Richmond at the bottom of the seas ' &c. in the best style imaginable."

Saunders and Otley refused to print *Paracelsus* ; and intervening once more, Fox persuaded Effingham Wilson, of the Royal Exchange, to take on the task of publication. His services to the young poet did not, however, stop there. It is generally accepted that John Forster wrote his long and enthusiastic review of *Paracelsus* without knowing anything whatsoever of its author. The review, it is true, was published in September, and Browning and Forster did not meet until the end of December. But it is also true that in 1835, Forster was not only writing for the same paper as W. J. Fox, but he occupied chambers at Lincoln's Inn Fields in the same house. Is it so difficult, then, in spite of the more picturesque version later circulated, to conclude that it was a timely hint from Browning's " literary father " that directed the attention of a fellow critic to the work of this hitherto unknown poet ? [1]

3

Robert Browning, who was always ready, in youth, to submit the idiosyncrasies of his cranium to the attentions of a phrenologist, appears to have been less willing to expose the secret of his personality to the professional portrait-painter. It was not until 1837, or thereabouts, that he consented to sit for his portrait : and even then his reserve was such that he surrendered half his face only to the light of publicity. It was a similar profile of the poet, later engraved for R . H. Horne's *A New Spirit of the Age*, that Elizabeth Barrett pronounced a " vulgarized caricature ". It " has not your character, in a line of it ", she wrote ; " something in just the forehead and eyes and hair, . . but even *that*, thrown utterly out of your order, by another bearing so unlike you ! " But Elizabeth Barrett had never known the Browning of 1837 ; or, familiar with the text, she might have recognised in the engraving the features and bearing of the young Sordello who, like the poet himself, is presented to us in profile :

His face
—Look, now he turns away ! Yourselves shall trace
(The delicate nostril swerving wide and fine,

[1] Fox had a high opinion of Forster's ability as a journalist. On April 2, 1840, Forster's birthday, he sent him, with the gift of a pen, a poem of which the following are the concluding lines :

But put *the Pen* in Forster's hand,
Sword, sceptre, wand ; to strike, to sway :
One touch—and through a barren land
Fountains of Truth and Beauty play.

MS. Forster Collection : Victoria and Albert Museum.

A sharp and restless lip, so well combine
With that calm brow).

Sarah Flower put it more bluntly : Robert Browning's appearance, she said, would have been " unexceptionally poetical if Nature had not played him an ugly trick in giving him an ugly nose ".

It was not, however, on aesthetic grounds that Eliza Flower was ready to find fault with the young poet.   Already, a new and vigorous egotism—(" the self-display he meant to compass ", perhaps)—had damaged, irreparably, the substance of her esteem for him.   To a friend, familiar with the earlier relationship, she confessed that his manner was such that he had " twisted the old-young shoot off by the neck ".   The current of sympathy thus deflected, she was able to observe, but not to understand, the nature of the change that had taken place in him.   It was the inexplicable division of a once unified nature that puzzled her most.   " If he had not got the habit of talking of head and heart as two independent existences, one would say he was born without a heart ", she wrote.   The words carry their own echo.   For is not this precisely Sordello's " accustomed fault of breaking yoke, Disjointing him who felt from him who spoke " ?   *Sordello*, it is true, was at the time not yet published, but it had lain on the poet's desk since 1833 ;   where it remained, a continuous record of his own development over seven critical years.   No other work of Browning's dwells so openly on the plight of a divided nature, the " internal struggles to be one That frittered him incessantly piece-meal ".

> Weeks, months, years went by ;
> And lo, Sordello vanished utterly,
> Sundered in twain ;   each spectral part at strife
> With each ;   one jarred against another life ;
> The Poet thwarting hopelessly the Man . . .

The most obscure of Browning's poems, *Sordello*, is also the most illuminating ;   for it was upon the deepest foundations of his own nature that he erected this remarkable edifice whose labyrinthine architecture seems calculated deliberately to outwit the ingenuity or the perseverance of his readers.   We need not, however, venture very deep into the maze in order to discover that what, at one angle, this elaborate Renaissance front conceals is the conflict between Robert Browning and the age in which he lived. This is typified plainly enough in the relationship of Sordellò to the inhabitants of Mantua. For if Goito, the " slim castle ", is the stronghold of the poetic vision, Mantua, on the other hand, is armed with the whole weight of early Victorian opinion. And to the force of that opinion, its prohibitions as its awards, Browning could not, he found, remain indifferent.

> The obvious if not only shelter lay
> In deeds the dull conventions of his day
> Prescribed the like of him : why not be glad
> 'Tis settled Palma's minstrel, good or bad,
> Submits to this and that established rule ?

Like Sordello, " Born just now—With the new century ", Browning inherited an age of transition : but whereas Sordello emerged from barbarism into the " glow and efflorescence " of the Renaissance, Robert Browning (" Fool, who spied the mark Of leprosy upon him, violet dark Already as he loiters ? "), heir to a revolution, succeeded only to a territory bounded on all sides by reactionary and Evangelical opinion. " To the age of revolt which runs from Rousseau to Shelley succeeds the age of acquiescence ", wrote G. M. Young ; " the Titans are dead or they have been tamed . . ." There is no doubt that in Robert Browning the age produced a Titan of authentic stature : and there is no doubt, too, that the age was successful, if not in taming, at least in partially muzzling him. The question remains. Why did he accept the process ? " Who were The Mantuans, after all, that he should care About their recognition, ay or no ? " But the truth was that he did care : infected, fatally, with the " stain O' the world ", his " will swayed sicklily from side to side ". For if indeed it were nobler, as he felt, to " be unrevealed Than part revealed ", then, accepting a solitary position, he must " leap o'er paltry joys, yearn through The present ill-appreciated stage Of self-revealment and compel the age Know him." Unequal to the austerity of such a course, a single alternative faced him : conformity and all that it implied.

45

better think
Their thoughts and speak their speech, secure to slink
Back expeditiously to his safe place,
And chew the cud—what he and what his race
Were really, each of them.

The bitterness here is outspoken.   For it was by his domestic
virtues, the most amiable qualities of his own nature, that he
was finally and effectively trapped.   Son of Sarah Anna, subject of Victoria, what other choice could he have made ?
Inevitably, compromise became the solution ; and no less
inevitably, compromise exacted its price.   The effect on his
work we may see : the massive effort simultaneously to release
and suppress the sum of his own inspiration—(" let it writhe
Never so fiercely he scarce allowed a tithe to reach the light
—his Language ").   The effect on character ? Faced with
two alternatives, Sordello—Ghibelline by blood, Guelf by
sympathy—finds in death the only release from his predicament.   This was not a solution congenial to the temperament
of Robert Browning.   Tenacious and robust, he lived through
" the ignominious years beyond " : and though he who once
had flung away his youth's chief aims seemed now to barter
his " attributes away for sordid muck ", in reality he redeemed
himself effectively enough from an ignominy of his own
choosing, since, forcing " joy out of sorrow ", it was " from
that very muck " that he managed triumphantly, as he put it,
to " educe Gold ".

But the complete Sordello, Man and Bard,
John's cloud-girt angel, this foot on the land,
That on the sea, with open in his hand
A bitter-sweeting of a book—was gone.

The small house at Craven Hill has long ago been pulled
down : but if bricks and mortar have been reduced to dust,
memories are not so effectively dispersed ; and it is still possible, by refraction, to catch momentarily the impact of a
voice, a smile, a gesture belonging to another age.   Thus we
recover, at varying levels, not only material fragments of the

life at Craven Hill, but a whole sequence, intact at times, of some quite trivial episode ; the very breath and presence, perhaps, of a human personality. " There, I feel like an honest man who earns his bread by the sweat of his brow " : the voice is that of W. J. Fox : back from a day at the office, he takes off his coat and slips into the dressing-gown held up to him by Eliza Flower. Briskly, to a dutiful rattle of applause from the audience, the folding-doors in the sitting-room are pulled apart, and Sarah Flower Adams, wreathed in veils, stands ready to act a scene from *Lord Ullin's Daughter*. One eye tight shut, his manuscript clapped to the other, short-sighted eye, Robert Browning, at the window, sits reading *Paracelsus* to Eliza and Fox, accompanied by the intermittent lowing of cows in the meadow at the end of the garden. There is the sprightly twang of a guitar : " determinedly picturesque " with his dead white complexion and " coxcombical curling whiskers ", Richard Hengist Horne sings sea-shanties to Sarah, tells Eliza long stories of his life in the Mexican Navy or, thrusting his head through the rambling roses at the window, indulges in a prolonged whistling match with Jetty, the tame blackbird.[1] The evenings draw in ; the lamp is lit : Leigh Hunt reads the last page of his play, the *Legend of Florence* ; " free, cheery, idly melodious as bird on bough ", he showers kisses and witticisms on all within reach. A creak of a chair-back, a great " horse laugh ", and there is the pug-nosed John Forster, mimic of the Macready voice, the Macready manner, swinging an eye-glass on a broad black ribbon and turning a glance of admiration on the temperate Eliza Flower. And here, characteristically, is Eliza herself, in the rôle of mediator. Once again, Forster and Browning (always an unstable, an explosive combination of personalities) have quarrelled : unwilling to accept the onus of " making the first advance ", each waits, dignified, for the other to apologise. Effectively, a reference on Eliza's part to " roman-nosed grandeur " punctures the pose, restores to its true proportions a friendship on which Forster, at least, claimed to place " no indifferent value ".

In all these glimpses of life at Craven Hill, one aspect, a

---

[1] In 1877, Horne told Alfred Domett that he, Horne, was sometimes considered to be the original of Browning's *Waring*.

central one, is consistently denied us. No clear light is thrown on the inner nature of the relationship of William Johnson Fox to Eliza Flower. With regard to Fox, we have his biographer's assurance of the purity of that relationship without his analysis of the motives responsible for such abstinence. Why, it may be asked, when Eliza loved Fox " most fervently and tenderly ", and he was aware of her devotion, were they willing, year after year, to endure the penalties of their position without availing themselves of its privileges ? What principally concerns us here, however, is not the emotional predicament of Eliza and Fox, but the effect of an irregular association upon the tender social conscience of the young Robert Browning. For, in contrast to the principle expressed in much of his poetry, (" All or nothing, stake it ! ", " Better sin the whole sin ", etc.) throughout his life the poet himself adhered scrupulously to what he called " the steady symmetries of conventional life ". (It was not the sheltered Elizabeth Barrett Browning, but her husband, who in 1852 avowed himself reluctant to meet, in her company, " the sort of society rampant " about George Sand.) How, then, did he view the ménage at Craven Hill : the association of the man whom he was pleased to call his " literary father " with a woman he had at one time regarded as nothing less than his spiritual mother ? From the fact that he continued to frequent their home, that —more significant—his affection for Fox remained unbroken, we may conclude that he accepted unquestioningly that which Harriet Martineau was ready to doubt : the platonic nature of the relationship. It was of precisely such a relationship that the Fox-Flower circle harboured, at the time, a second, and ultimately more notorious, example. For over twenty years, John Stuart Mill and Harriet Taylor were to drift, somnambulistically linked, between London and its environs : a Victorian Paolo and Francesca, whose sin was not that they were willing to " subject reason to lust " but lust, or its equivalent, to reason. Although they did not, as the years went by, relinquish the motive of their attachment, slowly, " gleam by gleam The glory dropped from their youth and love." Mill appeared to his friends to be " pining away into desiccation and nonentity ", while partially estranged, now, from a tolerant and affectionate husband, Harriet lay on a sofa at Walton-on-Thames, the victim both of a spinal injury and of disease of the lungs. " They are innocent, says Charity ; they are guilty, says Scandal : then why in the name of wonder are they dying broken-hearted ? " The query is Thomas Carlyle's : the theme, it may be said, that of *The Statue and the Bust* : and since the gossip of literary circles cannot have failed to reach Browning's ears, one is led to wonder if it was not, perhaps, of this ironic waste of youth and life—" the lip's red charm . . . the blood that blues the inside arm "—that Browning was thinking when, a few years after Mill had finally married his Harriet—middle-aged, now, and a confirmed invalid—he published in *Men and Women* this moral fable of the " Unlit lamp and the ungirt loin ". *De te, fabula !* For in the life of the poet a similar peril had been narrowly enough averted. All the seeds of it lay in his original offer to Elizabeth Barrett, to marry her, and be to her " no more than one of your brothers ". There was, indeed, a strong similarity between the rôle played by Elizabeth Barrett and that by Harriet Taylor : frail women, both, they shared not only the same physical disabilities, but an identical influence over the men they loved. " I do, dearest, feel confident that while I am in your mind—cared for, rather than thought about—no great harm can happen to me ", wrote Robert Browning : while John Stuart Mill, describing his wife as a " sort of talisman ", confessed that he felt " as if no really dangerous illness could actually happen to me while I have her to care for me ". . . .

For nearly five years, from January, 1835, to November, 1839, Eliza Flower may be said to have conducted at Craven Hill something in the nature of a minor *salon*. But if the presence of Count D'Orsay at Gore House did not impair the more glittering activities of Lady Blessington, the " peculiar and delicate relation " (as James Martineau had it) of Fox to Eliza had the effect of restricting her, socially at least, to the margins of contemporary life. It is a testimony, then, to some exceptional quality in both Eliza and Fox alike, that throughout the ten or eleven years of their public association, their hearth remained so constant a centre of political and literary activity. And as such, it played in the life of Robert Browning a rôle whose importance cannot be exaggerated. It is possible to say that every significant contact, social or professional, that Browning made in London between the publication of *Paracelsus* and his marriage to Elizabeth Barrett is to be traced back, by one way or another, to the house at Craven Hill. Leigh Hunt, R. H. Horne, John Kenyon, Macready, Talfourd, Forster, Mrs. Jameson, B. W. Procter, Carlyle, Harriet Martineau, Fanny Haworth—the ramifications are many, but the root is always the same. Little wonder, then, that a quarter of a century later, writing to Fox, and moved, still, by the " old gratitude and loyalty ", Browning should dwell so insistently on that which he had every reason to remember —" the good and kind hand you extended over my head how many years ago ! "

But good and kind as were the intentions of his patron, the immediate effect upon the poet was beneficial neither to his work nor to his character. In marked contrast to the life— " so pure, so energetic, so simple, so laborious, so loftily enthusiastic "—that the young man led under his parents' roof at Camberwell or at New Cross, is the manner of his existence in London during those years in which, night after night, in the wake of Macready, he was to be found haunting the stage-doors and dressing-rooms of Covent Garden, the Haymarket or Drury Lane. There is no sadder or less credit-able phase in his early life than that which saw the steady degeneration of the relationship between him and Macready : the long history of frustration and exacerbated vanity that lay between Macready's approval, in 1836, of the young poet's " simple and enthusiastic manner " and his no less whole-hearted dismissal of him in 1843 as a " very disagreeable and offensively mannered person ". Nor is it possible, in this connection, choleric and over-sensitive as he undoubtedly was, to lay the whole weight of the blame upon Macready. A man, in Carlyle's opinion, of " scrupulous veracity, correct-ness, integrity ", his difficulties were many. It was at his suggestion that Browning had written, in 1837, his first tragedy for the theatre : and struggling now to levitate, as best he could, the dense unactable mass of *Strafford*, exhausting both his " spirits and strength " in the attempt, he was determined that " *coûte que coûte* " as he wrote, Browning should not " have the power of saying that I acted otherwise than as a true friend to his feelings ". Browning's feelings, however, were not so easily assuaged : driven by a " sickly and fretful over-estimate of his own work ", he followed Macready about, expressing an " irritable impatience " with every defect of the play's production, or summarily demanding that the actor restore to the text an entire scene which he himself had pre-viously agreed to delete. Looking " very unwell, jaded and thought-sick ", he hurried backwards and forwards between Covent Garden and Lincoln's Inn Fields, complaining, to John Forster of Macready's bad faith : and to Macready, of John Forster's bad temper. By the time *Strafford* was produced, the poet was emphatic in his determination that he would " never write a play again " as long as he lived. After which, to our surprise, two months later we discover him once more in the throes of " thinking a Tragedy ". In 1839, the manu-script of that tragedy was in Macready's hands. This second play of Browning's, *King Victor and King Charles*, deficient as it may be in dramatic tone, is of considerable interest as a study in a father-son relationship : a situation, moreover, in which " the extreme and painful sensibility, prolonged immaturity of powers . . . and vacillating will " of the son, is corrected, in marriage, by the " noble and right woman's manliness of his wife ". (With regard to the poet's choice of such a subject—the persecution of a weak son by a brutal and unscrupulous father—it is curious to observe that Browning, whose father can without exaggeration be described as the mildest and most unaggressive of men, was all his life as sensitive to tyranny, to what he called the " execrable policy of the world's husbands, fathers, brothers and domineerers in general ", as if he had suffered under a father of the " fiery and audacious temper, unscrupulous selfishness " of King Victor himself.) Macready read the play : in his opinion, the whole thing was, he said, " a *great mistake* ". He declined to produce it ; as he subsequently declined *The Return of the Druses*, an involved drama in which a weight of his-torical matter overlays and effectively smothers the subtlety of the central situation. (" Read Browning's play," wrote Macready, " and with the deepest concern, I yield to the belief that he will *never write again*—to any purpose. I fear his intellect is not quite clear.") And indeed a smoke screen,

as dense at times as in *Sordello,* is laid between the public and
the motives of characters who, while adhering secretly to the
rites of their own faith, are permitted " to make outward
profession of whatever religion is dominant around them ".
Browning, however, was so convinced of the merit of his play
that he refused to accept Macready's decision. Again and
again he returned to the attack : in the privacy of his own
bathroom the actor was not free from the expostulating voice.
" Browning came before I had finished my bath," he wrote
plaintively on August 27th, " and really *wearied* me with his
obstinate faith in his poem of *Sordello,* and of his eventual
celebrity, and also with his self-opinionated persuasions upon
his *Return of the Druses.*" [1] Such an exhibition on the part of
a young and neglected writer is pardonable enough : what is
less easy to accept is the burden of the entry that follows.
" He speaks of Mr. Fox (who would have been delighted and
proud in the ability to praise him) in a very unkind manner,
and imputes motives to him which on the mere surface seem
absurd." If the revelation disconcerts, it is because it is
uncharacteristic, wholly, of a generous nature. And indeed,
Browning's conduct during those years in which, as he confessed, he saw " monstrously ambitious thoughts begin to rise
like clouds within me ", is so manifestly at variance with the
normal tenor of his life, that one is led to suspect that on the
evening when he met Macready at Craven Hill he suffered,
in the contact, a secret flare-up of all those old schemes for
self-aggrandisement first ignited by Edmund Kean on the
night of October 22, 1832.

But the life of the theatre, however absorbing, did not
engage his entire creative activity, and in 1842, between the
publication of *King Victor and King Charles* and the *Dramatic
Lyrics,* Browning found time to write, at the request of John
Forster, the only prose work other than the essay on Shelley
which is now to be attributed to him. This article, whose
re-discovery in the pages of the *Foreign Quarterly Review* we
owe to the vigilance of Professor Smalley, is headed only by

---

[1] Forty-one years later, Browning was asked by Irving to write him a play in
verse. " I have just answered his letter ", Browning told Gosse. " I have said
that it is very kind of him, very civil and all that, but that if he wants to act a
play of mine, there is *The Return of the Druses* ready waiting for him."

Robert Browning, 1855, a painting by D. G. Rossetti

The Guardian Angel by Guercino

the name of the book under review : *Conjectures and Researches concerning the Love Madness and Imprisonment of Torquato Tasso* by Richard Henry Wilde. Seven paragraphs are allotted to the problem of Tasso ; after which the main body of the article is devoted to a train of thought provoked by quite another book : the new Willcox edition of the works of Thomas Chatterton. " All these disputed questions in the lives of men of genius," wrote Browning, " —all these so-called calamities of authors—have a common relationship, a connexion so close and inalienable, that they seldom fail to throw important light upon each other." The truth of this statement is demonstrated, effectively, in an essay which throws a revealing light, not upon " the marvellous Boy " alone, but upon the motives and conduct of his self-appointed advocate. In this essay, Chatterton, Professor Smalley writes, " is for the first time defended in the courts of evangelical Christianity " : and it is there, in defence of the youth who " sold, Esau-like, his birthright—the vision and the faculty divine—for a mess of pottage ", that Browning has elected simultaneously to plead his own case with that of his client. There, in an attempt to prove that " poor Chatterton's life was not the Lie it is so universally supposed to have been ", and to mitigate the enormity of the Rowleian forgeries, Browning dwells at length on the need of every poet to obtain " a free way for impulses that can find vent in no other channel " ; and goes on to affirm that " so instinctively does the Young Poet feel that his desire for this kind of self-enfranchisement will be resisted as a matter of course, that we will venture to say, in nine cases out of ten his first assumption of the license will be made in a borrowed name ". Or anonymously, perhaps, as in the case of the author of *Pauline*, whose ambition, like Chatterton's, was " to assume and realise I know not how many different characters :—meanwhile the world was never to guess that . . . the respective authors of this poem, the other novel, such an opera, such a speech, etc., etc., were no other than one and the same individual ". If Browning had, thus, an intuitive understanding of Chatterton's need for imposture, it was a knowledge gained from the experience of one forced, spiritually, to lead a double life ; a knowledge put to work alike in his portrait of Djabal, the false messiah, and of Sludge, the false medium.[1] " It is old as the world itself," he wrote, " the tendency of certain spirits to subdue each man by perceiving what will master him, by straightway supplying it from their own resources, and so obtaining, as tokens of success, his admiration, or fear, or wonder." (This is the same Robert Browning who, having unmasked a perfidious woman and thereby " gained a victory " which " was as easy to me as ' kiss my hand ' ", added, revealingly: " Well, I like *knowing*, at any price : also I like the power that comes of it.") What, however, Browning is mainly concerned to do in this essay, is to demonstrate Chatterton's genuine desire to free himself from " the falsehood of the mediocre " and let " true works . . . silently take the place of false works ". His aim is to prove, conclusively, that the young poet " really made the most gallant and manly effort of which his circumstances allowed to break through the sorry meshes that entangled him". The adolescent boy, he clearly felt, was trammelled much as he himself had been. " All his distress ", wrote Browning compassionately, " arose out of the impossibility of his saying any thing to the real purpose." It is only, however, when Chatterton's self-inflicted death is described in terms of a struggle between his " intellectual " and his " moral " nature, that there is brought home to us the fact that once again, as in *Paracelsus*, as in *Sordello*, as in *The Return of the Druses*, what Robert Browning has chosen to investigate in the tragedy of Thomas Chatterton is the basic, the always unresolved problem of his own inner life.

4

" Our old wooden Battersea bridge takes me over the river ; in ten minutes' swift trotting I am fairly away from the monster and its bricks. All lies behind me like an enormous world-filling *pfluister*, infinite potter's furnace, sea of smoke, with steeples, domes, gilt crosses, high black architecture swimming in it. . . . I fly away, away, some half dozen

[1] In 1885, at their first meeting with him, the Michael Fields were struck by the " strange admiration " which the aged poet professed for Chatterton.

miles out. . . ." The rider is Thomas Carlyle : and it is for
Camberwell, home of his new acquaintance, Robert Browning,
that he is at that moment bound. Mounted on his mare
Citoyenne, he trots along, emerging gradually from " an
infinite Cockneydom of *stoor* and din " into the peace and
silence of a world lying " green, musical, bright " under a
pure sky. This contrast between the city and its environs
reinforces vividly the distinction between the turmoil of
Browning's life in London, and the tranquillity of his days at
Camberwell or New Cross. It was, perhaps, because Carlyle
had been privileged to see him in the circumstances of his
home life, that during those very years in which the poet's
reputation was declining amongst his other friends (" met
Mrs. Procter," wrote Macready, " and talked long with her
about Browning, of whom she and all think as I do ") his
presence at Cheyne Row was always regarded as a " pleasant
phenomenon ".

The phenomenon, it is true, was more pleasing to the host
than to the hostess. Jane Welsh Carlyle, (who might have
shared, with Mrs. Procter, the title of " our Lady of Bitterness "), shared also perhaps with her the opinion that what
the young man lacked was " seven or eight hours a day of
occupation ". An inexplicable hostility had early established
itself between Browning and the wife of Thomas Carlyle.[1]
Mrs. Carlyle, it seems, suspected the poet's integrity ; (" I
wouldn't give sixpence ", she said, " for his regard for me ");
and she considered him, in spite of his cleverness, " a considerable of a ' fluff of feathers ' ". Browning, on the other hand,
who was ready to overlook the " extraordinary limitations "
of his " dear old friend ", was not prepared to be so indulgent
to the failings of " his ' woman ' " ; and the poet who once,
in the middle of a dinner party, got up and strode from the
house because a friend of his had spoken brusquely to his
wife, appears in this case to have regarded Thomas, and not
Jane, as the true martyr of the marriage. There could be
no greater proof of the depth of his attachment to Carlyle
than this determined partiality. The attachment was compounded equally " of love and gratitude ". " Your friend-

[1] " No, you would not have liked her much," Browning told the Michael
Fields in 1889. " She would have tried to pick holes in you."

ship ", he wrote to Carlyle, " will always seem, as it does now, enough to have lived for." For forty years this attitude persisted : and one cannot but contemplate with curiosity the spectacle presented : the prolonged hero-worship on the part of an energetic optimist for a no less confirmed and vociferous pessimist. What, one wonders, was the motive force of this incongruously-geared relationship ? Certainly not sympathy of outlook : no views could have been more calculated to outrage the susceptibilities of Robert Browning than those advanced by a man so " abundantly contemptuous ", John Stuart Mill said, " of all who make their intellects bow to their moral timidity by endeavouring to believe Christianity ". Nor could Browning, with his deep-laid hatred of tyranny, have shared Carlyle's philosophy, his predilection for " Power —irresistible and eternal Power ". On what, then, was the admiration based ? Conscious as Browning always was of his own secession, did he admire the older man for rejecting compromise, and pronouncing, fearlessly, the darker side of the human predicament ? It was, perhaps, because he saw in Carlyle's attitude the mirror-image of his own that he felt so closely, so peculiarly bound to him. (Both shared, inescapably, the impress of a Scottish, an evangelical mother.)[1] Like Leigh Hunt, Browning " knew what honey there was in the jaws of Samson's lion " ; of such stuff, he too recognised, the man's " inner nature was altogether made ". As for Carlyle, who had begun by disliking Browning for his smart green riding-coat and the " element of Charles Lambism, British-Museum Classicality and other Cockney encumbrances " in which he dwelt, it was not long before the philosopher—poet *manqué*—discovered in the friendship of the poet who was, no less, certainly a philosopher *manqué*, alleviation from some of the sterner rigours of his own company. Browning was one of those men who could successfully " unwrap the baleful Nessus shirt of perpetual pain and isolation " in which all his life, " lamed, embated, and swathed as in enchantment ",

---

[1] Carlyle's religious scepticism caused his mother to lie " awake at night for hours praying and weeping bitterly ". *Cf.* Browning's " momentous " discovery, under similar circumstances, that " the soul is above and behind the intellect, which is merely its servant ", with Carlyle's doctrine that the " healthy Understanding . . . is not the logical, argumentative, but the Intuitive ; for the end of Understanding is not to prove and find reasons, but to know and believe ".

Carlyle had struggled. Pleasingly, then, between the years 1839 and 1846, we may see the poet descending from his Surrey hills in order to play the rôle of David to Carlyle's gaunt and pain-racked Saul. Arriving at Cheyne Row, he would find the philosopher, wrapped in a plaid dressing-gown, wrestling " drear and stark " with the evil spirits of melancholia and dyspepsia ; spirits that were exorcised readily enough by the warmth and generosity of Browning's affection. It was a feat worth performing. Restored to equanimity, Carlyle would talk " *constringingly, bracingly* " on the topics of the day, recite couplets from an old Scottish ballad, or indulge, in discussion of his contemporaries, the brilliant power of verbal caricature which has sketched for us, indelibly, the " short, angry, yet modest nose " of Lord Holland ; the " toothless horseshoe mouth " of Samuel Rogers : outlined Thackeray as a " *big*, fierce, weeping, hungry man ", Monckton Milnes as " a pretty little robin-redbreast ", and Albany Fonblanque, editor of the *Examiner*, as " a long thin flail of a man with wintry, zealous-looking eyes ".

The relationship—the " love and gratitude "—survived the hiatus of Browning's years in Italy. " *When* we go to England again ", wrote the poet, " I shall try and live near you " : and in 1851, arriving in London with wife, child and a " five years' hunger " for the sight of his friend, one of his earliest visits, with Mrs. Browning, was to the Carlyles at Cheyne Row. (" It was a very dull thing indeed," wrote Mrs. Carlyle later—" and I like Browning less and less ; and even *she* does not grow on me.") The death of Mrs. Browning, the residence at Warwick Crescent, brought a resumption of intimacy : for twenty years, the two men, grey-haired now, continued amicably to exchange their books, their opinions and their prejudices. Intellectually, it is true, the rift between them was becoming daily more pronounced. As talkative as Carlyle himself, Browning was no longer prepared to accept, without protest, the more dogmatic assertions of his " venerated friend ". Throughout the greatest provocation, however, his affection remained unimpaired : and—" If he were standing here before me—I'd hug the old man ! " he once exclaimed. An old man, indeed, Carlyle already was. In his eighties now, day by day, perceptibly, the desire to live was leaving him : and this celebrated insomniac (who once said of sick children that what " they so want, I suppose, is to get to sleep well on their mother's bosom ") now spent his days dozing against the cushions of his brougham, or lying remote and silent on a sofa in the drawing-room at Cheyne Row. (" Ah, Mother, is it you ? " he was heard to murmur when a hand touched his.)   One wintry day Browning received the message that Carlyle would " like to see him once more ". He went at once to Cheyne Row.   It was the last time he was to do so.   The door was opened to him by Mary Carlyle : a niece of the philosopher's.   She told me, Robert Browning said, that her uncle " was not speaking to any one, but I might go up and see him.   He was lying on a sofa, wrapt in a shawl. I stooped over him and said a word or two, and he put an arm round my neck.   That was all."

5

Upon the fly-leaf of a copy, in an American edition, of Carlyle's *Sartor Resartus*, there stands the inscription *Robert Browning, Esq. from H. Martineau, July 10th, 1837*.   If the date does not mark the inauguration of the friendship so recorded, the latter cannot, by all accounts, have been more than a few weeks old : for Harriet Martineau tells us that she first read *Paracelsus* at Macready's house, spending the whole night, in consequence, " without sleeping a wink " : and Macready, in turn, informs us that the occasion of this exalted insomnia was the night of June 5th–6th, 1837.   Miss Martineau's enthusiasm for the poem, says Professor Griffin, " led her to seek its author's acquaintance through Fox, their common friend ".   But here, surely, the admirable Griffin errs.   Fox, it is true, introduced Browning into a circle where such an encounter was possible ; but he could not himself have made the introduction, since, from 1834, when she went to America, until 1846, when the death of Eliza Flower removed the obstacle, Harriet Martineau expressed an unrelenting disapproval of the ménage at Craven Hill by refusing all personal contact with her former friend and benefactor.   It was, then, to Macready that Robert

Browning owed this friendship ; as he owed to him a more protracted relationship with Macready's neighbour, the mildly aspiring, mildly endowed Euphrasia Fanny Haworth. Eliza Flower had long receded from her original position in the life of the poet : it is at this point that her successors emerge, reticently to claim the distinction of being the only female figures, other than those of his mother and sister, to occupy the curiously deserted landscape of Browning's emotional life in the interval between the publication of *Paracelsus* and his first meeting, ten years later, with the woman who was to become his wife.

It is instructive to compare the temperate tone of these relationships with the uninhibited warmth of his male friendships. No woman, at this time, was capable of rousing in him the deep emotional regard he felt for Alfred Domett, for Thomas Carlyle, or for his cousin James Silverthorne : nor were his relationships with women agitated by those violent reversals of feeling, from the most exaggerated loyalty to the most unrestrained resentment, that characterised his friendship with Macready and with John Forster. We have seen that the poet confined himself in early life to the company of women older than himself : it is possible further to observe his preference for women invested already with the attributes of their own future spinsterhood. (Eliza Flower did not marry : nor did Harriet Martineau, or Fanny Haworth.) It was only, it seems, under the guarantee of sexual neutrality that he felt free to accept the privileges of a feminine friendship. And Harriet Martineau, ten years his senior, deficient " in three senses out of five ", presented to the world a buoyant sexlessness whose candour disarmed the most prejudiced. Overburdened as she professed herself to be by the Teutonic weight of his metaphysics, she was relieved to find that in conversation " no speaker could be more absolutely clear and purpose-like " : a fact confirmed by Crabb Robinson, who pronounced this notoriously " crazy poet " to be " a sensible man in prose conversation ". (Only at the level of poetic creation did genius, strangulated, wrestle despairingly with some powerful and residual inhibition). Miss Martineau enjoyed Browning's company, and confided the fact to her diary. Appreciating as she did the " good sense and fine feeling " of the young man, she was ready to make allowances for the " occasional irritability " which she also observed : while certain " little affectations " of his provoked, irresistibly, what Samuel Rogers once called " the freshest laugh you could hear out of a nursery ". Between two o'clock and four o'clock every afternoon, she was at home to visitors in the small house in Fludyer Street which she shared, to the detriment of her own nervous stability, with a domineering mother, an ageing aunt and an inebriate brother. In her little sitting-room, which afforded her a view of less conscientious members of society lolling idly at the windows of the Foreign Office, she would patch the household linen, or darn her own black stockings ; over the needles and cottons offering to young Mr. Browning her considered advice upon his " worldly concerns "—(" and not ", he said gratefully, " before I need it "). It was December, 1837 : a lively fire crackled in the grate : under brown hair dressed low on her brow, Harriet Martineau's face bore a " gentle and motherly " expression. Only a few hours before, she had written the final sentence in her three volume book, *Retrospect of Western Travel* ; and it was, consequently, in a relaxed and tranquil mood that she was able now to pour out tea for her visitor, and discuss with him the favourite literature of her own childhood. A sequel to this conversation, a few days later Robert Browning sent her, as she records in her diary, *Robinson Crusoe* : " an original copy, very venerable." [1] Miss Martineau was delighted : " I am going to sit down to it and be a child again," she wrote. A week or two went by, and the poet was once more in Fludyer Street. Drawing his chair close to hers, he confided to the ear-trumpet (that his powerful voice might well have rendered superfluous) his difficulties in the composition of *Sordello*. Was it wise, he wanted to know, to deny the reader the aid of preface and notes ? He must choose between being historian or poet : the danger lay in splitting the interest. Harriet Martineau advised him to " let the poem tell its own tale " : a critical boomerang that returned home to roost when *Sordello* was published, and Miss Martineau found herself so " wholly unable to understand it," that, she confessed, " I supposed myself ill." Meanwhile, however,

[1] On April 10th, 1837, Mr. Browning gave his son a copy of *The Life and Strange Surprizing Adventures of Robinson Cruso*, published in 1719.

under the impression that the much-discussed poem was on its way to completion, she did her best to engage on its behalf the good-will of other writers and critics. Robert Browning was invited to dine at Fludyer Street to meet Chorley, of the *Athenaeum*, and John Robertson, Mill's assistant on the *Westminster Review*. Henry Fothergill Chorley, described by his hostess as "the most complete specimen of the literary adventurer of our time", was a mannered young bachelor who compensated for the lack of feminine interest in his life by a prolonged and deferential attendance on the buxom Lady Blessington. Looking across the dining-room table at the odd, nervous, red-haired young man, Robert Browning would have been surprised to be told that he was facing not only, as he thought, a potential reviewer, but a future trustee to his own marriage settlement. For a warm friendship developed between the two men, which lasted, with one major hiatus, until 1872, when, in a coffin lined with cedar branches from the garden of Dickens's house at Gad's Hill, this strangely pathetic, strangely thwarted "literary adventurer" went to his grave, leaving all he possessed to the young nephew and namesake of the man ("my one true friend") whose loss all these years he had never ceased to mourn.

In marked contrast to the sensitive Chorley was John Robertson, former cooper's assistant, a "burly Aberdeen Scotsman, full of laughter, vanity, pepticity, and hope". An admirer of *Paracelsus*, he was eager to welcome its successor : and flattered by this attention, Browning kept him informed of the progress of the poem. It was Robertson that he hoped to see when he called at Fludyer Street on April 11th, 1838, two days before leaving for Italy ; and he was disappointed, on that occasion, to find with his hostess only that "polite, good, quiet man", Erasmus Darwin. It was Robertson, too, that the poet wrote to on the morning that he sailed, in order to inform him of the purpose of his journey ; which is, he said, "to finish my poem among the scenes it describes". There was good reason for this assiduity, since the young editor of the *Westminster Review* had promised "careful attention" for the new poem when it appeared. Prematurely, however, he demanded prior rights in reading and reviewing which Browning felt unable to grant : a refusal that offended not only

Robertson, but Harriet Martineau as well. There are no more records of the poet's visits to the household at Fludyer Street : and indeed, only a few months later, that household itself was suddenly and radically dismantled. Under the " extreme tension of nerves " produced by the life-long domination of a selfish mother, Harriet Martineau had collapsed. Carried to Tynemouth, for five years, a protracted lie-down strike, she remained on her " couch of pain ", awakened, nightly, by vivid dreams that her mother had " fallen from a precipice, or over the bannisters, or from a cathedral spire ". It was during this, the " passive phase " of her existence, that she entered into a correspondence with another initiate of the sick-room : as familiar as herself both with " the intense enjoyment of pleasures independent of the body ", and, enhancing these, the " lazy, hot ease of opiates ". Earnestly, she exhorted Elizabeth Barrett, (who had " long been a believer, *in spite of papa* "), to submit her case to mesmerism ; and with a fascinated reluctance, Elizabeth Barrett—" the most excitable person in the world, and nearly the most superstitious "—declined the experiment on the grounds that it must imperil the stability of one born, as she said, " with a double set of nerves, which are always out of order ! "

During the months that Robert Browning was calling at Wimpole Street, Elizabeth Barrett was disturbed from time to time by rumours of the poet's association with other women. A Miss Heaton, of Leeds, fixed her large black eyes on the invalid one afternoon, and informed her that a " friend of hers who had known Mr. Browning *quite intimately*, had told her that he was an infidel " : and when Miss Barrett, " a little more warmly, perhaps, than was necessary ", questioned her on the subject of this " intimate friend ", Miss Heaton was able to furnish her with the news that " her informant about Mr. Browning ... was a lady *to whom he had been engaged* " ; adding that " there had been a very strong attachment on both sides, but that everything was broken off by *her* on the grounds of religious differences—that it happened years ago and that the lady was married ". Confronted with this statement, Robert

Browning found it necessary to seek through " the favourable dimness and illusion of ' a good many years ago ' " in order to furnish Miss Heaton's story with " a local habitation and name ". Despite the fact that Miss Heaton was also a friend of Fanny Haworth's (with whom she later set up house), the attempt can have led him, as it leads us, to one source only ; for at no time could Browning have been described as an " infidel " except in the years when he was visiting the Flower sisters at Dalston ; and since, as we are told, the lady in question subsequently married, it becomes plain enough that this disclosure of an early and interrupted intimacy originated, characteristically indeed, not with Eliza, but with her less reticent and more volatile sister, Sarah Flower Adams. Only a few weeks later, however, gossip had it that " Mr. Browning was to be married immediately to Miss Campbell " : and this time, angrily disclaiming all knowledge of Miss Campbell, Browning was able to inform Elizabeth Barrett that in one case only might his friendship with a woman have afforded substance for such gossip : and that, he said, " to avoid mistake ", was in the case of Miss Haworth.

Euphrasia Fanny Haworth, Mrs. Orr would have us believe, shares with her friend Harriet Martineau a measure of responsibility for some of the more singular obscurities of the pervadingly obscure *Sordello*. For it was she, so tradition has it, who brought to the attention of the poet John Sterling's censure of the " verbosity " of *Paracelsus* : a censure which, conveyed to her in a letter from Caroline Fox, and communicated in turn to Robert Browning, produced in him such a " dread of being diffuse ", that, using henceforward " two words where he would rather have used ten ", he evolved that " chinese-like condensation of style " that was to baffle the wits and exhaust the patience of readers for generations to come. A pretty story, in its way. Since, however, John Sterling did not meet Caroline Fox until the middle of February, 1840, and *Sordello* was published a few weeks later, it is difficult to see how his comments can have influenced, appreciably, the composition of the poem. *Sordello* was seven - years in the making : in as many weeks it had become what, largely, it has since remained : a subject for literary witticism ; and of this, Mrs. Carlyle's statement, that she had read the poem through without discovering whether Sordello was a man, a city or a book, may be taken as sufficient example. Miss Haworth, however, would admit no blemish in the virtue of this unique poem, over the progress of which, since 1836, she had in a sense presided : and smarting, still, under the barbs of his critics, Browning was avowedly grateful for so emollient a response. " You say roses and lilies and lilac-bunches and lemon-flowers about it," he wrote, " while everybody else pelts cabbage stumps after potato parings." Timidly, nevertheless, she was driven to ask him to explain the reference to her at the close of book three, where, cryptically, she is addressed as " My English Eyebright "—the latter being, said the poet, " a simple and sad sort of translation of ' Euphrasia ' into my own language ". It was only by the licence of poetry, however, that he presumed thus to address her ; and in a relationship conducted otherwise wholly in terms of prose, this very English Eyebright was to remain for close on fifty years the formal Miss Haworth of her first introduction to the poet. This took place early in 1836 in Macready's house at Elstree. Robert Browning was then twenty-four, and Miss Haworth, remote already from " the flush of my spring-time hopes ", was in her thirty-sixth year. Nathaniel Hawthorne has described her as " a mature demoiselle, rather plain, but with an honest and intelligent face enough " : her talk, he wrote in 1853, " was sensible, but not particularly brilliant or interesting ;—a good, solid personage, physically and intellectually ". Sitting on the lawn at Elm Place, or strolling with Macready, his children and the dogs round the reservoir at Elstree, they discussed the poetry and drama of the day : Miss Haworth, it emerged, wrote poetry herself, and illustrated, in lithograph or line, her own verse and that of her contemporaries. She lived with her parents in an Elizabethan house at Barham Wood, where Mr. Haworth devoted himself to the pursuit of toxophily, and his wife—" an empty vessel," sighed Macready—elected to entertain her guests with psychic phenomena : (" lobster salad ", on one occasion, combined with " Oremus, spirit of the sun "). Small wonder, then, that " from this dreary weight of worldliness " as she put it—from an environment in which her own preoccupation with the arts was dismissed as one of " Fanny's crotchets "—the daughter of the family should turn with pleasure to the resources of this new friendship that was offered her. Her own talent was of the slightest ; but there is no doubt that she recognised the full stature of " the author of *Paracelsus*," to whom, under that title, she addressed two sonnets in the *New Monthly Magazine* of September, 1836. Did Browning communicate to her his own sense of being under-valued by his contemporaries ? " Perchance ", she wrote, " his musing spirit is the guest Of future ages, who shall prize him best." The suggestion was an attractive one : and in virtue of her faith in him, as of an overt maturity that accom-panied, reassuringly, the diffuse sensibilities of the artistic temperament, Fanny Haworth became over the years the correspondent, the confidante, the friend, even the " dear friend of mine " whose function Robert Browning was sum-marily to disavow in the moment when he addressed Elizabeth Barrett as " my dear, first and last friend ". But nine years were to elapse, almost to the day, before those words were written : and meanwhile it was to Miss Haworth, of Elstree, that the poet's letters were addressed : it was to her that he confided his literary projects ; with her that he discussed the problems and the pleasures of composition : the technical difficulties of one who could, as he said, " tie and untie English as a Roman girl a tame serpent's tail ". The critical standard of his " gentle audience " was not, however, always satisfactory to the poet : nor was the warmth of her admiration sufficient compensation for a " sad trick " as he described it, " of admiring at the wrong place—enough to make an apostle swear ". That she was conscious of her own inadequacy, we may gather from the second of the two sonnets addressed to Robert Browning, in which, confessing herself " unskill'd wholly to comprehend Thy scope of genius ", she begged of him no " splendours ", but the simple permission to " call thee *Friend* ". It is sufficient, today, to glance at the limpid in-sipidities of her published verse to see how very shallow was the soil in which, in order, as he said, to take " away my reproach among men ", Robert Browning endeavoured, like " each and all ", to cultivate a sentimental friendship. Endeavoured without success : neither morally nor intellectu-ally could Fanny Haworth be considered " better than my-self " ; between them that essential " disproportionateness in

a beloved object " which was to him the very law and condition of love, did not exist.   Unskill'd wholly to comprehend
Robert Browning's scope of genius, Miss Haworth was equally
incapable of inspiring the sense of worship which, in his case,
must precede and accompany love.   And frustrated once
again in his attempt to discover the necessary dimensions
in a relationship, the man who could love only " from
beneath, far beneath " was forced, conclusively this time,
to make up his mind " to the impossibility of loving any
woman ".

It was in this conviction, with " a mind set in ultimate
order ", as he thought, " for the few years more ", that Robert
Browning made his second journey to Italy.   He had first set
foot in that country six years before ; and the contrast in
mood and purpose between the journey of 1838 and that of
1844 is as striking as it is significant.   In 1838, Browning was
still enjoying the literary reputation and the social enlargement
that followed upon W. J. Fox's skilful exploitation of *Paracelsus* :
he had in preparation a companion piece which he hoped
would sustain, if it did not surpass, the reputation built by the
earlier poem.   It was, therefore, on a rising tide of self-
confidence (technically, a member of the freighting party in
charge of a " *locomotive* entire " that Rothschild was sending
" with all its appurtenances " to Trieste), that he sailed from
St. Katherine's docks on the afternoon of Good Friday, April 13,
1838.   Seven weeks later, the poet was sitting " on a ruined
palace-step " in Venice surveying a scene encountered previously in the poetry of Shelley, who, like Browning himself,
was twenty-six years old on the occasion of his first visit to
that city.   Inevitably, the newcomer was seduced by the
beauty of " temples and palaces " which seemed " Like fabrics
of enchantment piled to heaven " ; as he was stirred by the
suggestion of a world, gondola-borne, of passion and intrigue,
a world reflected, poignantly, in the music of a *toccata* of
Galuppi's, which on summer evenings he heard whistled or
sung at every street corner in Venice.   (" It is all to the tune
of the Toccata of Galuppi," wrote Florence Nightingale, who,

with her family, had arrived in Italy three or four months before Robert Browning).[1] But the beauty of the city did not blind him to the condition of its inhabitants. " I had no conception ", wrote Shelley on October 8, 1818, " of the excess to which avarice, cowardice, superstition, ignorance, passionless lust, and all the inexpressible brutalities which degrade human nature, could be carried, until I had passed a few days in Venice." Twenty years later, Venice was to provoke an equally vivid reaction in another young poet : one who, stifling within himself his " youth's chief aims ", had hitherto

> Preferred elaborating in the dark
> My casual stuff, by any wretched spark
> Born of my predecessors, though one stroke
> Of mine had brought the flame forth !

Now, the sight of " the whole poor-devildom one sees cuffed and huffed from morn to midnight " served, as he said, " to prick up my republicanism and remind me of certain engagements I have entered into with myself about that same " : and, the stifled flame bursting forth anew, Browning decided to make a love for suffering humanity become, thenceforward, the motivating force in Sordello's life.

But if Venice left its mark upon the composition of *Sordello*, Asolo—" one step just from sea to land "—was to produce an enduring impression upon the poet himself. Robert Browning had gone to Italy in order " to finish my poem among the scenes it describes ". He did not expect, amongst those scenes, to find the wholly subjective Goito ; the slim tower, hill-encircled, which, a symbol of the poetic vision, was also a symbol of the " still life I led, apart from all," before contact with the world of men had caused him " to turn My mind against itself". But when, arriving on foot from Venice, he " first found out Asolo ", it seemed to him that he had walked straight into the country of his own creative experience. For

---

[1] This tune—" What the children were singing last year in Venice, arm over neck " is how Browning refers to it—was set down for the benefit of Miss Haworth in a letter of April, 1839. It appears on p. 17 of the *New Letters of Robert Browning*, where the musical expert is cordially invited to identify it.

there, in the small hill-city, amongst encircling hills, he found
the ancient walls of the palace in which Queen Caterina
Cornaro, like his own Adelaide at Goito, had held, in exile,
her " graceful, poetic little court ".   The tower ; the dungeons,
the walls overgrown with wild flowers and weeds " made
gradually up The picture "—

>   'twas Goito's mountain-cup
> And castle . . .
> Ah, the slim castle ! dwindled of late years,
> But more mysterious ; gone to ruin—trails
> Of vine through every loop-hole.

And with this act of recognition, " Back rushed the dream,
enwrapped him wholly."   For three days, Browning wandered
about the court of Queen Caterina ; he mused in solitude
upon the Asolan hills that served to elevate him " far, far
above " those living in the plain beneath : for three days,
bathed, like Sordello, in " the fantastic glow of his Apollo-
life ", " inspiration seemed to steam up from the very ground ",
while—" Terror with beauty "—on every side the young poet
saw before him " the Bush Burning but unconsumed ".

For forty years after that experience, Robert Browning
" used to dream of seeing Asolo in the distance and making
vain attempts to reach it—repeatedly dreamed this for many
a year ".   In waking life, he made no effort to return there.
As if some intolerable memory or association lay in wait for
him in this " my very own of all Italian towns ", he turned
his face from Asolo, to sojourn precisely forty years in the
wilderness before he permitted himself a second glimpse of
the promised land.

Very different from the exaltation of that first journey was
the mood in which the poet disembarked at Naples in the
autumn of 1844.   He was then thirty-two years old.   In the
interval between his two Italian journeys he had witnessed the
resounding failure of *Sordello* : the repeated frustration of his
own ambition to write for the theatre : the " blight ", as he felt
it to be, which " had fallen upon his very admirers ".   That
he suffered socially as well as emotionally from these set-backs
is evident in the letters written at this time to Alfred Domett ;

Elizabeth Barrett Browning and 'Pen'—
Robert Wiedeman Barrett Browning,
Rome, 1860

Robert Browning, Rome

Robert Browning, Rome, May 22, 1859, from a portrait by
Rudolf Lehmann

(letters which he likens to mere scratches ; to so many kickings of the feet " such as those by which John Lilburne ' signified his meaning' when they gagged his jaws at the pillory " ; Browning evidently had a strong fellow-feeling for John Lilburne in his plight). Despite the friendly warmth of their tone, the letters betray a persistent undercurrent of apathy, even of despondency. " My own health is none of the best. I go out but seldom . . . So glides this foolish life away ; week by week " . . . " here everything goes flatly on " . . . " I make no new friends " . . . " I am dull, in every sense, this dull evening " . . . " my *head*, which sings and whirls " . . . It was finally because, as he complained, " my head is dizzy and wants change " that he decided, once more, to visit Italy. The journey lasted four months: and of what must have been, psychologically, its capital experience—the visit paid by Robert Browning to the grave of Shelley at Rome—no written record remains. Meagre enough, both poetically and emotionally, is the harvest of this very autumnal excursion—(" The lambent flame is—where ? Lost from the natural world . . . The Bush is bare ")—and out of all that he saw and experienced on this second journey, the poet brought back to England material for a poem or two ; a shell picked up on one of the Syren Isles ; and a sprig of hemlock gathered, in mistake for fennel, at the grotto of Egeria. One important thing, however, he did discover on this occasion—" which is," he wrote a few months later, " that all you gain by travel is the discovery that you have gained nothing, and have done rightly in trusting to your innate ideas—or not done rightly in distrusting them, as the case may be. . . . After this, you go boldly on your own resources, and are justified to yourself, that's all."

In other words, he was back where he had started from. As everything served to remind him. For, restored to the domestic circle at New Cross, it was not so easy to go boldly on his own resources ; and he soon found that the same intimate dissatisfaction which had driven him abroad, had also waited, faithfully, to claim him upon his return. What was the source of that self-dissatisfaction ? A sense of aimlessness ; an inability successfully to co-ordinate and assert the resources of his own personality. Other men, he felt,

had some core
Within, submitted to some moon, before
Them still, superior still whate'er their force,—
Were able therefore to fulfil a course,
Nor missed life's crown, authentic attribute.

What he, in his turn, needed in order to secure that crown
was some

outward influence,
A soul, in Palma's phrase, above his soul,
Power to uplift his power,—this moon's control
Over the sea-depths,—and their mass had swept
Onward from the beginning and still kept
Its course : but years and years the sky above
Held none, and so, untasked of any love,
His sensitiveness idled. . . .
So had Sordello been, by consequence,
Without a function.

A few weeks after his return to England, the poet picked
up from a table at Hatcham two green-covered volumes : the
Poems of Elizabeth Barrett Barrett. Published while Browning
was out of the country, these volumes had created an immediate
impression. Between the poetry of Miss Barrett, wrote one
critic, " and the slighter lyrics of most of the sisterhood, there
is all the difference which exists between the putting-on of
' singing-robes ' for altar service, and the taking up lute or
harp to enchant an indulgent circle of friends and kindred ".
Robert Browning had long resigned himself to the slighter
lyrics, the attenuated harpings and flutings of Fanny Haworth
or the Flower sisters : startling indeed was the impact upon
him of this new and fully modulated voice. In his old room
at the top of the house, ignoring his own " half-done-with
' Bells ' ", he continued, day after day, to " read, read, read " :
and progressively, as he did so, " the fresh strange music, the
affluent language, the exquisite pathos and new true brave
thought " entered into him, enlarging, with " octaves on
octaves of quite new golden strings ", the compass of his
own experience. This enlargement, moreover, came to him
through the personality of a woman : in this " fresh strange

music " he detected a note long lost to him : the overtones of maturity, of a high spiritual range in the voice of a woman. Overwhelming was the instinct which guided his response : which told him that in this direction, and in none other, lay the promise of a fulfilment which, specifically, the years had hitherto denied him. And when at last he drew towards him pen and paper, the man who was " incapable of loving any woman " was able, with the surpassing assurance of an action undertaken in a dream, to write to a woman he had never seen, but whom all his wants had long anticipated—" I do, as I say, love these books with all my heart—and I love you too."

2

A Room in Wimpole Street

"Turning the wonder round in all lights," wrote Elizabeth Barrett to Robert Browning, "I came to what you admitted yesterday . . yes, I saw *that* very early . . that you had come here with the intention of trying to love whomever you should find. . . ."

The accusation was retrospective in intent : nearly a year had gone by since, yielding to the implacable patience of his desire, the front door of number 50, Wimpole Street had opened for the first time to admit him : and although limited, week after week, to the relevant hallways and landings, to a single, a fabulous room on the second floor, he was as familiar already with the atmosphere of Mr. Moulton-Barrett's household, its concealments and its submissions, its sobrieties and its secret gaieties, as he was with the more limpid domesticities that governed the pattern of his own home life at New Cross. Armed, then, as Elizabeth Barrett suggested, with the intention of falling in love, or, as he himself put it, with the " premonition " that he might be about to do so, what manner of woman was it that the poet discovered under the twilight of an established invalidism, whose glance—" I fancied you just what I found you—I knew you from the beginning "—was sufficient to convert anticipation into a full and abiding certainty ?

Had it been the " delightful young creature " encountered nine years previously by a susceptible Miss Mitford, the most exigent requirements of popular taste might have been fully satisfied. At thirty, according to Miss Mitford, Elizabeth Barrett had " a slight girlish figure, very delicate, with exquisite hands and feet, a round face, with a most noble forehead, a large mouth, beautifully formed, and full of expression, lips like parted coral, teeth large, regular, and glittering with healthy whiteness, large dark eyes, with such eyelashes, resting on the cheek when cast down ; when turned upward, touching the flexible and expressive eyebrow ; a dark complexion, with cheeks literally as bright as the dark china rose, a profusion of silky, dark curls, and a look of youth and modesty hardly to be expressed ". But this tender and deferential girl, whose immaturity aroused the protective instinct of Mary Russell Mitford, was not destined, one might almost say, was not designed, for the eyes of Robert Browning—(" Besides, care-bit erased Broken-up beauties ever took my taste Supremely ")—and the woman who placed her hand in that of the poet on the afternoon of May 20th, 1845, had not only "totally lost the rich bright colouring which certainly made the greater part of her beauty", but "dark and pallid ", appeared now in her fortieth year " as much beyond her actual age as, formerly, she looked behind it ".

To this material loss of beauty, Elizabeth cannot have been indifferent. The " rust of time, the touch of age, is hideous and revolting to me ", she wrote. " I hate it ; put it far from me. Why talk of age, when it's just an appearance, an accident, when we are all young in soul and heart ? " There is no doubt that, bound up with the more complex manifestations of a morbid sensibility, it was also a " worse than womanly weakness about that class of subjects ", that caused her during her years in Wimpole Street resolutely to screen her face from the assessing eye of the newcomer : to shut her door against all but the most familiar or the most indulgent visitor. But if the door of the sickroom remained curtained, sealed-off from the outer world, one channel of communication at least was left open—a vent, like that enabling a diphtheria patient to breathe : the mouth of the letter-box that, five years earlier, the introduction of the penny post had caused to be cut in the front door of number 50, Wimpole Street. Through this, the stale airs of the sickroom, the staler airs of an ingrown family affection, were vicariously renewed ; and, a practised, an addicted letter-writer, Elizabeth Barrett was able continuously to extend, in the variety of her correspondence, the range of her own experience. Committed to this type of relationship which reproduced the climate of intimacy with none of its obligations, she would have been content, adding Robert Browning to the list of " unknown friends with whom I am intimately acquainted all except their faces ", to protract indefinitely the pleasure of " talking on paper ". (" No, no ! " she wrote to Miss Mitford, " you can't possibly send me too many letters. For now, I will confess to you !—I like letters *per se* . . and as letters. I like the abstract idea of a letter —I like the postman's rap at the door—I like the Queen's head upon the paper—and with a negation of queen's heads (which doesn't mean treason) I like the sealing wax under the seal and the postmark on the envelope.") [1] Uneasily, therefore, as

[1] May 24, 1843. Wellesley College Library.

Robert Browning wrote her letters " praying to be let in, quite heart-moving and irresistible ", she deferred the prospect of an actual encounter : and it was only because she felt, in the last resort, " ashamed of having made a fuss about what is not worth it " that she consented, after months of procrastination, to summon to her side the man who, as she confided to Miss Mitford, " writes letters to me with Attic contractions, saying he ' *loves* ' *me* ".[1] Even then, at the thought of that man's eyes upon her, she would " shrink and grow pale in the spirit " ; and conscious, to her own distress, of the exaggerated brightness with which he invested her image, she was at pains to forewarn him of the disillusionment that it was her fate to inflict. " There is nothing to see in me," she wrote, " nor to hear in me. . . . If my poetry is worth anything to any eye, it is the flower of me. I have lived most and been most happy in it, and so it has all my colours ; the rest of me is a root, fit for the ground and the dark." But if, when the moment was upon her, the timorous heart " beat itself almost to pieces " at the sound of the " knock at the door, followed by the footstep on the stair ", if she could scarcely bring herself, as he crossed the floor, to acknowledge the glance of her visitor, it must nevertheless have been made plain to her that there was nothing to fear in the judgment of the grey eyes that sought her own ; that, mysteriously, in the confrontal, she suffered no depreciation, she inflicted no disillusionment. For the young man who came to see her, (" Younger looking than I had expected and looking younger than he *is*, of course "),[2] believed that it was a " spinal injury, irremediable in the nature of it ", that had sentenced to her sofa this woman who had long " been a very by-word among the talkers, for a confirmed invalid ". He neither sought nor expected, therefore, the coral lip, the silky curl, the cheek as bright as the dark china rose. He saw on the contrary, as he was prepared to see, a woman darkened by deprivation and suffering : a frail woman bowed, it seemed, under the burden of an omnipresent grief, since she confronted him (as in her portraits she confronts us) " with a head that hangs aside Through sorrow's trick ". And at that first glimpse of her, small and dark, lying in her worn black velvet dress amongst the pillows and shawls, the

---

[1] March 18, 1845. Ibid.   [2] Monday. Ibid.

bottles and the rugs, the whole elaborately mounted structure of her own physical dependance, Robert Browning discovered that it was precisely in that depleted beauty, the " dear, dear pale cheek and the thin hand ", that he found irresistible confirmation of all the emotion that continuously until that moment he had vested under her name.

Upon his return to New Cross that evening the poet sat down and addressed an anxious note to Wimpole Street. He was afraid, he said, that he had stayed too long : that he had spoken too loudly. For the impression remained : that by his impetuousness he had jarred or jeopardised in some way the tranquillity of the sickroom. That tranquillity was of an exceptional order. A room upon which " the door of the future seemed shut and locked ", the silence, wrote Elizabeth, " is most absolute. Flush's breathing is my loudest sound, and then the watch's tickings, and then my own heart when it beats too turbulently. Judge of the quiet and the solitude ! " Admission there, direct from the busy streets of the capital, gave the effect of a sudden secession, not from the broad light of day alone, but from the total traffic of contemporary life. No room was more admirably equipped to achieve its own purpose : the incubation of a climate independent at all times of conditions prevailing in the world outside. To this end, for seven or eight months of the year, the edges of the three large windows were pasted over with paper : " every crevice sealed close " against the raw breath of the east wind. Similar precautions were taken against light and air : a dark-painted blind, a tangled web of ivy leaves whose progress across the pane the invalid regarded with satisfaction : " I should like ", she said, " not to be able to see out of any one of my three windows for the thickness of the ivy." The entrance to the bedroom was no less carefully insulated : for, dissatisfied with a mere curtain as protection, in the autumn of 1844 Mr. Moulton-Barrett had caused a green double door to be constructed : a reinforcement of her privacy with which his daughter proclaimed herself well pleased. Vitiated by her constant presence there, the supply of oxygen was still further depleted by the fact that both Arabel and Flush slept in the room with her at night. Not until May was it possible " to have the windows opened and a little dusting done " ; a capital occasion on which Elizabeth moved for the day into her father's bedroom, the room adjoining her own. The spring cleaning which followed was a major one. " The consequence of living through the winter in one room, with a fire, day and night, and every crevice sealed close ; you may imagine perhaps by the help of your ideal of all dustlessness latent and developed," Elizabeth wrote to Miss Mitford. " At last we come to walk upon a substance like white sand, and if we don't lift our feet gently up and put them gently down, we act Simoons, and stir up the sand into a cloud.—As to a duster or a broom, seen in profile even, . . calculate the effect upon us !—The spiders have grown tame—and their webs are a part of our own domestic economy,—Flush eschews walking under the bed." [1]

Progressively, all the while, the insulating character of the sickroom cut her off, not only from the life of the outer world, but from the sense of time itself. I might, she mused, be living in the depths of the desert, " so profound is my solitude and so complete my isolation from things and persons without ". Amid the noiseless sedimentation of dust, the " amreeta draughts " of ether and morphine, the intimate ministrations of her maid or her physician, she lived season after season in this sealed-off room at the back of the house : the days slipping past in a continuous dream, in which time, she said, seemed " to go round rather than forward ". She had no means of measuring its progress : long ago—two years, was it, or three ?—the mainspring of her watch had broken ; and the clocks in the neighbourhood all struck " out of hearing, or, at best, when the wind brings the sound, one upon another in a confusion ". Not only did she lose count of the hours, but of the months and the years. She dated her letters vaguely, tentatively ; often not at all. At Hope End, in the days of " past joys and holiday times and family unwounded affections ", she had greeted every birthday with its mock-heroic ode : now, she confessed, " I could not tell you the age of one of my brothers or sisters . . unless it were my younger brothers,—and when I told you his once I discovered after-

<hr/>

[1] May 4 [1844]. Wellesley College Library.

wards that I had made a mistake by a year or more. Nay,
you may open your eyes,—but I could not tell you off-hand,
and without reference to my books, as they ' calculate ' over
the Atlantic, how old I myself am." [1]   Shut up, year after year,
in a single room " face to face " with her own spirit, Time had
lost its sequence, almost its significance ; and earth itself had
come to seem

> As strange to me as dreams of distant spheres
> Or thoughts of Heaven we weep at.   Nature's lute
> Sounds on, behind this door so closely shut,
> A strange wild music to the prisoner's ears,
> Dilated by the distance, till the brain
> Grows dim with fancies. . . .

Between Elizabeth's bedroom and the bedroom of Edward
Moulton-Barrett, her father, there was a communicating door.
Very late, sometimes at eleven or twelve at night, that door
would open, and Mr. Moulton-Barrett would make his way
across the room to his daughter's bedside.   " Papa ", she
wrote, " is my chaplain,—prays with me every night,—not
out of a book, but simply and warmly at once,—with one of
my hands held in his and nobody besides him and me in the
room." [2]   During the years of her incarceration in Wimpole
Street, the only sound that had " the power of quickening my
pulse ", the only joy which she felt herself capable of supporting
was, as she confessed, the sound, surprisingly light and youthful
still, of her father's " footstep on the stair, and of his voice
when he prayed in this room : my best hope, as I have told
him since, being to die beneath his eyes ".

In order to gain access to the presence of Elizabeth Barrett,
it was necessary each time resolutely to negotiate " the strange
hedge round the Sleeping palace keeping the world off " ; a
barrier reinforced within the house itself by " the cold dead
silence all round, which is the effect of an incredible system ".
It was in keeping with the fairy-tale atmosphere of the whole
situation that Robert Browning never met, that he never was
to meet, the man who imposed the system, although for nearly

[1] November 18, 1842. Wellesley College Library.   [2] October 27, 1842. Ibid.

two years he was a constant visitor to that man's house. Throughout the whole of that time, the ogre remained absent ; and the intruder was able to assess his stature only through the words and gestures of those he kept subservient to his will. To Browning, however, it did not seem inappropriate that the treasure-house should be so carefully guarded. " I wholly sympathise," he wrote to Elizabeth, " however it go against me, with the highest, wariest pride and love for you, and the proper jealousy and vigilance they entail." For if Mr. Moulton-Barrett found in the darkened room on the second floor an unfailing source of emotional replenishment, to the poet the sealed-up windows opened onto an incomparable vista ; since there, obscurely ensconced as in " chapel or crypt ", he had found his own " world's wonder " : a woman he could love.

To Elizabeth, more clear-sighted at times than her lover, it seemed that, wilfully, Browning chose to take for a high road what could be in his life nothing more than a cul-de-sac. But the vehement young man, the restless talker, the rapid and energetic walker, discerned in the very limitations of the sickroom a novel, an irresistible, appeal : I should like, he declared, to " shut myself in four walls of a room with you and never leave you and be most all *then* ' a lord of infinite space ' ". Neither the dust, nor the dimness, nor the staleness of the air, could mitigate his desire to linger on in this room—" the dearest four walls that I ever have been enclosed by "—and very early Elizabeth received the impression, which she found distasteful, that the poet was attracted in some way by her very " infirmities " : that " without them, you would pass by on the other side :—why twenty times I have thought *that* and been vexed—ungrateful vexation ! " For she could not forget the fact that, having seen her only once, Browning had written a wild, an " intemperate " letter telling her that he loved her : that he had been ready, no less irresponsibly, she felt, to propose marriage to a woman whom he believed " to labour under an incurable complaint ". She was too fastidious not to " recoil by instinct and at the first glance " from the implications of such a suggestion : as unbecoming, she said, " to the humilities of my position, as unpropitious (which is of more consequence) to the prosperities of yours ". The prosperities of his position !

81

—Browning was bewildered. This was reversing the situation as he saw it ; a situation in which, as he said, my " uttermost pride and privilege and glory above all glories would be to live in your sickroom and serve you ". And he was in haste to explain to her—although he could scarcely bring himself to write the word, he said—" so incongruous and impossible does it seem ; such a change of our places does it imply "—that " from the beginning and at this moment I never dreamed of winning your *love* ". This last, her love, was a gift " which, I shall own, was, while I dared ask it, above my hopes—and wishes, even, so it seems to me. . . ." He went on to define the limits of his aspirations. " Now while I *dream*, let me once dream ! I would marry you now and thus—I would come when you let me, and go when you bade me—I would be no more than one of your brothers—' *no more* '—that is, instead of getting tomorrow for Saturday, I should get Saturday as well —when your head ached I should be *here*. I deliberately choose the realisation of that dream (—of sitting simply by you for an hour every day) rather than any other, excluding you, I am able to form for this world, or any world I know—And it will continue but a dream."

" You see in me what is not ;—*that*, I know : and you over-look in me what is unsuitable to you. . . ." It was a cry of despair on Elizabeth's part. From the first she was startled, made uneasy, by the emotion she inspired, whose excess, as it seemed to her, she attempted vainly to repudiate. She found the expression of it all the more bewildering in that it grated, point for point, against an obstinate preconception of her own. A " great hero-worshipper ", Elizabeth had long admired the poetry of Robert Browning ; and it is curious to see how constantly in her letters she feels impelled to defend him against the accusations and strictures of Miss Mitford. " Mr. Browning is no imitator. He asserts *himself* in his writings, with a strong and deep individuality—and if he does it in Chaldee, why he makes it worth our while to get out our dictionaries. . . . This is for *you—I do not know him*." [1] A few weeks later : " Browning is a true poet—and there are not many such poets —and if any critics *have*, as your critical friend wrote to you, ' flattered him into a wilderness and left him ' they left him

[1] July 15, 1841. Wellesley College Library.

alone with his *genius*,—and where those two are, despair cannot be." [1]   Again : " I always believed that Mr. Browning was a master in clenched passion, . . concentrated passion . . burning through the metallic fissures of language . . . Promise me not to say again that it was a pity he missed being . . an attorney . . an engineer . . a merchant's clerk . . what trade was it ? " [2]   But if Miss Mitford continued to speak disparagingly of the man who was later to " steal " her beloved friend from her, accusing him alternately of " silver forkism " and of " effeminacy ", from Mr. Kenyon, her cousin, Elizabeth heard nothing but favourable comments on the work and character of the young poet. " Do you know ", Elizabeth wrote triumphantly to Miss Mitford, " that Mr. Browning is a great favourite (I mean as a man) of Mr. Kenyon's ? Mr. Kenyon spoke to me warmly of his high cultivation and attainments, and singular humility of bearing. And he is weak in health too ! " [3]   For ten years, from the obscurity of her " prison ", her " dungeon ", she had followed with a peculiar interest the vicissitudes of his literary career : regarding him, not without a certain romantic interest, as one who had " drunken the cup of life full, with the sun shining on it ".   To her, as to many of her contemporaries, he was the author of *Paracelsus* : and it was with Paracelsus himself, philosopher and physician, that she chose spontaneously to identify him. " You are Paracelsus," she wrote, " and I am a recluse with nerves that have all been broken on the rack, and now hang loosely— quivering at a step and a breath." This identification enhanced, immeasurably, her awe of Robert Browning. " Shall I have the courage to see you soon, I wonder ! If you ask me, I must ask myself. . . In the meantime, you do not know what it is to be . . a little afraid of Paracelsus." Having, however, " influenced " her " in a way which no one else did ", Paracelsus succeeded, after four months' siege, in gaining admittance to the sickroom : and Elizabeth found herself, as she had fully expected to be, frightened of him ; " frightened in this.   I felt as if you had a power over me and meant to use it, and that I could not breathe or speak very differently from what you chose to make me."

[1] July 16, 1841. Ibid.   [2] Valentine's Day, 1843. Ibid.
[3] Friday, October 19, 1842. Ibid.

Quite simply, what Robert Browning chose—(and " when did I once fail to get what I had set my heart upon ? As I ask myself sometimes, with a strange fear ")—was that Elizabeth Barrett should live and not die. He had recognised early his most intimidating rival : it was Death. " Only do you stay here with me in the ' House ' these few short years," he wrote on March 12 ; on first detecting in Elizabeth a disquieting desire, never wholly to be overcome, to " lie down and sleep among the snows of a weary journey ". This " pernicious languour " went very deep. " Sometimes ", she wrote, "—it is the real truth—I have haste to be done with it all. It is the real truth. . . ." Over and over again during the months to come, a sober, an indefatigable Orpheus, he was to lure Eurydice to the very brink of the upper world ; only to feel her, at a word, melt from his grasp ; drawn down once more into a region whose " morbid and desolate " spells he was powerless to combat. Patiently each time he renewed his efforts (" you will take exercise, go up and down stairs, get strong ") ; and subjected day by day to this prolonged, this sustained act of resuscitation, Elizabeth could not suppress the feeling that, like Paracelsus himself, her lover was indeed in possession of an occult method of restoring life ; a " secret " that would " cheat the grave ". For, within its limits, the process was a successful one ; progressively, Elizabeth learnt to stand upright ; to open the door of the sickroom ; to admit and tolerate the light of common day. " I have been drawn back into life by your means and for you," she wrote to Browning. It was an acknowledgement : not a cry of gratitude. " I had done *living*, I thought, when you came and sought me out. And why ? And to what end ? " The answer, however, was clear enough. " Think ", wrote Robert Browning, " what happiness you mean to give me, what a life ; what a death ! " She had been called back, she saw, in order to perfect and prolong that anticipated happiness. Unflinchingly as she accepted the transaction—" What should I be if I could fail willingly to you in the least thing ? But I *never will*, and you know it "—she could not conceal how heavily, at times, it taxed the inmost resources of her nature. " My life was ended when I knew you, and if I survive myself, it is for your sake. . . ." " I have come back for you alone . . at

your voice and because you have use for me : I have come
back to live a little for you——"

> As brighter ladies do not count it strange,
> For love, to give up acres and degree,
> I yield the grave for thy sake, and exchange
> My near sweet view of Heaven, for earth with thee !

" I *know*," wrote Browning, " if one may know anything,
that to make my life yours and increase it by union with yours,·
would render me *supremely happy*, as I said, and say, and feel.
My whole suit to you is, in that sense, *selfish*. . . ." This
selfishness of which he convicted himself gave him, it seems,
a strange confidence. " I never ask myself, as perhaps I
should,—will *she* be happy too ?—All that seems removed
from me, far above my concernment—she—you, my Ba, will
make me so entirely happy, that it seems enough to know . . .
my palm trees grow well enough without knowing the cause
of the sun's heat." This, in the end, was the argument that
was to prevail. For, an invalid in her fortieth year, " Behold-
ing, besides love, the end of love ", Elizabeth was reassured,
not by the young man's passion for her, but by his need, which
drove firmer roots into the future than the most fervent pro-
testations of love could hope to do. It was this, the persuasion
that she had it in her power to create happiness, that caused
a woman long reluctant to " put out my finger to touch my
share of life ", to accept tremulously " the precious deposit of
' heart and life ' " that was placed now between her hands.
" All the other doors of life were shut to me, and shut me in as
in a prison, and only before this door stood one whom I loved
best and who loved me best, and who invited me out through
it for the good's sake which he thought I could do him." For
the good's sake which he thought I could do him. . . . In
the final resort, it was not to the " mastery " which it had once
pleased her to detect in every " word and look " of the poet
that Elizabeth Barrett responded, but to something more
compelling still : his weakness.

" Talking of happiness," wrote Elizabeth, "—shall I tell
you ? Promise not to be angry and I will tell you. I have
thought sometimes that, if I considered myself wholly, I should

choose to die this winter—now—before I had disappointed you in anything." It was December, 1845 : a bare three months after she had consented to be his " for everything but to do you harm." This recurrent, this persistent fear of harming him in some way was to Browning one of the most puzzling features in his relationship with Elizabeth Barrett. It had first disclosed itself when, unaccountably, he could not but feel, she declined to choose for him the day on which he was next to visit her. Through " a weakness, perhaps of morbidness, or one knows not how to define it, I *cannot help* being uncomfortable in having to do this," she said. It was not, she went on to explain, merely the feminine fear " of asking you to come when you would rather not ", but the effect ," the influence of a peculiar experience over me and out of me ". Her fear was, he discovered, that if it was her will and not his that brought him to Wimpole Street on a certain day, he would suffer in the journey some disaster for which she must then account herself personally responsible. " Ah," she said, " if you knew how dreadfully natural every sort of evil seems to my mind, you would not laugh at me for being afraid." Robert Browning did not laugh. A man singularly free of superstition of any kind, he was disturbed only by the fact that the evil which she apprehended seemed to have its source in nothing less than the operation of her own will. " What an omen you take in calling anything my work ! " she wrote. " If it is my work, woe on it—for everything turns to evil which I touch." She was at pains, constantly, to remind him of " the law of my own star, my own particular star, the star I was born under, the star *Wormwood* ". (" *I* ", she wrote to Miss Mitford, " who own a fatal star ! ") Incautiously, on one occasion, Browning admitted that his health had not improved during the time that he had known her. Instantly : " What if it should be the crossing of my bad star ? " she demanded. Even in the " surpassing " wonder of his love for her, she found a source of anxiety, of self-torment. " It is my especial fairy-tale," she said, " from the spells of which, may you be unharmed." What possible harm, the poet patiently asked, could come from one who was to him the source of all goodness and all truth ? In the grip of a strange distress, Elizabeth Barrett could only cry out : " May God turn back the evil of me ! "

" Of all fighting ", wrote Browning grimly, " the warfare with shadows—what a work is *there*." For the shadows seemed on such occasions not to recede but to multiply in his path. Where did they spring from ? What events, deposited in a past he could not know, cast their reflection so menacingly, at times, between himself and the woman he loved ?

2

The picture of the impetuous young Elizabeth of Hope End days is so different from that of the " religious hermit " of Wimpole Street, that it is difficult, at first glance, to reconcile one with the other. Robert Browning, doubtless, was more entertained than alarmed by Elizabeth's assertion that passion —" the good open passion which lies on the floor and kicks "— was " the born weakness of my own nature " : how could he be expected to believe that even in childhood the gentle Ba had " upset all the chairs and tables and thrown the books about the room in a fury " ?

Elizabeth Barrett, however, was speaking the simple truth about herself. Such " demonstrations ", she added, " were all done by the ' light of other days ' " : and it is beneath those refracted beams that we are permitted, now, to discover the vehement quality of a child small enough to " take refuge from the cruelties of the world in a *hat-box* ", and determined enough to assert by physical force if necessary her right to absolute dominion in the nursery. " I was always of a determined, if thwarted violent disposition," she wrote in an early auto-biography.[1] " My actions and temper were infinitely more inflexible at three years old than now at fourteen. At that early age I can perfectly remember reigning in the Nursery and being renowned amongst the servants for self-love and excessive passion." The desire, however, that there should be " no UPSTART to dispute my authority " suffered an early set-back, since the usurper had already appeared : Mr. Moulton-Barrett's first son, Edward, the " crown of his house " and focus

[1] *Glimpses into My Own Life and Literary Character. Hitherto Unpublished Poems etc.* Bibliophile Society, Boston. 1914.

of his patriarchal pride. It must have been about the time that the newcomer was taking his first, tenderly applauded steps across the nursery floor that the " excessive passion " of the dispossessed became manifest in Elizabeth : and as the years went by, the privileges accorded to his masculinity aroused in one " inconsolable for not being born a man " a tempestuous " spirit of emulation ". The delicately built girl with the eager eyes and the dark cropped hair became an uncontrollable tomboy : " much more wild and much more mad " than any of her brothers and sisters. Despite her hated petticoats, no wall was too high for her to climb, no ladder too steep, no tree too perilous : she was ready to jump out of the ground floor window in order to stand bareheaded beneath a heavy downfall of rain : to throw off her shoes and stockings and wade in the dew, or plunge herself headlong " into a bath of long wet grass ". Refusing contemptuously the embroidery and the hem-stitching proposed to her sisters, she refused, too, the offices of the governess engaged for their instruction. Edward was to have a tutor : Edward was to learn Greek : scorning that " subserviency of opinion which is generally considered necessary to feminine softness ", she insisted on sharing with her brother the benefit of Mr. McSwiney's Latin and Greek. As a small child, she had once cried " very heartily for half an hour because I did not understand Greek ". Translating into intellectual force the ardour of her own emotion (" At twelve . . . metaphysics were my highest delight and after having read a page from Locke my mind not only felt edified but exalted "), she became now a confirmed pedant : and the woman who wrote in 1838 that she did not like the " constant carrying about of an intellect rampant, like a crest ", may have been thinking of her own early years ; years of stress in which the conduct of daily life was governed by " a steady indignation against nature who made me a woman, and a determinate resolution to dress up in men's clothes as soon as ever I was free of the nursery, and go into the world ' to seek my fortune ' ".[1]

It was impossible, of course, to go out into the world, even to become, as she wished to be, Lord Byron's page. The gates of Hope End remained securely shut, protecting its inhabitants

[1] July 22 [1842]. To Miss Mitford. Wellesley College Library.

alike from the intrusion of neighbours and the temptations of a world " where vices roam ". Nevertheless, the moment was fast approaching in which a necessity from within was to force those gates apart. " Bro " was nearly thirteen : it was time, Mr. Barrett decided, that his son and heir should attend a public school. On a long-remembered morning in April, 1820, the lodge gates of Hope End opened to permit a small round-faced boy to pass through them, carriage-bound for London and his first term at Charterhouse : after which the gates closed themselves resolutely once more upon the less privileged members of a highly sequestered community. The effect upon Ba of this enforced separation was a curious one. In the midst of the anguish, duly celebrated in verse, " of Bidding Farewell to My Beloved Bro ", she was seized with a passionate anxiety for the moral welfare of one remote, now, from the restraining influence of Hope End. Ringing in the ears of the adolescent girl was " the laugh of dissipation " ; in all earnestness, mixing tears and exclamation marks, she implored her absent brother not to " stray from the path of honorable rectitude ! " : to " spare that heart which your degradation would break ! " " Grant," she wrote in her autobiography-cum-diary, " Grant my Father that ere I behold my beloved Brother ! my valued friend whose upright and pure principles my soul now glories in, deviating from honour, I may have breathed my last sigh and preserve the ideal vision of his virtue to my grave ! " What could not however be confided to the diary was the sense, bitter and deep, of her own frustration. So far, her insistence on sharing the privileges of her brother had been successful : now, however, summarily, the real difference in their station was brought home to her, for she who had followed with him the ascending incline of Mr. McSwiney's tuition—" Together many a minute did we wile On Horace's page, or Maro's sweeter lore "—could not follow him through the gates of Hope End ; could not follow him into the world of men where he belonged. " The Dream has faded—it is o'er," she wrote. It was the dream of equality, of feminine emancipation first ignited in her relationship with Bro, and powerfully re-fuelled, at the age of twelve, by Mary Wollstonecraft and *The Rights of Woman*.

The marked change that came over Elizabeth must be

dated from this time ; when, together with the continued absence of Bro, she had to accept in herself the inescapable realities of her own femininity. My character, she wrote in her fifteenth year, " is still as proud, as wilful, as impatient of controul [*sic*], as impetuous, but Thanks be to God it is restrained. I have acquired a command of myself which has become so habitual that my disposition appears to my friends to have undergone a revolution. But," she was compelled to add, " to myself it is well known that the same violent inclinations are in my inmost heart and that altho' habitual restraint has become almost a part of myself yet were I once to lose the rigid rein I might again be hurled with Phaeton far from everything human . . . everything reasonable ! "

She did not " lose the rigid rein " : on the other hand, when the anniversary of Bro's first parting came round and it was time for him to return once more to school, Elizabeth lay on her bed, the subject of prolonged and spectacular paroxysms of pain : the hourly centre of her parents' attention and anxiety. (" When *I* was ill," she wrote later, " my father and mother, during two years, scarcely ever left me to go anywhere, not even to dine in the neighbourhood,—tho' I was in *immediate danger* for only a *few months*.") [1] It was, however, neither an injury to the spine nor " a common cold striking on an insubstantial frame " which, as she later claimed, " began my bodily troubles ". That Elizabeth Barrett's long history of " bodily troubles " began, and under the circumstances described, with a persistent " pain in the head ", we know from the evidence of her doctor, one of three called on that occasion into consultation on her case. (" The mind," observed one of them, " has ceased in a great degree to engage in those investigations and pursuits which formerly constituted its greatest delight, and there appears to be a degree of listlessness . . . even where the affections are concerned.") [2] What emerges clearly enough from their several reports is the fact that the case of Miss Barrett—" that prodigy in intellectual power and acquirements ! " [3]—was equally puzzling to all three of them. Thus, we find Dr. Carden suggesting a

---

[1] June 6, 1828. To H. S. Boyd. Wellesley College Library.
[2] June 24, 1821. Dr. William Coker to Dr. Nuttall. Illinois University Library.   [3] Ibid.

" cold shower bath " and the use of a " *tight* flannel binder round the abdomen " : [1] Dr. Nuttall, talking darkly of " flatus ", and attributing the root of the evil to the " dyspeptic complaints " [2] natural to her age : while Dr. Coker, who is candid enough to admit, after an examination, that " the positive proofs are wanting of the existence of a deseased spine," is not ashamed to put forward the suggestion that, all else failing, it might be as well, under the circumstances, to treat " Miss Barrett's case as for deseased spine ".[3]

Miss Barrett was acquiescent. Whatever the treatment proposed, it could only establish the strength of her own position : a position in which she was required to resign all domestic duties to others and blandly to ignore her sister's pointed reference to " the most useless person in the house ". The privileges of frailty, she discovered, were too rewarding to be lightly relinquished. Six years later, the former tomboy was writing languidly in reply to an enquiry about her health that " deficiency in strength makes me quite incapable of much exertion ". By this time, of course, Edward had already left school : brother and sister were re-united beneath the spires and minarets of Hope End. But with the passage of the years, there had come also a corresponding change in the relationship. The tenderness on both sides remained as imperative as before ; but in Ba's case the " rage for power " that had accompanied her early affections had been, if not resolved, at least re-absorbed. So deeply, indeed, had that hidden rivalry been buried that she was ready to deny its very existence. As she had once prayed to be allowed to preserve " the ideal vision of his virtue," so she now perpetuated a no less ideal vision of her brother's perfections. " Oh, my beloved friend," she wrote to Miss Mitford a year after Edward's death : " —there was no harsh word, no unkind look—never from my babyhood till I stood alone. A leaf never shook till the tree fell. The shade was over me softly till it fell." [4] We are offered, however, through another source, a more convincing glimpse of early life at Hope

[1] May 8, 1821. To — Barrett Esq. Ibid.
[2] [1821] To Elizabeth Barrett. Ibid.
[3] June 24, 1821. Dr. Coker to Dr. Nuttall. Ibid.
[4] June 14, 1841. Wellesley College Library.

End. "Now, my darling child," wrote Ba's grandmother reprovingly, "you must allow me to say I think you are too big to attempt fighting with Bro. He might give you an unlucky Blow on your Neck which might be serious to you. He is strong and powerful. I have seen him very rude and boisterous to you and Harry [Henrietta]. He is now a big Boy, fit only to associate with Boys, not Girls."[1] The days of fisticuffs, of open competition were over : the "violent inclinations" which it took so much energy to subdue lay buried now in the "darksome pit" of memory ; never again to be uncovered or acknowledged. But if Elizabeth Barrett was reluctant, after the age of fourteen, to commit herself to the candour of prose, her poetry offers an indirect but no less illuminating commentary upon the nature of her own predicament. Amongst the "fugitive poems" published in 1833 with her translation of *Prometheus Bound*, is "A Fragment" called *The Tempest*. Prefaced by a quotation from Lucan, *Mors erat ante oculos*, this poem was written during the emotional turmoil either preceding or following upon the departure from Hope End and her own final dissociation from the scenes and circumstances of childhood. Heavily charged in mood and phrase, the poem opens with a description of a violent thunderstorm in the Malvern Hills ; during the course of which a tree is stripped and blasted by lightning. (The same tree, apparently, as twelve years later she was to describe so vividly in a letter to Robert Browning.) *The Tempest* is written in the first person, and we can recognise clearly the voice and temperament of the young Elizabeth in one whose spirit is "gladden'd, as with wine, To hear the iron rain" ; who, exulting in the display of violence, runs "along the bowing woods to meet The riding Tempest". In a lurid flash of lightning she is arrested suddenly by "a white and corpse-like heap Stretch'd in the path". Despite the exclamation—" I knew that face—His, who did hate me, —his, whom I did hate ! "—the identity of the dead is not revealed ; but long arrears of emotion are uncovered in the

[1] Undated. To Elizabeth from Mrs. Moulton. University of Illinois Library. With this letter, shocked, apparently, by Ba's lack of modesty, her grandmother sends her "six slips to wear under your frocks, you are now too big to go without them ".

laconic phrase which follows. " The man was my familiar."
And as she looks at that dead face, open to the " white un-
blenching breath " of the storm, a reversal of mood takes
place in which exaltation is quenched like a taper " in a pit
wherein the vapour-witches weirdly reign In charge of
darkness ".

> I no longer knew
> Silence from sound, but wander'd far away
> Into the deep Eleusis of mine heart,
> To learn its secret things. When arméd foes
> Meet on one deck with impulse violent,
> The vessel quakes thro' all her oaken ribs,
> And shivers in the sea ; so with mine heart :
> For there had battled in her solitudes,
> Contrary spirits ; sympathy with power,
> And stooping unto power ;—the energy
> And passiveness,—the thunder and the death !

Day dawns at last : she awakens from a " deep unslumb'ring
dream ".

> Within me was a nameless thought : it closed
> The Janus of my soul on echoing hinge,
> And said ' Peace ! ' with a voice like War's.

And as the speaker in another curious poem, *Night and the
Merry Man*, hastens to bury before the break of day the secrets
of his own past, so now, with " feverish strength " she digs
with her bare hands a grave for the un-named dead.

> I gave it to the silence and the pit,
> And strew'd the heavy earth on all : and then—
> I—I, whose hands had formed that silent house,—
> I could not look thereon, but turned and wept !

Seven years later, Edward Moulton-Barrett was drowned
while yachting in Babbacombe Bay. The effect upon his
sister, who was responsible for his presence in Torquay, was
catastrophic. " Oh my dearest friend——" she afterwards
wrote to Miss Mitford. " That was a very near escape from
madness, absolute hopeless madness. For more than three

months I could not read—could understand little that was said to me. The mind seemed to myself broken up into fragments. And even after the long dark spectral trains, the staring infantine faces, had gone back from my bed—to *understand*, to hold on to one thought for more than a moment, remained impossible." [1]   Lying rigid and tearless beneath " the blanching vertical eye-glare of the absolute Heavens ", she waited to die in her turn : it was against her own will, as she felt, and through the agency of the morphine which she could never afterwards dispense with, that, after months and years of convalescence, she recovered a small measure of bodily strength.   What she was never to recover was peace of mind. The past, she wrote, " has left its mark with me for ever ". To the end of her life, there was " *one face* which never ceases to be present with me " : there was one name which she could not bring herself either to write down or to speak aloud.   Even in the intimacy of marriage, she confessed, she could not speak out, " in a whisper, even, what is in me ".   Nor could she tolerate, from another's lips, the slightest reference to the subject.   " Once at the Baths of Lucca I was literally nearly struck down to the ground by a single word said in all kindness by a friend whom I had not seen for ten years.   The blue sky reeled over me, and I caught at something, not to fall."

But the vigilance which sought, with so fanatical an insistence, to keep Edward's name unspoken, uninvoked, could not withhold his presence from her poetry.   The passions and rivalries of Hope End were to emerge once more, startlingly, in *Aurora Leigh*, a novel-poem in blank verse published when Elizabeth Barrett Browning was fifty.   Into this " fictitious autobiography ", wrote the poetess, " I have put much of myself " :   and if she also put into it much that was gleaned, involuntarily, from the field of contemporary fiction, *Jane Eyre* and *The Blithedale Romance* included, the opening sections of the poem, at least, derive wholly from the manner and circumstances of her own early life at Hope End.   The ardent, the bookish young Aurora is loved by her cousin and neighbour, Romney Leigh.   Wrapped up in his own political and social theories, Romney is a man who " sees a woman as the complement of his sex merely " :   he dismisses, slightingly,

[1] Undated.   Wellesley College Library.

the pretensions of Aurora, of any woman, to become a major poet.

> You write as well . . and ill . . upon the whole,
> As other women. If as well, what then?
> If even a little better, . . still, what then?
> We want the Best in art now, or no art.

This airy dismissal draws down upon Romney's head the deep-laid fury of the woman scorned, not in her sexual, but in her creative capacity. Passionately—" I too have my vocation "—Aurora refuses to marry the man whose contempt so belittles and humbles her. It is Romney, however, who at the end of a very long story indeed is humbled ; and most effectively so : not only is he forced to acknowledge his cousin's poetic genius, but, Job-like, he has to endure the resounding failure of his own social experiment, to witness the destruction of his ancestral home, and to accept, at the hands of his author, the culminating affliction of a sudden and irreparable loss of sight. His " calm, grand eyes, extinguished in a storm ", the erstwhile proud man turns to his cousin, and in an act of long-delayed abnegation and reconciliation—" I yield, you have conquered "—he beseeches Aurora to take over where he, through his own folly, has failed.

> Shine out for two, Aurora, and fulfil
> My falling-short that must be !

At the age of fourteen, it had once pleased Ba to select from *Lycidas* a line on which to base her *Verses to my Brother*. Twenty-one years later, when Edward was indeed drowned at sea, Elizabeth Barrett—(" May God turn back the evil of me ! ")—was ready to discover in the manner of his death the recoil of her own original intention. " The griefs that are incurable ", she wrote a few years before her death, " are those which have our own sins festering in them."

3

On January 6, 1846, almost a year after Robert Browning had addressed his first letter to her, Elizabeth Barrett was moved to make a confession. "You never guessed, perhaps," she wrote, "what I look back to at this moment in the psychology of our intercourse, the curious double feeling I had about you—you personally, and you as the writer of those letters, and the crisis of the feeling, when I was positively vexed and jealous of myself for not succeeding better in making a unity of the two. I could not ! And moreover I could not help but that the writer of the letters seemed nearer to me, long . . long . . and in spite of the postmark, than did the personal visitor who confounded me, and left me constantly under such an impression of its being all dream-work on his side, that I have stamped my feet on this floor with impatience to think of having to wait so many hours before the ' candid ' closing letter could come with its confessional of an illusion."

From the first, the relationship between the lovers was conducted at two levels : the level of the letters, irradiated so dazzlingly with the ardour of human passion ; and the level of the visits, in which, circumscribed, emotion expressed itself too often in stiffness, diffidence, and even in mutual misapprehension. Elizabeth, it seems, was so oppressed by shyness that, "like a little girl ", she could scarcely raise her lids to look her lover in the face ; and as for Browning— " I that stammer and answer haphazard with you—Have you not discovered by this time that I go on talking with my thoughts away ? " The division was carefully maintained : until the day of their marriage, there were certain matters— ("I could not speak it—to write it, is easier ")—that could be broached between them by letter only, and then on the strict understanding that the topic was not to be raised by either when next they met. "Do not notice what I have written to you my dearest friend . . ." "Do not speak of it when next we meet. . . ." Throughout the love letters the injunction abounds ; a trick of Elizabeth's, which Browning was later to catch. As a result, much was lost in the no-man's land between the two poles of communication. "When I am away from you ", wrote Browning, "a crowd of things press on me for utterance—' I will say them, not write them ' I think :—when I see you—all to be said seems insignificant, irrelevant, —' they can be written, at all events ' —I think *that* too. So, feeling so much, I say so little ! "

Nevertheless, despite these alternating modes of intimacy, each felt that it was in absence that they were able most clearly to discern the features of the other : in absence alone that the innermost qualities stood irrefutably revealed. So that when, after an interval, they met once more face to face, each was similarly disconcerted by an appearance which marred, momentarily, the image adopted and perfected in solitude.

If Elizabeth found that she could not, for all her efforts, succeed in " making a unity " of the two aspects of Robert Browning, she was none the less continuously on the alert for the clue, " some chance expression of truth " which might enable her to do so. For she was haunted by what he had once called " the horrible counterbalancing never-to-be-written *rest of me* " ; by the memory of an early letter of his in which, reminding her that she " knew nothing " of him, the poet went on to assert that " for every poor speck of a Vesuvius or a Stromboli in my microcosm there are huge layers of ice and pits of black cold water—and I make the most of my two or three fire-eyes, because I know by experience, alas, how these tend to extinction—and the ice grows and grows— still this last is true part of me, *best* part perhaps, and I disown nothing—only—when you talked of *knowing* me ! "

Elizabeth did, nevertheless, believe that she was possessed of " a sort of instinct by which I seem to know your views of such subjects as we have never looked at together ". Browning, too, was ready to acknowledge that " there are many things in which I agree with you to such a tremblingly exquisite exactness, so to speak, that I hardly dare cry out lest the charm break. . . ." Alas, only three days later, to the consternation of each, that charm had received its first serious jar ; and, shaken, Ba was writing to ask her lover why he and she must " see things so differently, ever dearest ? If anyone had asked me, I could have answered for you that you saw it quite otherwise. And you would hang men even —you ! " For Elizabeth, who thought Browning " free from conventional fallacies ", was distressed to find that he upheld not only capital punishment, but, even less defensibly, she felt, the purpose and practice of duelling. Agreeing with her that the latter custom was intended merely " to satisfy the world ", he insisted nevertheless that, living in society, men " must take such a course to retain the privileges they value ". It is difficult to discover which Elizabeth was more distressed by : the gusto of Robert's allusion to an opponent " writhing with a sword through him up to the hilt " ; or the abnegation of conscience that she detected in this resolute passion for social conformity. " You are wrong . . . ", she wrote sadly, " when you advocate the pitiful resources of this corrupt social life . . . and if you are wrong, how are we to get right, we all who look to you for teaching."

Elizabeth had stated her case as earnestly and as lucidly as her own " heartache " would permit. What she was far from expecting, however, in a letter received by return of post, was the *volte-face* therein presented to her. Browning made no further attempt to justify his own point of view. On the contrary : " I submit unfeignedly to you, there as elsewhere," he wrote. Nor was this all. " Oh, Ba, did I. not pray you at the beginning to *tell* me the instant you detected anything to be altered by *human* effort ? to give me that chance of becoming more like you and worthier of you ? . . . I won't repeat the offence, dear—*you are right* and I am wrong and will lay it to heart, and now kiss, not your feet this time, because I am the prouder, far from the more humble, by this admission and retraction."

Elizabeth was perhaps more shocked by this withdrawal of a point of view than previously she had been by the upholding of it. " You cannot," she wrote, " you know, you know you cannot, dearest . . ' submit ' to me in an *opinion*, any more than I could to you, if I desired it ever so anxiously." She was all the more taken aback in that, six months before, with every appearance of an impassioned sincerity, Browning himself had declared to her that " All passive obedience and implicit submission of will and intellect is by far too easy, if well considered, to be the course prescribed by God to Man in this life of probation—for they *evade* probation altogether, though foolish people think otherwise. Chop off your legs, you will never go astray ; stifle your reason altogether and you will find it is difficult to reason ill. ' It is hard to make these sacrifices ! '—not so hard as to lose the reward or incur the penalty of an Eternity to come ; ' hard to effect them, then, and go through with them '—*not* hard, when the leg is to be *cut off*—that it is rather harder to keep it quiet on a stool, I know very well."

From what level of experience did this knowledge spring? Elizabeth was unacquainted with the circumstances of Robert Browning's early life. She could not know what latent emotion inspired his statement that " the hard thing " in life was " to act on one's own best conviction—not to abjure it and accept another's will ". All she knew was that he who had denounced so forcibly the docile acceptance of " an infallible church, or private judgement of another ", sought now, through her, to " *evade* probation altogether " ; demanded of her, inexplicably, she felt, that she impose the weight of her own judgement upon his. Faced with these contradictory aspects of a single personality, how indeed, Elizabeth Barrett wondered, was she to succeed in " making a unity of the two " ?

4

For a whole year, Robert Browning came and went between New Cross and Wimpole Street without suspecting that he was shadowed by a concealed enmity : that a man he had never heard of watched in steadily mounting resentment the repetition of his visits. Like himself, this man was in love with Elizabeth Barrett ; like Browning, he, too, was a regular and privileged visitor to the sickroom. His devotion, however, had ante-dated by a good many years that of the poet : for it was in Sidmouth, at the end of 1832, that Elizabeth was first introduced to the Reverend George Barrett Hunter, minister of the Marsh Independent Chapel where she and her family worshipped. A firm friendship soon established itself between the minister and the eldest daughter of the family. " I wish you could hear Mr. Hunter," Elizabeth wrote to her friend Mrs. Martin. " He is very eloquent . . . And 'out of the pulpit I like so much to hear him talk. He has a *feeling* (not that cold word *taste*) for poetry and literature, which you meet with, or at least *I* meet with, very rarely. And so gentle and humble and simple-minded—— Oh—I wish you knew Mr. Hunter ! " [1]   Mr. Hunter, however, was by no means as quiet and humble, or even as simple-minded as in " our Sidmouth talks Beneath the elms and beeches " he had at first appeared.   Over the years, in the grip of an unrequited love, he revealed himself a moody, passionate and embittered man who, while professing for his " angel of heaven " a " pure principle of adoration ", molested her all the while with his jealous resentment of her poetry and of her friends.[2]   When, after thirteen years of stormy devotion, he became aware that he had been supplanted by the man whom he referred to, tauntingly, as Elizabeth's " New Cross Knight ", his behaviour became so ominous that Elizabeth had to beg Arabel to remain in the room with her during his visits— " otherwise *I am afraid*—he is such a violent man ".   What, however, taxed most highly the patience of Elizabeth was not the violence to which she was subjected, but the veneration. To Mr. Hunter, she was not a woman of flesh and blood : she was a principle of purity ; a disembodied inspiration ; " Guardian Angel " to his own lesser and altogether more reprehensible clay.   Under the merciless infliction of his idealism, she could only endure, helpless, an attitude whose effect was consistently to deny her own reality as a human being.   When, therefore, the prospect was opened to her of a friendship with Robert Browning, it was with alacrity that this confirmed " hero-worshipper " abandoned her pedestal ; eager not only to entertain at ground level the author of *Paracelsus*, but " sinking down " in happy obeisance, as she said, " to the feet of your spirit ".   All the more disconcerting, then, to find herself gently but firmly replaced on her eminence ; to watch a chivalrous Perseus conscientiously renewing the chains of her captivity.   The pedestal, she was to find, was not so easily discarded : and indeed for fifteen years it was to remain for Robert and Elizabeth Browning at once a keystone and a stumbling-block within the structure of their wedded lives.

Throughout the love-letters of the two poets, there is a

[1] September 7, 1833. Letter omitted from F. G. Kenyon's *Letters of E.B.B.* Unabbreviated Typescript : Brit. Mus. Add. Mss. 42228–31. Afterwards referred to as Kenyon typescript.

[2] For a fuller treatment of this relationship see " Miss Barrett and Mr. Hunter " : the *Cornhill Magazine*, Spring, 1951.

continual discussion, a gentle persistent wrangling as to " how the love-account really stands between us ". Over and over again, they tot up the items ; examine the debit and credit side of their relationship : disconcertingly, nevertheless, the sum persists at times in cancelling itself out. " I have just so much logic," Elizabeth wrote, " as to be able to see . . . that for *me* to be too good for *you*, and for *you* to be too good for *me*, cannot be true at once, both ways." For Robert's fixed belief, that " There is no love but from beneath, far beneath ", encountered not a complementary, but a parallel attitude in Elizabeth, who " never could love ", she asserted, " except *upward* very far and high ". A stalemate was thus produced : a predicament born of the very similarity of their needs. " One's ideal must be above one, as a matter of course " : it was necessary, therefore, to raise yet higher the spiritual ceiling of love. Thus—" I *know* you are immeasurably my superior," Browning will write : only to be assured in his turn, and with no less resolute a humility : " I know you are too high and too good for me." Throughout the five hundred and sixty seven pages of the love letters this continues, strophe and anti-strophe, until the disadvantages as well as the advantages of agreeing with one another, " to such a tremblingly exquisite exactness " became apparent, at times, to both. In despair, finally—(his own praises, he complained, were continually blown back in his eyes)—" Why do you not help me," Robert exclaimed, " rather than take my words, my proper word, from me and call them yours, when yours they are not ? You said lately love of you ' made you humble '—just as if to hinder *me* from saying that earnest truth ! "

" If it were not that I look up to him," wrote Elizabeth confidentially to Mrs. Martin, " we should be too alike to be together, perhaps, but I know my place better than he does, who is too humble." We cannot agree, she said to Robert, " because we stand in different positions ". But it was, on the contrary, because they stood, or attempted to stand, in the same, wholly reverential attitude that the collision continued to occur. One or other, it was plain, must retire from this coveted position : must consent, self-sacrificingly, not to worship but to be worshipped. Elizabeth perceived that in her ability to accept this rôle lay the whole future of her relationship with Robert Browning. Before consenting, however, to the process of beatification—a process in which, as she reproached her lover, " you slew and idealised me "—she made a final effort to present herself to him at the level of plain human reality. " Without seeing me at all, you love me," she warned him ; and, " disquietedly sure that you are under an illusion ", she did her utmost to open his eyes to the series of disadvantages and drawbacks that he courted in her name. " Besides, the *truth* is, that I am *not* worthy of you," she said : how then could his repeated " exaggerations, idealizations " flatter or even reassure her ? On the contrary. " Ah,—if you could know—if you could but know for a full moment of conviction, how you depress and alarm me by saying such things, you never would say them afterwards, *I* know." For listening to him, perceiving that he addressed himself in her to a woman of his own creation, she had a strange and desolating impression of being supplanted. " It seems to me as if you were in the dark altogether and held my hand for another," she wrote sadly. And with all the earnestness of which she was capable, she made a final appeal to him to establish the relationship on a truer and more equable basis. " Have pity on me, my own dearest, and consider how I must feel to see myself idealized away, little by little, like Ossian's spirits into the mist . . till . . ' Gone is the daughter of Morven ! ' And what if it is mist or moon-glory, if I stretch out my hands to you in vain, and must still fade away farther ? "

. For that it was in vain, she saw clearly enough even then. Robert Browning could not relinquish his ideal conception of love without relinquishing at the same time love itself. And earnestly as she might implore him to " give me liberty to breathe and feel naturally . . . according to my own nature ", she had not the courage more fundamentally to impair the basis of their relationship. Reproach herself as she might for " seeming to love your love more than you ", she was ready, none the less, to accept a devotion that came to her, as she felt, blindly and by proxy. Was there not, even, an added reassurance in the fact that this love was dependent upon no accidental quality or virtue of her own ? For if the motive of love should lie " in the feeling itself and not in the object

of it ", how much stronger, she felt, must be the guarantee of
its durability. Useless, then, by her own action to disturb
an equilibrium so established. There was a time when, as she
admitted, " I used to be more uneasy, and to think that I
ought to *make* you see me. But Love is better than Sight, and
Love will do without Sight. Which I did not understand
at first. I knew it was enough for *me*, that you should love
me. That it was enough for *you*, I had to learn afterwards."
And in final submission to the fixed necessities of the situation
—" May God grant that you *never see me*," she wrote, " for
then we two shall be ' happy ' as you say. . . ."

Robert Browning had no such misgivings. On the contrary.
He had rediscovered, re-activated through the power of love, a
sealed-off mine whose veins, bright with a forgotten happiness,
had lain unexploited all the while, beneath the indifferent
surface of the years. And he recognised now by touch, by
memory, by the un-named senses of the soul, the contours of a
long-lost felicity. " And now, my love—I am round you . .
my whole life is wound up and down and over you . . I
feel you stir everywhere." Within the blind intimacy of such
a union—" I should like to breathe and move and live by your
allowance and pleasure "—was the security he sought : a
security in which he was permitted not only to lie beneath
the " mind supremacy " of the woman he loved, but also, to
his own " unutterable delight " beneath the dominion of " your
eye, your hand ". So deep in him was the need for self-
abnegation (" —I desire . . . to be yours and with you and,
as far as may be in this world and life, YOU——") that he
begged her to envisage him as " living wholly in your life,
seeing good and ill only as you see,—being yours as your
hand is,—or as your Flush, rather ". In the position thus
allocated to him, lay a long-term guarantee against the perils
of independence. " I shall grow old with you and die with
you—as far as I can look into the night I see the light with me.
And surely with that provision of comfort one should turn with
fresh joy and renewed sense of security to the sunny middle
of the day." Above him, once more, was the ministering
presence ; the guiding, the correcting hand : was not Ba his
" very, very angel ", the " dear angel of my life ", and must
he not, in " contented lowness ", turn and " look up into your

eyes for all light and life ? " And even as he did so, as he
abased himself in " a worship of you that is solely fit for me,
fit by position ", solicitously, all the while, the tender countenance brooded over his own, the tender eyes gazed down,
" understanding and pardoning all ".

5

Whenever they found themselves discussing together the
circumstances, domestic and financial, of their future lives,
there was one subject which produced between these Victorian
lovers an inevitable constraint. But if this—the question of
sharing a bedroom—was hedged about with reticences and
evasions of all kinds, it was because Robert, and not Elizabeth,
exhibited a shrinking timidity at the thought of the intimacies
therein involved. Elizabeth was once surprised to find that a
man who had lived " in the midst of this London of ours, close
to the great social vortex ", where he must have met " tempta-
tion more than enough, I am certain, under every form "
should have kept himself " so safe, and free, and calm and
pure from the besetting sins of our society ". She was no less
surprised, now, to discover that this " same mild man-about-
town " who had confessed to knowing " what most of the
pleasures of this world are ", should reveal so little worldly
aplomb in a discussion of this nature. For here, despite his
earnest, his oft-avowed desire to live " in one room " with his
beloved, he had to confess, reluctantly, to " a weakness " of
his own which was, he admitted, " hardly reconcilable to that
method of being happy ". With the utmost embarrassment,
imploring Ba to put her hand before his two eyes—" I shall
begin ", he wrote, " by begging a separate room from yours—
I could never brush my hair and wash my face, I do think,
before my own father—I could not, I am sure, take off my
coat before you *now*—why should I ever ? . . ." It was left
to Elizabeth, as tactfully as she could, to placate this affrighted
modesty. " Dearest, what you say is unnecessary for you to
say—it is in everything *so* of course and obvious ! You must
have an eccentric idea of *me* if you can suppose for a moment

such things to be necessary to say. If they had been *unsaid*, it would have been precisely the same, believe me, in the event."

What Elizabeth could not yet know was how tenaciously rooted into the very sub-soil of his nature was this curious " male prudery " of Robert Browning's. To the poet, the most humiliating of all imaginable situations was that in which " some clownish person had thrown open the door of a bathing machine in which I was undressing ", with the result—(" and a very young lady would be mortified enough ")—that " the whole company on the beach stare and probably laugh ". Even in childhood, Mrs. Orr tells us, " his sense of certain proprieties was extraordinarily keen. He told a friend that on one occasion, when the merest child, he had edged his way by the wall from one point of his bedroom to another, because he was not fully clothed, and his reflection in the glass could otherwise have been seen through the partly open door." This early reticence, the need to cover up what must on no account be seen, remained with him to the end of his days ; taking, in its several manifestations, an extreme and sometimes even a violent form. We have seen the effect on his work : after the inadvertent self-exposure of *Pauline,* the search for a denser, a more adhesive disguise : the adoption of the dramatic form, in collusion with which he was enabled for so many years effectively to outwit the proctors of society. The most successful disguise of all, of course, was language itself : there can be little doubt that much of the obscurity of Robert Browning was an involuntary form of self-protection. (Browning himself put it otherwise. I write " ugly things ", he said, " in order to warn the ungenial and the timorous off my grounds at once ".) He was not always so peremptory. Conformity is itself a form of disguise : the poet was scrupulously careful, all his life, to avoid the censure or the derision of society. It was only in the privacy of his own room at Camberwell or New Cross that he permitted himself the Bohemian ease of " a blouse and a blue shirt " : despite his avowed contempt for " all manner of dress and gentlemanly appointment ", whenever he made the descent into town, it was not in the " distinctive blouse and Louis II hat " of the artist, nor even with " his hair as picturesquely disordered as the best of them ", but dressed and groomed, on the contrary, with a scrupulous neatness and correctness that impressed itself on all who saw him.[1] Even the " lemon-coloured kid gloves " of which, in youth, the poet was inordinately fond, served to complement the total disguise : a fact one may gather from the history of yet another pair, older and more battered, which daily, in " gales and snow " as in " burning heat ", Browning wore on board ship while on a journey of seven weeks from London to Trieste. " Mr. Browning might, on such an occasion," wrote Mrs. Orr, " have dispensed with gloves altogether ; but it was one of his peculiarities that he could never endure to be out of doors with uncovered hands."

Tortuous as were the manoeuvres, from one corner of the bedroom to another, of a child who sought to shield from the parental glance the secrets of his own body, they were exceeded, in later years, by the efforts of the grown man to conceal the conditions of his inner life from the fixed, the all-expectant eye of public enquiry. The biographer who embarks on his task in face of this unrelenting prohibition, has all the sensations of a surgeon about to perform an operation without first having obtained the written consent of the patient. Only partially immobilised, moreover, the patient kicks obstreperously throughout the whole of the proceedings.

> Which of you did I enable
> Once to slip inside my breast,
> There to catalogue and label
> What I like least, what love best,
> Hope and fear, believe and doubt of,
> Seek and shun, respect—deride !·
> Who has right to make a rout of
> Rarities he found inside ?—

is a challenge which retains, across the years, the force of its original and by no means unreasonable resentment. Nor is the timid investigator reassured by the proviso that

[1] Many years later, an observer was struck by the contrast between Browning —" extremely well dressed " in a " very new and very good top hat "—and Tennyson who, in a " long Inverness cape and soft wide-brimmed wideawake . . . looked rather like an old beggar man ".

whoso desires to penetrate
Deeper, must dive by the spirit-sense—

since, instantly, the poet snarls in his face

No optics like yours, at any rate !

Most disconcerting of all, as if goaded by the eyes " so curiously, so pryingly " trained upon him, Robert Browning rebukes the biographical methods of a generation yet unborn, and turning towards the future, advises " nobody who thinks nobly of the Soul, to give, if he or she can help, such a good argument to the materialist as the owning that any great choice of that Soul . . . may be scientifically determined and produced, at any operator's pleasure . . . with the same certainty and precision that another kind of operator will construct you an artificial volcano with so much steel filings and flower of sulphur and what not."

Eighteen years later, in dedicating a partially revised *Sordello* to his friend Milsand, Browning put on record his much-quoted belief that " little else is worth study " save the " incidents in the development of a soul ". The incidents in the development of his own soul, however, he was determined should be studied by no one : and to this end, from 1833 onwards, he set himself actively to frustrate the needs of contemporaries and successors alike. For it was the publication of *Pauline*, with its repercussions, that first brought to the surface the peculiar fear of exposure which was to haunt for the rest of his life this " most pattern of citizens ". From then on, every letter, every scrap of paper left unaccounted for, was a menace to his own security. Stupefied with grief after the death of his wife, he could still experience " nervous apprehensions " about the " papers and letters " so " hastily packed away in that miserable time : even then ", he said, " I was anxious for their safety." He was not to be pacified until he had gathered into his own keeping or, better still, destroyed, documents which he chose for some reason to regard as in-criminating evidence. Elizabeth Barrett, who valued letters as " the most vital part of biography " detected with surprise this desire to " efface all autobiography and confession— tear out a page bent over by many learners ". It was not only letters, however, which Browning distrusted : all juvenilia was equally suspect. Imagine, wrote the author of *Pauline*, the feelings of a man who " finds that some bookseller has disinterred and is about publishing the raw first attempt at a work which he was guilty of in the outset ! " It was an ordeal that he was determined to spare himself : into the grate at Warwick Crescent went not only all the letters " which, while his parents lived, he had written to them by way of minute daily journals from Russia, Italy and England ", but a whole collection of boyish poems once intended to compose a volume called *Incondita*. Again the question arises : why these elaborate precautions ? Why this unsleeping anxiety on the part of a man whose public and private life alike were of a quite exceptional rectitude ? A letter written by Browning on March 19, 1864, to his friend William Wetmore Story, brings us as close as we shall get, perhaps, to the root of the matter. Angrily, in this, the poet complains of the action of Thornton Hunt in printing without permission a joint letter to Leigh Hunt from Elizabeth and himself ; knowing all the while, Browning wrote, that " I should have refused leave to print such a thing in the most energetic terms possible ". And he goes on to say, inadvertently uncovering as he does so what can only be the original site, long obscured, of this deeply based prohibition : " There's nothing in my letter I care about except the indecent nature of the exposure—it's just as if, being at my toilette, some clownish person chose to throw the bedroom door wide——" But here, apparently, the poet realised, suddenly, upon what brink he stood ; and some imprudence contained in the following four words has been vigorously erased by his pen. Instead—" there's enough of it ", he concluded ; and hastily, before the reflection in the glass can be glimpsed by the Peeping Tom of posterity, Robert Browning has slammed the bedroom door in our faces.

6

Only one letter is missing out of the five hundred and seventy-two that passed, before their departure for Italy, between Elizabeth Barrett and Robert Browning : and that is the letter which, after their first meeting, the poet wrote to an incurable invalid, as he then believed her to be, asking her to become his wife. Barely had he posted the letter, however, before panic broke in upon him. " The moment after that inconsiderate letter, I reproached myself bitterly with the selfishness apparently involved in any proposition I might then have made—for though I have never been at all frightened of the world, nor mistrustful of my power to deal with it, and get my purpose out of it if once I thought it worth while, yet I could not but feel the consideration, of *what* failure would *now* be, paralyse all effort even in fancy."

Elizabeth's unequivocal refusal can only have come, then, as a relief to this impetuous but wholly impractical wooer, who, however confident he might feel of his own power to deal with the world, had never yet made an effective attempt to do so ; and was still, in his thirty-fourth year, living a life of naïve and child-like dependence within the family circle at New Cross. As a poet, Browning rightly felt he could afford to be indifferent to material success

> —since verse, the gift,
> Was his, and men, the whole of them, must shift
> Without it, e'en content themselves with wealth
> And pomp and power, snatching a life by stealth.

While, however, one can have nothing but admiration for this indifference to success " in the worldly sense ", it is necessary to remember that until the day Robert Browning married, the burden of this independence was borne by shoulders older and more submissive than his own. That the situation at New Cross had attracted the comments of the outside world, we already know : and it was, perhaps, because he felt himself responsible for the friendship of the two poets, which he had done so much to bring about, that Mr. Kenyon undertook, now, to keep a watching brief on the development of that concealed relationship. He continued, as always, to speak with amiability of the character and the poetic achievement of Robert Browning. Nevertheless, the day arrived in which, " after talk upon other subjects, he began a long wandering sentence, the end of which ", said Elizabeth, " I could see a mile off, about how he 'ought' to know better than I, but wished to enquire of me ' . . what, do you suppose ? why, ' what Mr. Browning's objects in life were '." For Mr. Kenyon, it seems, had been discussing the case of the poet with Mrs. Procter, and once again—(" Mrs. Procter ", Browning said grimly, " is very exactly the Mrs. Procter I knew long ago ")—the " seven or eight hours a day of occupation " or the lack of it, had come prominently into the foreground. Elizabeth was distressed by the insinuations of this " worldly woman ". She took refuge in indignation. Robert Browning, she told Mr. Kenyon, " did not *require* an occupation as a means of living . . having simple habits and desires . . and if Mr. Procter had looked as simply to his art as an end, he would have done better things." Browning, however, was alarmed to hear of Mrs. Procter's open " bitterness of speech " : of Miss Procter's assertion that she, for her part, would rather " commit suicide " than live as he chose to live. Despite the secret key which, he claimed, enabled him to " lock out the world, and then look down on it ", it frightened him to think that this worldly criticism should have seeped through the double doors of the sickroom and reached the ears of Elizabeth Barrett. For, he said, " if *here* the world plucked you from me by any of the innumerable lines it casts, with that indirectness too,—*then* I should simply go and live the rest of my days as far out of it as I could." Elizabeth, in reply, repudiated with scorn the idea that it was possible for the world to catch her " with a ' line ' so baited " ; or, indeed, for any " such motives to divide me from you ". On the contrary, she said : " With a hundred a year between us, I would have married you, if *you* had not been afraid." Browning's relief, on hearing this, was as spontaneous as it was overwhelming. " You only, only adorable woman, only imaginable love for me ! " he wrote : " —how must I love you and press closer to you more and more, and desire to see nothing of the world behind you, when I hear how the world thinks, and how you think ! "

Elizabeth's courage, however, was not without its limitations. It was she who suggested with many circumlocutions and much painful embarrassment that, since " it is not of the least importance to either of us, as long as we can live, whether the sixpence we live by, came most from you or from me ", they should " join in throwing a little dust in all the winking eyes round ", and conceal, not only from the world at large, but from the members of her own family, the true facts of Browning's financial position. Those facts were simple enough. Robert Browning was penniless.[1] And the necessity of a union between poverty on the one hand and a private income on the other produced between them almost as much embarrassment as the prospect of sharing a double bed. " My own Ba, *do not refer to what we spoke of*—the next vile thing to the vilest is, being too conscious of avoiding *that*—painfully, ostentatiously, protesting and debating . . . you understand what I expect at your hands." Nevertheless, the subject continued to cause uneasiness between them ; so much so, that resolutely, from time to time, Browning found it necessary to present himself to her in the rôle of breadwinner. Whenever I make up my mind to it, he told her, " I can be rich enough and to spare." Therefore, he said, " when the only obstacle is only that there is so much *per annum* to be producible, you will tell me ". Stung, suddenly, by this " one possible occasion of calumny ", he went further still. " Does anybody doubt ", he demanded fiercely, " that I can by application in proper quarters obtain quite enough to support us both in return for no extraordinary expenditure of such faculties as I have ? If it *is* to be doubted, I have been greatly misinformed, that is all." And his own indignation gaining, suddenly, upon him : " *Let me do so, and at once, my own Ba !* And do you, like the unutterably noble creature I know you, transfer your own advantages to your brothers and sisters . . . making if you please a proper reservation in the case of my own exertions failing, as failure comes everywhere. I am ", he went on, " entirely in earnest about this, and indeed had thought for a moment of putting my own share of the project into immediate execution—but on consideration,—no ! "

An equally timely consideration checked similar plans to sell his own copyrights, to apply for a pension or seek a diplomatic post. Elizabeth, as he knew, was determined not to allow " a superfluousness of devotion " on such grounds. It would have been the more difficult for her to do so, in that

---

[1] When it was realised that Elizabeth could not, without attracting suspicion, divert to him a sum of money sufficient for the journey to Italy, the poet was forced to borrow £100 from his father.

Browning himself had made plain to her at the outset a certain
reluctance to prove his devotion in this form. " I shall own ",
he once wrote to her, " *that would be* the *one* poor sacrifice I
could make you—one I would cheerfully make, but a sacrifice,
and the only one . . . this absolute independence of mine,
which, if I had it not, my heart would starve and die for. . . ."
Elizabeth, not unnaturally—" I would not bear or dare to do
you so much wrong "—refused with dignity to " accept *such* a
sacrifice " from the poet. Nor in any case was it necessary,
she told him. For " if I *wished* to be very poor, in the world's
sense of poverty, I *could not*, with three or four hundred a
year of which no living will can dispossess me ". Upon hearing which—" all my solicitude was at an end ", Browning
frankly declared. A new form of discomfort, on the other
hand, was about to begin : the thought that he might be
regarded, like his friend Horne, in the light of a fortune-
hunter ; and it was, finally, to ease his mind of this burden
that Elizabeth put forward to him the suggestion that, after
he and she had both died, such capital as she possessed should
return to her own family, whence it came. Browning immediately countered the suggestion with a more quixotic one of his
own, whereby he refused, in effect, to retain a single penny of
hers after her death. It distressed Elizabeth that he should
" disinherit " himself in this fashion ; and " after a long pause
and much irresolution ", he consented to change his mind.
For, he said, " if the saddest fate I can imagine should be
reserved for me . . . I should need distraction, the more
violent the better " ; and in order, therefore, " to live the
days out worthily ", as he put it, " I return nothing to your
family, be assured. You will not recur to *this* ! "

It was necessary to recur to it, however, for the discomfort
persisted : and this time, to dispel it, Elizabeth had recourse
to a different suggestion. " Would you be easier, dearest,"
she enquired, " if a *part* were relinquished *now* ? " Robert
Browning answered the letter by return of post. No, he said,
" I do not ask you to ' relinquish a part '—not as our arrangements now are ordered : for I have never been so foolish as
to think we could live without money, if not of my obtaining,
then of your possessing, and though, in certain respects I
should have preferred to try the first course . . . yet, as that

is not to be, I have only to be thankful that you are not dependent on my exertions,—which I could not be *sure* of, particularly with this uncertain head of mine." And with so much admitted, it was easier for him to go on, as he now did, to ask her, " at once, or as soon as practicable," to " ascertain what you certainly possess—what is quite yours, and in your sole power to take or to let remain—what will be just as available to you in Italy as in England ? I want to know, being your possible husband . . . so tell me how much will be found in the purse. . . ." For, he went on to say, " in spite of a few misgivings at first I am not proud, or rather, am proud in the right place. I am utterly, exclusively proud of you—and though I should have gloried in working myself to death to prove it, and shall be as ready to do so at any time a necessity shall exist, yet at present I shall best serve you, I think, by the life by your side, which we contemplate."

The young Robert Browning was genuinely indifferent to money. His whole concern, it will be realised, was not to acquire a fortune, but to re-create, as far as possible, the circumstances in which, " free and poor ", he had lived hitherto under his father's roof at Camberwell and at New Cross. It was no pleasure to him to know that, after she married him, Elizabeth Barrett must relinquish all rights in her own property ; that, the wedding ceremony concluded, every penny she inherited or earned became his by right of law. On the contrary. His one desire was to evade altogether the responsibilities and cares attached to the management of property. " My notion of the perfection of money arrangements is that of a fairy purse which every day holds *so* much, and there an end of trouble." The fairy purse now placed at his disposal was not altogether dissimilar to that on which he had, up till then, so trustingly relied. As to " a humiliating dependence in money matters ", I should be, the poet confessed, " the first to except myself from feeling *quite* with the world there ". The reason he offers is a characteristic one. " I hate being *master*, and alone, and absolute disposer in points where real love will save me the trouble . . . because there are infinitely more and greater points where the solitary action and will, with their responsibility, cannot be avoided." If Elizabeth and not he, therefore, was to guarantee the security of their

wedded lives, there could be no real humiliation in the fact.
On the contrary. Was it not the purest of privileges that,
for the satisfaction of his deepest needs, material and spiritual
alike, he should be permitted to turn in future to the woman
he loved ?

7

" Always," wrote Elizabeth a few weeks after her marriage,
" he has had the greatest power over my heart, because I am
of those weak women who reverence strong men." It was
not, however, of her husband that the bride was thus speaking, but of her father. Edward Moulton-Barrett, his daughter
confessed, " might have been king and father over me to the
end, if he had thought it worth while to love me openly
enough ". In which case, Robert Browning would not have
been given the opportunity to come close enough to prove his
love for her. " So the nightshade and the eglantine are
twisted, twined, one in the other . . and the little pink
roses lean up against the pale poison of the berries—we cannot
tear this from that, let us think of it ever so much ! " For
there was much in her nature that yearned, still, for the very
domination which she was about to reject : the sternness ;
the resolute handling ; the steel-like tenacity in decision.
" Papa ", she often said, " is stronger than most men " ; and
this pre-eminence called out a corresponding " gratitude and
reverence " in one whose " immoral sympathy with power "
had more than once drawn down upon her the disapproving
comments of her cousin, John Kenyon. Susceptible as she
might be to the " divine patience and tenderness " of Robert
Browning, it was none the less the " inflexible will " of the
tyrant that continued, to the end of her life, to inspire in the
invalid the deepest emotional response. Once upon a time,
Elizabeth Barrett had had a very strong will of her own :
thwarted, she had thrown the books about the room, and
upset tables and chairs in a fury. But since then, she had seen
the exercise of that will bring down a lasting desolation upon
her own head : and in a violent revulsion of feeling, she had

retracted all overt expression of it : withdrawing into a " state of neutralised emotion ", in which she lay " tranquil unto death " beneath the ministrations of hands more capable than her own.   But if this neutrality was accepted without question by every member of the household, it did not mislead Robert Browning.   Some intuition, some necessity of his own, divined the will, latent still, within her ; and presumed, in spite of every resistance, to call it forth.   Nothing could have been more disconcerting to Elizabeth than to discover in Browning the curious conviction that " women were as strong as men " : [1] or to be faced, as she now was, with the earnest invitation to exercise, at his expense, the full resources of that reputed strength.   " I submit to you and will obey you implicitly— obey what I am able to conceive of your least desire, much more of your expressed wish."   It was in these, as it might be wifely, terms, that the poet made to her a proposal of marriage. More bewildering still, to a daughter of Edward Moulton-Barrett, was his refusal to inflict upon her the weight of his own will.   On the contrary : " I wish your will to be mine, to originate mine, your pleasure to be mine only," he wrote. A suggestion exquisitely calculated to frustrate the established needs of her own nature.   As, vainly, she tried again and again to make him see.   With the utmost earnestness, preferring in every case to " be vexed " than to " vex ", she begged him to " consent to be selfish in all things " ; for his continual deference and solicitude, like a trough of low pressure, denied her the very conditions that her peculiar state of health required.   " Have so much faith in me, only beloved, as to use me simply for your own advantages and happiness, and to your own ends without a thought of any others. . . ." Browning, however, declined with finality the invitation to assert himself.   " My own will has all along been annihilated

---

[1] Thirty-five years later, Browning was to express unbounded enthusiasm for *Dorothy, A Country Story in Elegiac Verse*, a poem by A. J. Munby, celebrating the fitness, in women, of physical labour.

> " Stalwart and tall as a man, strong as a heifer to work :
> Built for beauty, indeed, but certainly built for labour—
> Witness her muscular arms, witness the grip of her hand !

This poem, Browning read " with a surprise of delight as rare as it was thorough . . . it is literally years since I have admired and enjoyed a poem *so much*," he told Kegan Paul.

before you—with respect to you—I should never be able to say ' she shall dine on fish, on fruit ', ' She shall wear silk gloves or thread gloves '—even to exercise in fancy that much ' will *over* you ' is revolting ; I *will this,* never to be ' over you ' if I could ! ''

With an almost perceptible sigh, Elizabeth spoke once of her lover as '' too perfect, too overcomingly good and tender ''. '' You grow awful to me sometimes with the very excess of your goodness and tenderness,'' she told him. '' Indeed,'' she confided to her sister, '' all women might not like *the excess* . . I do not know.'' For there were moments when she found this '' pleasure in obedience '' more trying than any '' of the common rampant man-vices which tread down a woman's peace ''. It displaced her own preconceived notion of Robert Browning ; a notion which, wistfully, all the while, she sought to retain : the masterful character who had forced his way into her life in order to take her under the protection of an all-powerful will. It was true that he had forced her to accept a resurrection which she had long ceased to wish for : that he had turned her face, once more, towards the light of day. Barely was the life-giving process complete, however, before he laid himself, in his turn, inert at her feet. '' Will you not do what you can with me who am your very own ? '' he asked. '' I am yours to operate on.'' And humbly—'' my life lies before you to take and direct,''—he implored her to '' take me and make me what you can and will '' : assuring her that beneath her ministrations he was ready '' to lie quietly and let your dear will have its unrestricted way.'' Gradually, it became clear to Elizabeth that if Robert Browning had demanded her hand in marriage, it was in order that this same hand should exert, for the rest of his life, a guiding pressure upon his own. '' Leading me up and onward,'' Elizabeth Barrett, '' my audience, my crown-bearer, my path-preparer '', was to '' hold me by the hand till the end ''.

> we will go hand in hand,
> I will go with thee, even as a child,
> Looking no further than thy sweet commands.

Thus he had written, at the age of twenty, in *Pauline* : poem of conflict and capitulation. Obscurely, once more, the poet rediscovered the happiness of that acquiescent handclasp. " So, is your hand in mine, or rather mine in yours again, sweetest, best love ? All will be well."

The idea of casting herself, " a dead burden, on the man I love " had once produced in Elizabeth " a long struggle and months of agitation ". Many more months were to pass before she realised that, far from being passive, against all appearances and probabilities, the active rôle in this marriage was to be taken by her and not by Robert Browning. The prospect was not one to fill her with pleasure. It placed a grave burden upon a woman who for many years had lived " under circumstances of confinement and total personal dependence " : who, in her fortieth year, still looked on her father as the " natural source of counsel and strength ". Out of her love for Robert Browning, however, and her gratitude to him, she found the courage to accept what she saw to be a necessary condition of their marriage. For that such it was, Browning himself did not hesitate to make plain to her. There was " one thing " only, he confessed, which he had hitherto regretted, and that (he wrote to her from his room at New Cross), was the idea of losing, in marriage, " the pro- longed relation of childhood almost . . nay altogether— with all here ". Now, however, through her, this state of protracted childhood in which he had always taken such " a great delight ", would not be lost : it was " only modified— transferred partly and the rest retainable ". Wherefore—" I hope if you want to please me especially, Ba, you will always remember I have been accustomed, by pure choice, to have another will lead mine in the little daily matters of life. If there are two walks to take (to put the thing at simplest) you must say, ' *This* one ' and not ' either ' . . because though they were before indifferently to be chosen—after *that* speech, one is altogether better than the other, to *me* if not to you. When you have a real preference which I can discern, you will be good enough to say nothing about it, my own Ba ! Now, do you not see how, with this feeling, which God knows I profess to be mine without the least affectation,—how much my happiness would be disturbed by allying myself with a woman to whose intellect, as well as goodness, I could *not* look up ? —in an obedience to whose desires, therefore, I should not be justified in indulging ? It is pleasanter to lie back on the cushions inside the carriage and let another drive—but if you suspect he cannot drive ? "

8

On January 27th, 1846, Robert Browning wrote to Elizabeth Barrett : " I claim your promise's fulfilment—say at the summer's end : it cannot be for your own good that this state of things should continue. We can go to Italy for a year or two and be happy as day and night are long." Acquiescent in tone, Elizabeth's reply to this presents, nevertheless, a characteristic reservation. " If in the time of fine weather, I am not ill . . *then* . . *not now* you shall decide, and your decision shall be duty and desire to me, both—I will make no difficulties." In the time of fine weather, she was not ill ; she was strong enough, in May and June, to walk under the trees of Regent's Park, and to witness, in Mr. Kenyon's company, the " strange new sight " of the Great Western arriving in " earth-thunder " at its destination : at the same time, enervated as much by emotional inbreeding as by morphia, she could not control, wholly, the vacillation of her own will : and it was in some such moment of irresolution that she wrote to enquire of her lover whether, instead of precipitating their departure, they might not gain, perhaps, " by remaining quietly as we are, you at New Cross, and I here, until next year's summer or autumn ? " This " simple experimental question ", the sudden outcrop of weeks and months of procrastination, touched the poet to " the very quick and core of the heart ". His reply has an unmistakable emphasis. " Every day that passes before *that day*," he wrote, " is one the more of hardly endurable anxiety and irritation, to say the least ; and the thought of another year's intervention of hope deferred—altogether intolerable ! " There was good reason for this anxiety on his part : for as the time approached when she must redeem her promise to him, there became evident in the invalid a growing reluctance to translate into terms of reality the content of that long-deferred dream. " I scarcely ever do think of the future," she confessed ; " scarcely ever further than to your next visit, and almost never beyond . . . the future never seemed to belong to me so little— never ! " Continuously Browning sought to release her from a dangerous complacency : to awaken her to the perils and realities of her own situation. There were moments, too, when he found it necessary to remind her that what he felt for her was something more than " a dreamy abstract passion for a phantom of my own creating " : that, grateful as he might be for the spiritual intimacy which she afforded him, his no less impassioned desire was to confirm at yet another level of experience the unity between them. " And if *now* you do not understand—well I kneel to you, my Ba, and pray you to give yourself to me in deed as in word, the body as the heart and mind,—and *now* ! "

But there was " no getting rid of these mistakings before the time . . . the hoe never cuts up all their roots " ; and ten days later, after a night of insomnia and low spirits, Elizabeth was writing again to ask her lover to release her from a promise just given : that she would never allow the opinions of others to dissuade her from marrying him. It is impossible not to sympathise with Browning during the course of these critical days ; his qualities as lover and friend have never been better exhibited than in his patient, tender and desperate attempts to pacify anxiety, to rally a flagging will-power. " Do not for God's sake," he implored her, " introduce an element of uncertainty and restlessness and dissatisfaction into the feeling whereon my life lies. To speak for myself, this matter is concluded, done with,—I am yours, you are mine, and not to give use to refinements upon refinements as to what is the being most of all each other's, which might end in your loving me best while I was turned a Turk in the East—or my—you know the inquisition does all for the pure love of the victim's soul. Let us have common sense. . . . If you dare make the effort, we will do as we propose,—if not, not : I have nothing to do but take your hand. . . ."

If you dare make the effort. . . . But how great that effort must appear to the recluse, even he could not be expected to realise. " I have ", Elizabeth confessed, " lived so in a dream, for very long !—and everything, all undertakings, all movements, seem easy in dream-life. The sense of this has lately startled me." For, despite the precision of a finely-geared intellect, this haziness had intervened of late increasingly between herself and the external world, causing her to resent at times the presence of her own relatives, whose conversation jolted her sharply " out of my dream-life with you —into the old dreary flats of real life." With solitude, however, the dream was reinstated : all-sufficient as before. How then, dream-bound, was she to prepare herself for the future, for a future that seemed at once so remote and so improbable ? Even the plans for their suggested journey to Italy—alluring enough " by the dreamlight we look at them by "—all seemed to her, she languidly confessed, " too earnest for the mere dream I have been dreaming all this while ".

Disquieted by the persistence of this attitude, the poet was no less disturbed, as the weeks and months went by, to find that old fears and superstitions, long dormant, were working their way once more towards the surface. The " black intervals ", rare in the April of that year, reappeared in June, and darkened much of July. Misunderstandings sprang up again and multiplied : Browning tried to bring home to her how rapidly " the ground is crumbling from beneath our feet " : Elizabeth, reverting suddenly to the theme of her own unworthiness, told a weary lover : " You had better give me up " : Mr. Kenyon, encountering Browning on the stairs of Wimpole Street, brandished his eye-glass from one flushed face to another and embarked on a series of searching, inconvenient questions : even Flush, infected by the general irritability, went berserk and bit the poet on the ankle. The uncertain weather—" at noon, so oppressively hot—this morning a wind and a cold,"—brought the month to a close ; and on the first day of August, 1846, Browning sat the whole afternoon behind the closed doors and windows of the sickroom, while one of the greatest thunderstorms in living memory burst over London and the suburbs. Giant hailstones rattled down the chimneys, and shattered thousands of panes of glass which fell with a ringing clash into the flooded streets below. For three hours, in that darkened room overhanging the mews, he sat at the side of a ghostly-looking Ba, feeling with joy the " dear hand press mine closer while the thunder sounded." But Elizabeth was not thinking of Robert : she scarcely saw him. " When you sate there yesterday," she wrote, " I was looking at Papa's face as I saw it through the floor." She was listening for the sound of Mr. Moulton-Barrett's footstep on the stair, of his voice at the brusquely-opened door ; awaiting, mute with terror, a scene whose violence was more redoubtable, far, than that of the thunderstorm itself. An hour later, when she was " lying on the sofa and had on a white dressing-gown, to get rid of the strings ", he did in fact come into the room. " Looking a little as if the thunder had passed into him," he demanded : " Has this been your costume since the morning, pray ? " : adding, ominously, " It appears, Ba, that *that man* has spent the whole day with you." " Think," said Elizabeth piteously, " how it must have been a terrible day, when the lightning of it made the least terror." Then, hesitating a little—(" What is the use of telling you this ? I do not know ") —she went on to make a confession. " Before yesterday's triple storms," she wrote, " I had a presentiment which oppressed me during two days . . a presentiment that it would all end *ill*, through some sudden accident or misery of some kind." A few days later, there was another storm ; and it is in a letter of this same date that there recurs an expression which had been absent for many months from her vocabulary. " *May* I be yours, not to do you harm, my beloved." It was, like her talk of her own " ill luck ", her evil star, " a word of my old life ".

One evening, Elizabeth Barrett received a letter from Robert Browning. When she broke the seal, she discovered inside the envelope three or four withered leaves. " Dear brown leaves," she wrote in surprise, " where did they come from, besides from *you* ? " For she did not recognise, at once, a symbol of despair, of frustration. Nor did she recognise, perhaps, what an ardent nature suffered in the protracted deferment of its own most cherished hopes. " I will be yours ", she promised her lover, " at the summer's end." Amongst the flowers and fruit trees of his mother's garden at New Cross, Browning watched, for the second year in succession, the steady rise and decline of the seasons. First, " the spring passes away without the true spring feeling," he wrote, " and then the summer itself ". Once, already, he had lit a fire in his room. Walking in the garden, he saw " all the roses fast going, lilies going . . autumnal hollyhocks in full blow ". " Would it be profane ", the poet wrote to her, " to think of that lament . . . ' the Summer is ended and we are not saved ' ? "

Elizabeth, in reply, sent him a " green little branch " plucked, through the carriage window, from a lane in Hampstead. " Oh—there is time," she said lightly,—" full time." She wished to believe so, indeed. For whereas she lingered, now, " on the edge of a precipice in a position full of anxiety and danger ", what lay before her, she could not help feeling, presented a danger more formidable still. Robert Browning had never yet seen her outside the walls of this one room— never looked upon her face by the broad light of day. What if he started back, dismayed ? " Tomorrow and tomorrow and tomorrow, what will *you* do ? " she wrote. " Nay, but it is rather reasonable that when the hour strikes, the fairy-gold should turn back into leaves, and poor Cinderella find herself sitting in her old place among the ashes, just as she had touched the hand of the king's son." This humility, these fears were incomprehensible to Browning. To him, on the contrary, Elizabeth—" my Lady, my Queen "—was not only the central prop of his existence, but upon her, he had felt from the first, " every instant of my life depended . . . for its support and comfort ". What, then, above everything else he needed, he told her, was to feel that " *you* will go on to the end, that the arm round me will not let me go ". For, without that support, where would he be ? Panic rose in him at the very thought. " You would undo me in withdrawing from me your help, *undo* me, I feel ! "

The cry of distress had its effect. " *I* will not fail to you," Elizabeth wrote. " If the arm you talk of *drops*, it will not be for weariness nor even for weakness, but because it is cut off at the shoulder." This docile reliance on her reputed " strength of arm " was scarcely calculated, however, to reassure one as " sublimely helpless and impotent " as Elizabeth Barrett believed herself to be. " I rest on you, for life, for death, beloved," Browning assured her. But she, too, required a like support : was not her need, at such a juncture, even

greater than his own ? " For after all," she said reprovingly,
" this is rather a serious matter we are upon, and if you think
you are not to have your share of responsibility, that you are
not to consider and arrange and decide, and perform your
own part, you are as much mistaken as ever *I* was." And,
replacing her hands once more in her lap, " For my part,"
she said, " I have done, it seems to me, nearly as much as I
can do." It was the old, the familiar deadlock : two natures
equally reluctant to command ; eager, each, to obey. " Think
for us both ! " was Browning's constant request. No less frequently : " You must think for both of us," Elizabeth implored
him. " My whole life," Browning reminded her, " is bound
up with the success of this measure . . . therefore, think and
decide, my Ba ! " " Don't," Elizabeth begged him, " don't
above all, refuse to think for me, and decide for me, or what
will become of me, I cannot guess." But she did guess : she
knew that now and hereafter the thinking, the deciding, would
have to be done by her : that the poet married her in order
to place himself, unreservedly, under the dispensation of her
will—" you whom I implicitly trust in to see for me," he said.
In this " second year of our reign " Elizabeth Barrett understood a little, if not all, of the nature of Robert Browning's
need for her. " Ah—I have my ' theory of causation ' about
it all—but we need not dispute, and will not, on any such
metaphysics." For as long as it was " *love* " she said, " should
I accept it less gladly, do you imagine, because of the root ? "

September came, and nothing had been decided upon,
neither the date of the wedding nor the manner of their
departure from England. Browning suffered increasingly from
irritability and a " sick vile headache " ; while Elizabeth was
low in spirits, and so apprehensive that the sound of " my
own footsteps startle me ". Her fear was, she admitted, that
she would break down, " in nervous excitement and exhaustion ", for she belonged to that " pitiful order of weak women
who cannot command their bodies with their souls at every
moment, and who sink down in hysterical disorder when they
ought to act and resist ". However, she said with a sigh,
" where things *ought* to be done, they of course *must* be done.
Only we should consider whether they really *ought* to be done
—not for the sake of the inconvenience to me, but of the

consequence to both of us." With admirable control : " I *do* understand your anxieties, dearest," Browning wrote to her, "—I take your fears and make them mine, while I put my own natural feelings of quite another kind away from us both, succeeding in *that* beyond all expectation. . . . If you find yourself unable, or unwilling to make this effort, tell me so plainly and at once—I will not offer a word in objection—I will continue our present life, if you please, so far as may be desirable, and wait till next autumn, and the next and the next, till providence end our waiting."

> Meantime, worse fate than a lover's fate,
> Who daily may ride and look
> Where his lady watches behind the grate !

Elizabeth was stung by the reproach behind his words. " Now *is* it fair, ever dearest, that you should turn round on me so quickly, and call in question my willingness to keep my engagement for years, if ever ? . . . I do not," she assured him, " object nor hold back." At the same time, she admitted, she could not avoid the panic of pain and fear that assailed her, at the thought of the many risks involved in that leap into the unknown. " If you jump out of the window you succeed in getting to the ground, somehow, dead or alive . . . but whether *that* means ' ending well ' depends on your way of considering matters," she wrote. Browning's reply to this is characteristic of a philosophy of life magnificently to be expressed by him in poetry as yet unborn. " I would ' run the risk '," he said, " rationally, deliberately,—knowing what the ordinary law of chances in this world justifies in such a case ; and if the result after all *was* unfortunate, it would be far easier to undergo the extremest penalty with so little to reproach myself for,—than to put aside the adventure,—waive the wondrous possibility of such best fortune, in a fear of the barest possibility of an adverse event. . . . *Now*, jump with me out, Ba ! "

> But next day passed, and next day yet,
> With still fresh cause to wait one day more
> Ere each leaped over the parapet.

In the end, it was Mr. Moulton-Barrett himself who pushed them both summarily over the edge.

At midnight on Wednesday, September 9th, 1846, Elizabeth Barrett wrote a hurried letter to Robert Browning. " This night ", she told him, " an edict has gone out, and George is tomorrow to be on his way to take a house for a month either at Dover, Reigate, Tunbridge, . . Papa did ' not mind which ' he said, and ' you may settle it among you !! ' but he ' must have this house empty for a month in order to its cleaning '—we are to go therefore and not delay." Breathlessly : " If we are taken away on Monday . . what then ? . . . It seems quite too soon and too sudden for us to set out on our Italian adventure now—and perhaps even we could not compass——" She did not finish the sentence. But Robert Browning chose, this time, to finish it for her. " We must be *married directly* and go to Italy. I will go for a licence today and we can be married on Saturday." For he recognised in this emergency an " intervention of Providence " on his behalf ; and one without which he might never have found it possible to make Elizabeth Barrett his wife. He took full advantage of the " little brief authority " offered him. " Your words, first and last, have been that you ' would not fail me ' " he wrote : with significant emphasis,—" you will not," he told her. Elizabeth was lulled at once into a hypnotic acquiescence. " I will act by your decision and I want you to decide," she said. Mere passivity, however, was not sufficient. " *Now your* part must begin," Browning reminded her. " It may as well begin and end, both, *now* as at any other time." Once more Elizabeth agreed : she was too bewildered, nevertheless, by this sudden acceleration in the pace of events to understand or even to believe in what she was about to do. " Will not this dream break on a sudden ? " she wrote. " Now is the moment for the breaking of it, surely." But the dream did not break ; and it was with the mien of a somnambulist that, supported on the arm of Wilson and fortified by inhalations of sal volatile, Elizabeth Barrett mounted the steps of St. Marylebone Church at a quarter to eleven on Saturday morning, September 12th, 1846. " What a wild, dreadful, floating vision it all looks like, to look back on it now ! " she afterwards wrote to her sister. " Three times I tried to write my name and could not form a letter, and someone said, I remember, ' Let her wait a moment,' and somebody else thrust in a glass of water." [1] A year later, in Florence, she was able to smile a little at the " ridiculous side " of this " dream marriage " of hers. " Always it *does* make us laugh, for instance, to think of the official's (the man with the wand in the church) attitude and gesture of astonishment as he stood at the church door and saw bride and bridegroom part on the best terms possible and go off in separate flies. Robert was very generous and threw about his gold to clerk, pew-openers, etc., in a way to convict us of being in a condition of incognito —and this particular man with a wand had hazarded, between two bursts of gratitude, a philosophic sentiment about ' marriage being a very serious event in one's mortal life ' ;—this as we left the church. And there he stood in the door way, his speech scarcely ended on his lips ; . . mouth wide open in surprise ! ' Never had he seen anything more remarkable than *that*, in the whole course of his practice ! ' " [2] There was no smiling on the day itself, however : indeed the pallor of his bride's face, as, " more dead than alive ", she struggled up the steps to meet him at the church door, was something that Robert Browning was to remember for the rest of his life. In a passion of gratitude : " Oh, I know the effort you made, the pain you bore for my sake ! " he afterwards wrote to her. " How you have dared and done all this, under my very eyes, for my only sake." And in words filled with the deepest emotion—" I exult," he said, " in the irrevocability of this precious bestowal of yourself on me—come what will my life has borne flower and fruit—it is a glorious, successful, felicitous life, I thank God and you."

Once more, Elizabeth received an enclosure in a letter from Robert Browning. When she opened the envelope, she found, not withered leaves this time, but a " dear, dear little *bud* ". Gathered so late in the season, would it ever flower ? " I shall keep it to the end of my life, if you love me so long . . ." She was pale and her eyes were smudged with tears : again and again, that morning, she had tried to write a letter to her father, but, she said, " I am paralysed when I think of having to write such words as . . ' Papa, I am married ; I hope you will not be too displeased.' " She was paralysed,

---

[1] Florence. July 9, [1847]. Huxley typescript.
[2] September 13, 1847. Ibid.

too, before the thought of the packing and planning necessary before Wilson and she could leave Wimpole Street at the end of the week. " I must break from the dream-stupor which falls on me when left to myself for a little, and set about what remains to be done," she wrote. And here she could only contemplate, dismayed, an ever-widening range of responsibility. " You know more of the world and have more practical sense than I," she once told Browning : an assumption that she was forced, now, regretfully to abandon. For this practical man of the world, she found, was nonplussed before the simplest task : he could not frame a marriage announcement or get a card engraved without her guidance and authority. More alarming still, he was incapable of reading a timetable correctly. " All shall be cared for," he wrote to her. " Depend on me." But how could she ? On Wednesday, he informed her that the " Havre-boat leaves Southampton, *Wednesdays* and Saturdays." On Thursday, she received one letter telling her that the days of sailing had been changed to Tuesdays and Fridays : and another, later in the day, contradicting that same statement. " In the flurry," Browning explained, he had inadvertently " noted down the departures from *Havre* instead of Southampton ". The next day, more consultation with timetables. " My own Ba—forgive my mistaking ! I had not enough confidence in my own correctness. The advertisement of the Tuesday and Friday Boats is of the South of England Steam Company. The Wednesday and Saturday is that of the South Western. . . . Perhaps you have seen my blunder." Yes ; Ba had seen it ; and Browning could not but be " thankful ", as he said, for her perspicacity. It was now Friday, September 18th : the last night that she was ever to spend under her father's roof. And at this, the eleventh hour, Browning blundered again : he mistook the departure of trains from Vauxhall Station. Dazed and exhausted, Elizabeth picked up a timetable and worked the matter out for herself. " Surely you say wrong in the hour for tomorrow," she wrote. " Also there is the express train. Would it not be better ? " It was an Andromeda half in love with the monster she fled from, who was forced to teach an inexperienced rescuer the most efficient method of achieving his own happiness.

"Do you confide in me, Ba?" Browning wrote. "Well, you *shall* !—in my love, in my pride, in my heart's purpose ; but not in anything else. Give me your counsel at all times, beloved : I am wholly open to your desires, and teaching, and direction. Try what you can make of me. . . ." For all its determined lightness of tone, is there not, in Elizabeth's reply to this, a hint of some half-submerged exasperation? "In your ways towards me", she wrote, "you have acted throughout too much ' the woman's part ', as that is considered. You loved me because I was lower than others, that you might be generous and raise me up :—very characteristic for a woman (in her ideal standard) but quite wrong for a man, as again and again I used to signify to you, Robert—but you went on and did it all the same. And now, you still go on—you persist—you will be the woman of the play, to the last ; let the prompter prompt ever so against you. You are to do everything I like, instead of my doing what *you* like, . . and to ' honour and obey ' *me*, in spite of what was in the vows last Saturday,—is *that* the way of it and of you? and are vows to be kept *so*, pray? after that fashion?" Whereupon, implacable now, Robert Browning was driven to assert over his wife the full force of his authority. "You shall think for me," he wrote, "that is my command !"

3

Casa Guidi Windows

It was raining when Robert Browning and his wife arrived in Pisa.

The chill rain is falling, the nipt worm is crawling,
The rivers are swelling, the thunder is knelling
         For the year ;

wrote Shelley ; watching, twenty-six years earlier, another autumn descend on the " quiet, half-unpeopled town ". It continued to rain, steadily, for the next ten days. There were " about forty-seven doors and windows ", Browning said, on the front of the great Collegio Ferdinando in which they lived : and from the window of their sitting-room, they could contemplate the equinoctial rains that, slanting over the " strange silent old city ", confined them day after day within the boundaries of an unremitting intimacy. It was not until nightfall, when Wilson brought in a kettle of hot water to bathe her mistress's feet, that they retired to their separate bedrooms ; only to resume, the next morning, with coffee and eggs and toasted rolls, the day-long vigil over a re-kindled fire. Now that the long and difficult journey was accomplished, that they had reached at last the city that months of procrastination had rendered fabulous to both of them, they found themselves upon an alien hearth, marooned, suddenly, not only from all contact with the outside world, but from the whole scheme of ties and duties and obligations that had upheld until that moment the structure of their daily lives. Nor did the climate of this " Paradise of Exiles " provide at once the incentive to renewed growth. Pisa, " so beautiful and so full of repose, yet not *desolate* ", lay in the repose rather " of sleep than of death " : a torpor fatal, nevertheless, to intellectual activity since, as Elizabeth already discerned, the " roots of thought here in Italy, seem dead in the ground. It is well that they have great memories—nothing else lives." Would the same desuetude descend upon them ? In their rooms in the " great college house built by Vasari ", husband and wife lived " the quietest and most tête-à-tête of lives, knowing nobody, hearing nothing, and for nearly three months together never catching a glimpse of a paper ". This undifferentiated liberty was as unnerving, at times, to the newcomers as the silence which surrounded them on all sides :

a silence which, lest it press too heavily on the heart, Browning did his best to dispel ; making himself, to that end, " an inexhaustible companion ", who, Elizabeth wrote, " talks wisdom of all things in heaven and earth, and shows besides as perpetual a good humour and gaiety as if he were—a fool, shall I say ? or a considerable quantity more, perhaps ". For Browning was anxiously aware of the strain placed upon one who had been forced violently to uproot not only the familiar amenities and associations of the sickroom, but some of the earliest and tenderest affections of her own heart. Inevitably, the arrival of letters from England re-opened the wound, sometimes forcibly. To endure this, solitude was essential : and Elizabeth was reduced to begging a solicitous husband " to go away for ten minutes " in order that she might " meet the agony alone ". For what she had to accept here at Pisa was not only the sight of her own letters to her father returned to her unopened, but the manifestation, no less implacable, of a cold and enduring hostility on his part. " If I had committed a murder and forgery, I don't see *how* Papa could have shown his sense of it, otherwise than he has done. To have thrown the books out into the street, would have produced a crowd and some inconvenience to himself, but the act would not have been more significant than what he has done." [1] What Mr. Barrett had done, in a vengeful " painting out of one's footsteps in the old room ", was to bundle his daughter's remaining possessions into a couple of boxes, and despatch them to Tilbury's warehouse, with the instructions that the bill for storage was to be forwarded to her, and not to him. " Oh—how unkind it all is," she lamented. " I could not have had the heart to act so to any-one I had ever loved. . . . It is hard and cruel I think." [2] More painful in some ways, because less expected, was the attitude of her brothers, who, aligning themselves with Mr. Barrett, accused her of absconding from home, leaving " the weight of shame and sorrow ", as George put it, to be borne by her family. (As if, she said, bewildered, " I had run away without being married at all.") Surely, she wrote to Henrietta, Papa " cannot really think (nor can any of my family) that I have *disgraced* him or them by connecting myself as I have.

[1] December 19 [1846]. Huxley typescript.   [2] Ibid.

Throwing all considerations of literature and genius into the fire, I have married a gentleman in every sense of the word, a man of high principles and delightful manners—the whole world with its code of artificial morality can say nothing against him." [1] This, however, was not the prevailing opinion at Wimpole Street, as we may gather from the tone of Elizabeth's next letter on the subject. " Those insinuations about money and ' Mr. Browning ' being reiterated, are really ' de trop ' altogether," she wrote angrily. " Money, money, money . . nothing but money ! My brothers are all of them considerably younger than my husband and have seen less of the world ; . . but that he is infinitely less worldly than any of them, taking no thought of this filthy money, money ; . . is as *true* . . as that he would be no husband of mine if it were otherwise." [2] Of the unworldliness of Robert Browning, there was at that moment, in Pisa itself, a privileged witness. Anna Jameson, the art historian, Ottilie von Goethe's " verrückter Engel ", had encountered the runaway couple in Paris. Perceiving the exhaustion of the one, and the nervous apprehensions of the other, she took them both under her wing, and offered to escort them on their journey through France to Italy. Mrs. Jameson, in Ruskin's opinion, was " absolutely without knowledge or instinct of painting, and had no sharpness of insight for anything else ". It required, however, very little sharpness of insight to discover, as she now did, that for all his " bright intelligence, and his rare acquirements of every kind ", Robert Browning was " in all the common things of this life the most unpractical of men, and the most uncalculating, rash—in short the worst *manager* I ever met with ".[3] The naïveté was not likely to endear him to one who, from the age of sixteen onwards, had been ready to support not only herself but her whole family : and it was Mrs. Jameson's concern for the invalid—(" *she* is really charming ")—that compelled her to offer to the fugitive poets—" a pretty pair to go thro' this prosaic world together ! "—the benefit of her experience, both as a traveller

---

[1] November 24 [1846]. Ibid.
[2] December 19 [1846]. Ibid.
[3] Mrs. Jameson to Lady Byron. One of five letters written between September 22 and October 17, 1846. Baylor University.

and as a seasoned woman of the world. Her intervention was welcomed by the Brownings who, far from resenting it, appeared to derive from her presence a support that each required, and failed, under certain conditions, to find in the other. It was not long before Mrs. Jameson, who was accompanied on her travels by a seventeen-year-old niece, found that she had become " Aunt Nina " to a couple, " no longer in the first freshness of life ", who placed themselves under her authority with all the docility, if not the eagerness, of the wide-eyed Gerardine herself.

Many years before this meeting with the newly-wed couple in Paris, Anna Jameson had undertaken for a time the education of a pupil called Louisa Mackenzie. It was this dark-eyed girl who, as Louisa, Lady Ashburton, was later to claim the distinction of being the only woman, other than Elizabeth Barrett, to receive a proposal of marriage from Robert Browning.

I *intend*, Robert Browning once wrote to Elizabeth Barrett, " by God's help to live wholly for you ; to spend my whole energies in reducing to practice the feeling which occupies me . . . as you shall know in time and place ". During the solitude of that first winter at Pisa, he was able to fulfil his intention : to give free expression to an ambition restricted, hitherto, by the peculiar conditions attendant upon his own presence in Wimpole Street. Throughout the whole of that time, permitted to see the woman he loved for a few brief hours each week, the poet had solaced himself by recording not only the " date and duration " of each visit, but the " number of minutes " he had been privileged to spend in her company. Now, happiness was no longer parcelled out to him in minutes, nor was their intercourse at the mercy of the first comer who chanced to knock. (" One day ", Browning wrote grimly, " I shall not go away at any dear Mr. K's coming ! ") That day had arrived at last, and the poet set himself systematically to recover the arrears of intimacy denied to him in Wimpole Street by the intervention of others. For this experiment, Pisa provided the perfect setting. There were no bells in their rooms at the Collegio : nobody rang ; nobody knocked : day after day, in " the utmost seclusion and tête-à-tête " husband and wife sat before the pinewood fire, pursuing, through the ramifications of sense and spirit alike, the potentialities of an all-absorbing relationship. Elizabeth found that she could not persuade Browning to leave her side : what makes him " perfectly happy ", she wrote to her sister, is " to draw his chair next to mine and let the time slip by ". Unwilling to relinquish, even for a moment, a privilege so dearly won, he refused to move a step without her ; assuring her that never in his life, " from his joyous childhood upwards ", had he enjoyed such happiness as he found in this uninterrupted communion of two people with " one soul between them ". Months ago, in London : " I shall be satisfied to the full," he had written to her, " if you only live in my sight,—cross the room in which I sit,—not to say, sit down by me there. . . ." How little he had misunderstood the nature of his own need for her she was now to see, when, if she got up " even to move across the room ", promptly, resenting the hiatus in their intimacy, he got up too, to accompany her : when it had become for him " a matter of course to walk with me every night from this room to my bedroom door if Wilson has said that it is time for me to begin to undress ". The presence of a third person only accentuated this need : six months later, in Florence, Mrs. Jameson had cause to look on " in utter astonishment, while Robert ", Elizabeth said, " seized on the place next to me on the sofa, just as if he saw me once in three months at the uttermost ".

" We like our seclusion here in Pisa," Elizabeth wrote, " though rather extreme, perhaps, for people who want to see Italy and the Italians . . for I might as well almost (for the world-seeing) be shut up in my old room—so very, very quiet we are here . . knowing not a creature." [1] To Browning, however, who had no desire at this juncture to see either Italy or the Italians, the isolation was full of charm. Indeed, he said of his wife, " I cannot imagine any condition of life, however full of hardship, which her presence would not render not merely supportable but delicious " : and he continued as the weeks and months went by to derive an incomparable pleasure not only from the " divine goodness and infinite

[1] December 26, 1846. To Miss Thompson. Omitted letter. Kenyon typescript.

tenderness of her heart ", but from the no less " inexhaustible affluence and power " of " that wonderful mind of hers ". Subjected to an intimacy so searching, to a scrutiny that enlarged the most trivial word or gesture, Elizabeth became uneasy : we are living, she said, " in a way to *try* this new relationship of ours to the utmost " : and since " to talk for four and twenty hours together " was admittedly rather exhausting, she began to wish that Pisa was capable of offering some distractions in the way of mixed society. Browning was appalled at the suggestion. Working himself up " into a fine frenzy " at the very idea, he begged her to admit no one to their hearth. If we once let them in, he said, " these people ", as he called them, will " spoil all our happiness ". And pleading for a resumption of their former intimacy, he went on to assure her that, far from being a drawback, it was of " the greatest *advantage* to us to be shut up in this seclusion without any distractions " : that he for his part wished for no better fate in life than to be allowed to prolong indefinitely this entrancing, this comprehensive, this all-absorbing tête-à-tête, which restored to him, in a form so immeasurably enhanced, a happiness he had long believed to be irrecoverable.

By this time, although she did not know it, Elizabeth was pregnant. Plunged " in the deepest innocence of ignorance ", she attributed her symptoms to colic, and huddled over the fire, sipping hot coffee and brandy-water. Winter had descended upon Pisa : from her window she could see the Duomo lightly powdered with snow ; while in the streets outside Browning met passers-by " muffled up in vast cloaks, with little earthenware pots full of live embers to warm their fingers, besides ". Elizabeth herself no longer ventured out of doors ; undressing, morning and evening, by the sitting-room fire, she crouched there all day, with no other resource —" since one is not always in a humour for writing prose or rhyme "—than to plough through yet another translation into Italian of some third-rate French or English novelist. Browning, who did not share his wife's passion for novel-reading, had undertaken, it seems, the revision of some of his early work : for Elizabeth informed Mrs. Jameson that " Robert is very busy with his new edition, and has been throwing so much golden light into ' Pippa ', that everybody shall see her ' pass ' properly . . yes, and *sur*pass ".[1]   In the next room, meanwhile, dyspeptic, disorientated, Wilson contemplated the prospect of an unprecedented idleness in which her most onerous duty could be but to patch Mrs. Browning's clothes, lace up her stays, or comb out, twist and plait, morning and evening, the long dark hair of which, justly, her mistress was so proud.   Severed from a system of bell-wires whose jerks from floor to floor had regulated, marionette-wise, the attitude of her working-hours, Wilson was " unwell and out of spirits ".   She could not speak to the Italians, nor eat their food : and the only entertainment that Pisa offered her was the spectacle, frequent at this time of the year, of one or other of the " many ghastly funerals " that passed beneath her window, on the way to the nearby Campo Santo.   " The monks, sometimes all in black, and sometimes all in white (according to the order), chant in a train, carrying torches," wrote Elizabeth, " and on the bier comes the corpse . . openfaced . . except   just   a   veil."   The   " horrible hoarse chanting . . . like the croaking of death itself ", rose upon the air ; and, filled with her " old horror " at the sound, —" Oh, *don't* go to the window ! " Elizabeth would cry out. " I can't help it, Ba—it *draws* me," was her husband's reply : and despite her remonstrances, the poet would crane his neck to watch the last of the procession wind out of sight along the wind-swept corner of the Collegio.

Six months after their wedding-day, on March 12th, 1847, Elizabeth was taken ill.   The miscarriage, for such it proved to be, was " *of five months date*, says Dr. Cook, or nearly so ". Elizabeth was more astonished than alarmed by this revelation, and bore the ordeal " with so much bodily vigour " that those about her were confounded.   The agitation of Browning, on the other hand, was something painful to behold.   Dishevelled, exhausted, quite " overcome ", he could neither eat nor sleep : as soon as he was allowed into the room, " he threw himself down on the bed in a passion of tears, sobbing like a child. . . . ' We are rebellious children,' he said, ' and He leads us where He can best teach us.' "   For three days, Elizabeth was ordered by Dr. Cook to keep " one position in

[1] February 4, 1847.   Omitted letter.   Kenyon typescript.

bed . . not suffered to move ". With a " womanly tenderness " that made Wilson open her eyes, Browning spent the
entire day at his wife's bedside ; coaxing her to eat ; massag-
ing her limbs ; reading to her ; entertaining her and making
her laugh, she said, " till I refuse to laugh any more ".
Wonderingly : " I never saw a *man* like Mr. Browning in my
life," said Wilson, and Dr. Cook is said to have made a remark
" to the same effect ".

During the illness of her mistress, Wilson slept on the sofa
in her bedroom. Waking sometimes at night, and catching
sight of that hunched figure under the blankets, Elizabeth
was reminded sharply of Arabel who had shared in this fashion
her room at Wimpole Street ; and in the stillness, her heart
would ache suddenly for past intimacies, now sundered for
ever. At four o'clock in the morning, the nearby bells began
to toll. Inexorably, the deep rhythms " rang my dreams
apart ". The *Pasquareccia*, in particular, tolled on the occasion
of an execution, had " a profound note in it, which may well
have thrilled horror to the criminal's heart ". Hearing it,
Elizabeth would turn over on her pillows with a shudder.
Ghastly in its effect, it was a sound that " dropped into
the deep of night like a thought of death ".

Despite the publication of *Pictor Ignotus* in 1845, it does not
seem to be generally known (it is not mentioned, for instance,
in the standard biography), that previous to his marriage
Browning had visited both Pisa and Florence. And yet
Browning himself, in the love letters, alludes to the fact. " By
the way," he wrote, " Byron speaks of plucking oranges in his
garden at Pisa . . I saw just a courtyard with a high wall
—which may have been a garden . . but a gloomier one
than the palace, even, warrants." It was in Moore's *Letters
and Journals of Lord Byron*, published in 1830—(" I read this
book of Moore's too long ago," Browning told Elizabeth)—
that he had read of the oranges in Byron's garden : (" I can
walk down into my garden, and pluck my own oranges,—and,
by the way, have got a diarrhoea in consequence of indulging
in this meridian luxury of proprietorship," was what his
Lordship actually wrote.) " As for the travelling English,"

Browning added, " they are horrible, and at Florence, unbear-
able . . their voices in your ear at every turn . . and such
voices !—I got to very nearly to hate the Tribune for their
sakes." If, then, as it would seem, on his previous journeys
to Italy Browning had visited Pisa and Florence, as well as
Venice, the Euganean Hills, Naples and Rome, it is evident
that, guided on the second occasion by the *Essays, Letters from
Abroad*, as well as by Mrs. Shelley's elucidatory comments in
the *Poetical Works*, he had made something in the nature of a
pilgrimage to the principal places in Italy associated with
Shelley's life and with his poetry. Two years later, he found
himself once more in Pisa ; and with a wife who, like the
bride in Shelley's Campbell-esque poem *The Fugitives*, fled the
wrath of one who could no less be described as " the grey
tyrant father ". Of all places in Italy, Pisa carries the deepest
imprint of the domestic life of the Shelleys, as the poet himself
realised. " Our roots ", he told Mary, " never struck so
deeply as at Pisa " : and it was here, united in literary pursuits,
that husband and wife ("we do not enter into society ") led
in their apartment high above the Lung' Arno a life almost as
quiet and secluded as that of the Victorian couple who, a
quarter of a century later, were to warm themselves in their
turn over " fires from the Grand Duke's wood " in a corner
of the grave silent old Collegio Ferdinando.

Regularly each day, interrupting the hours of firelit communion, Elizabeth drove her husband out of doors to take
some exercise in Pisa or the surrounding countryside. Thus
compelled, Browning would take " his dreary hour's walk on
Lung' Arno (when it is wet he can go nowhere else) in ever
such an imprecative humour on the soul-less faces he meets
there." [1] It was not, however, with the soul-less faces of
the Pisans—" crawling and crab-like," wrote Mary Shelley,
" through their sapping streets "—that Browning chiefly concerned himself. He concerned himself, on these solitary walks
of his, with such matters, momentous to himself alone, as the
discovery that Shelley, in his poem *The Tower of Famine*, had
mistaken " the Pisan Torre Guelfa, by the Ponte a Mare,
black against the sunsets ", for Ugolino's tower—" the vestiges
of which ", Browning pointed out, " should be sought for in

[1] February 4, 1847. To Mrs. Jameson. Omitted letter. Kenyon typescript.

the Piazza de' Cavalieri ".[1] What he followed, what he
looked for in the streets of Pisa, were the footsteps of one who,
walking these pavements with " a fire in his eye, a fever in his
blood, a maggot in his brain ", had composed under this sky
lines that were to revolutionise, a few years later, the life of
the schoolboy who first encountered them in that " strange
edition of Shelley published by Benbow in 1826 ". Here, of
all places, did the air seem " bright with thy past presence
yet " : an air that quickened, inevitably, the memory of old
conflicts and old betrayals. " The poet and the man are two
different natures," wrote Shelley, " though they exist together,
they may be unconscious of each other, and incapable of
deciding on each other's powers and efforts by any reflex
act." In Browning's case (the process is fully described in
Sordello) some inescapable necessity caused the man to intervene continually upon the poet, restraining his full utterance.
It was Browning's tragedy, perhaps, that, unlike Shelley, it
had been his fate to revolt, not against the authority of the
" grey tyrant father ", but against the standards of an all-too-
tenderly loved mother. Unable to relinquish love, he had
relinquished freedom : and walking here, the stones and walls
of Shelley's Pisa seemed to reflect back to him the memory
of that early betrayal.

> I crossed a moor, with a name of its own
>   And a certain use in the world, no doubt,
> Yet a hand's breadth of it shines alone
>   'Mid the blank miles round about :
>
> For there I picked up on the heather
>   And there I put inside my breast ˙
> A moulted feather, an eagle-feather !
>   Well, I forget the rest.

---

[1] It is Mary Shelley's footnote which describes the tower of famine as " sit-
uated near the Ponteal Mare ". Browning assumed that the note was Shelley's.
He was to make a similar mistake, 26 years later, when he affirmed that
Shelley " mentioned . . . in a note to *The Triumph of Life* " the air *Stanco di
pascolar le pecorelle*. The note, once more, is not Shelley's, but Mary's.
According to Medwin, Shelley was aware that the tower was " erroneously called
Ugolino's ".

The impression made today on a visitor to Casa Guidi in Florence is predominantly a sombre one. In *The Ring and the Book*, Browning himself wrote of his former home that

> the black begins
> With the first stone-slab of the staircase cold,

and the gloom persists when, on the floor above, the door is opened on to the famous suite of rooms, sub-divided now into separate flats. It seems surprising that Elizabeth should have found delight in this grim-looking building, whose walls, with their massive stones and mask-like shutters can more reasonably be compared to " Newgate's turned inside out " than those of her former home in Wimpole Street. That which time has extinguished, however, on this celebrated hearth of hers, is to be rekindled still in her letters ; in which we find these sombre rooms illuminated, brilliantly enough, by the light of her own happiness. For it was here, in " Casa Guidi by Felice Church ", that she created for the first time a home of her own ; sharing with her husband the pleasure of selecting and assembling objects that were to complement their joint lives for many years to come. Outside, revolutions came and went : Elizabeth, who was capable of becoming " really *mad* " with anxiety over the welfare of her family in Wimpole Street, listened unperturbed to the reverberations that beat against the thick walls of Count Guidi's palazzo. " The whole edifice of political falsehood is crumbling down on all sides," she wrote. " I cannot but rejoice for my part, far more than I am frightened by the thunderous sound of the falling ruins." Out of those ruins, " the poorest and most prudent of possible poets " were able to furnish their home at a minimum of expense : five pounds for an elaborate gilt-framed mirror to hang over the fireplace ; three shillings and eightpence apiece for antique chairs of " black, carved wood " : a couple of pounds for a magnificent inlaid ivory and ebony chest, " with the curiousest gilt handles, Tritons holding masks ". Carpets were laid down in the bedrooms ; windows draped in " crimson satin with yellow flowers " : and " rococo chairs, spring sofas, carved bookcases, satin from Cardinals' beds " arrived at intervals to complete the domestic pattern. During the course of these months, Elizabeth had occasion to remark that Robert " really cares a good deal about external things. . . . For instance about houses, and furniture, and horses and carriages, he is far more particular than I ever was or can be . . he has a feeling about them, not altogether Spartan." (Two years later : " We never ask anybody to dinner, as a general rule . . ." she wrote. " Robert is shamefaced because we haven't silver forks ; about which, I don't care the least in the world. He's much more alive to those little things than I am, and ought really by rights to have been born to five thousand a year, as I often tell him.")[1] More austere was Browning's attitude towards the possibility of getting into debt. Elizabeth did not share his inhibitions in this respect ; having left behind her in Wimpole Street a number of " profligate debts ", the discovery of which outraged her brothers : she had borrowed, it seems, seventy pounds from Arabel, and another large sum from Minny, the housekeeper : a fact which, when we consider the hampers of fresh fish or of white grapes despatched regularly to Three Mile Cross, must be regarded simply as an indication of " how easy it is to spend money, and not on oneself ". Browning, however, being, as his wife said, " descended from the blood of all the Puritans, and educated by the strictest of dissenters ", had " a sort of horror of the dreadful fact of owing five shillings five days " which she called " quite morbid in its degree and extent ". " I laugh insolently sometimes at Robert and his accounts, and his way of calculating for the days and the weeks. . . . His horror is of having to apply ever to any human being for pecuniary help. . . . And *if* you were to see his little book, with our whole income accounted for to the uttermost farthing, week by week, and an overplus (yes, an overplus !) provided for casualties, or ' lest Ba should be ill ' you would smile as I do, or be touched as I often am besides." [2] She smiled too at the solemn ceremony every Monday morning when Wilson brought in the bills and laid them on his desk—(" all except

[1] November 15 [1850]. Huxley typescript.
[2] [August 2, 1847]. Ibid.

the *washing bill* which I never allow to be looked at and which is brought straight to myself, with any other private items " [1]). As for Robert, Elizabeth added, " his garments seem to me those of a wilderness-Israelite—never to wear out. The teazing I have to use before he will get anything for himself ! " [2] But she understood well enough the nature of his reluctance ; and had hastened from the first to make it plain to those in Wimpole Street. " Let my brothers learn, if they do not by their own hearts, guess it . . by their own hearts and sense of honour ; that precisely *in consequence* of the informality of our marriage, and of my money falling therefore into the unrestricted possession of my husband . . he shrinks from touching it, and forces me to consider and determine the manner of spending it, until I come to reproach him . . yes, *I* too ! Only that nothing, and least of all, matters of such vile interest, could ever produce a division between *us*." [3]

All this while, there had lain in a drawer in Elizabeth's bedroom a pile of garments whose folds she could not contemplate without pain. Two months before settling in Casa Guidi, on the anniversary, almost, of the first mishap, she had had a second miscarriage. The disappointment on this occasion was naturally more acute : to Elizabeth at least : as for Browning, he had more than once assured her, she told Miss Mitford, that " he never could love his child as he loves his wife, and that for himself he desires nothing more ". [4] Dr. Harding—" who is called by Murray and others the Locock of Florence "—attributed the disaster to port wine. The morphine, on the other hand, he considered " by far the safest help of the sort which I can take. . . . And I was bid beware of attempting to diminish, except by the slightest degree —say a drop at a time. ' If you do, the effect will be that you will be forced to recur to a still larger quantity than you make use of now.' Pray observe that the morphine is therefore irreproachable ! " [5] As before, she made a rapid recovery. " I am made at once of glass and iron, I believe—or rather altogether of willow . ., which springs up as quickly as it can be trodden down." Soon she was out in the carriage

---

[1] January 4-5-6- [1848]. Ibid.   [2] February 10-14-20 [1849]. Ibid.
[3] December 19 [1846]. Ibid.   [4] February 22 [1848]. Kenyon typescript.
[5] April 22 [1848]. Huxley typescript.

with her husband, driving through the Cascine, and seeing
" the elms as green as ever they mean to be, and the grass like
emeralds, and the pheasants all alive and flying ". " If you
did but see ", she wrote to Henrietta, " how delighted Robert
is to have me out with him again ! He is quite in an ecstasy
about it—which is only a fair recompense . . for the anxiety
he has had of late by my means." ¹ And she could not help
remembering Henrietta's prognostication that she " would
be afraid " of Robert Browning, once she married him.
" Afraid ! " she wrote now. " Oh, I should not like being
' afraid ' at all—it is better to be pert and impertinent, as I
am sometimes. I think aloud to him—and he to me. I am
sure that we have not an ' aside ' once a week from one
another " :² a state of intimacy perfected, as the world knows,
five years later,

> When, if I think but deep enough,
> You are wont to answer, prompt as rhyme
> And you, too, find without rebuff
> Response your soul seeks many a time
> Piercing its fine flesh-stuff.

By now, the ardours of a Florentine summer were sending
the thermometer up to eighty in the shade. Behind its sultry
blinds and shutters, it was stifling in the apartment. Flush
was seen to turn his head away from warm milk, and his tail
from soft cushions. Inert on the sofa, Elizabeth fanned herself
wearily, while Robert poured eau de Cologne into her hands
and on to her brow. Pregnant for the third time, she suffered
increasingly from nausea. (But what did that matter ? The
" sacred drawer " could be re-opened ; and the little gifts
from Wimpole Street, " which I never liked to look at ", she
said, " have come in to light and hope and prospect again ".)
Suddenly, in the early part of July, Browning developed
influenza, and was very unwell for some days.³ When he
recovered, it became evident that a change would do them
both good ; and, poring over Murray's guidebook, the
Brownings decided to make for Fano, on the Adriatic, " where

¹ March 7–April 7 [1848]. Huxley typescript.
² Florence, June 24 [1848]. Ibid.
³ Mentioned in deleted passage : letter of July 17 [1848]. Ibid.

we shall pitch our tent, for the benefit, as Robert says, of the sea air and oysters ".

In Fano, Robert Browning was to find inspiration for the only poem he is known to have written during the first three years of his married life.   In this small walled town, where, tradition had it, the earliest printing press in Europe was set up, they found the houses " uninhabitable from the heat, vegetation scorched with paleness, the very air swooning in the sun ". If they endured it for three days, it was because it was possible to escape from blanched pavements into the " purple glory " of one or other of Fano's numerous churches.   Robert, Elizabeth assured her friends, " knows a great deal about art ".   It was, then, something more than aesthetic respect that drove the poet, on three separate occasions, to return to San Agostino, in order to contemplate there Guercino's *L'Angelo Custode* : a mediocre picture, which in sentiment and execution alike may be said to have closer affinities with nineteenth than with seventeenth century standards of taste. Here, in a canvas blackened by taper-smoke, and through " a favourable darkness ", he saw Guercino's great winged angel bend solicitously over a kneeling child, helping it to fold its " little hands " in prayer.   In the situation thus presented— childhood's surrender to the ministering presence of a superior being—Browning found something which corresponded closely with an omnipresent need of his own nature.   Irresistibly, it aroused in him the old desire, the old nostalgia : the wish to creep beneath the shelter of the outspread wings, there to " feel thee guarding Me, out of all the world ".   And addressing himself to the angel, the poet begs him to " leave that child when thou hast done with him, for me ! " : to see in him, the erring adult,

> another child for tending,
> Another still, to quiet and retrieve.

And wilt thou, he asks,

> bend me low
> Like him, and lay, like his, my hands together,
> And lift them up to pray, and gently tether
> Me, as thy Lamb there, with thy garment's spread ?

Robert Browning had recently recovered from a sharp attack of influenza. The pervading lassitude of his poem, *The Guardian Angel*, is to be attributed in part perhaps to the after-effects of illness. But there are also undertones which spring from some deeper and less definable source of dissatisfaction. Over two years ago, in London : " I look forward to a real life's work for us both," Browning had written to Elizabeth Barrett. " *I* shall do all,—under your eyes and with your hand in mine,—all I was intended to do." The " greater works ", he assured her, were to follow : with Elizabeth to guide him, he would find at last the path of true self-expression. " If you take a man from prison' and set him free . . do you not probably cause a signal interruption to his previously all ingrossing occupation, and sole labour of love, of carving bone-boxes, making chains of cherry stones . . . does he ever take up that business with the old alacrity ? No ! But he begins ploughing, building—(castles he makes, no bone-boxes now)." Robert Browning sat in the church of San Agostino and looked at Guercino's *L'Angelo Custode*. In two years, as it soon would be, of married life, he had added nothing to the sum of his own poetic achievement. Where, then, were the castles ; where was the track of the plough ?

Not long after her marriage, Elizabeth discovered two things about her husband. One was the wholly " unmasculine freedom from pride " with which he showed himself ready to defer to her judgment : the other was the headache which so frequently accompanied this display of docility on his part. In a letter to her sister Arabel, Elizabeth has described one of the " great arguments " which took place from time to time between husband and wife. The subject under discussion is not, in this case, divulged to us : but during the course of the conversation Robert, " growing warmer and warmer ", got " quite into extravagances " ; until Elizabeth refused, cate-gorically, to discuss the matter further with him. A dead silence followed, which lasted " at least ten minutes ". Sud-denly, Robert spoke. " ' Ba, do you know one of the reasons why I love you ? . . . When I get into a petulant, irritable humour (*he !!*) and have the headache as I have now, and say unreasonable and improper things which my own reason would recoil at another time, you do not give up to me, and attempt

to soothe me by agreeing with me or letting it pass as so many
good tempered women do to the eternal injury of foolish men,
but you always tell me the truth plainly, Ba.' " [1]

That was nearly eighteen months ago, at Pisa. Now he
was at Fano, sitting in the church of San Agostino, contemplating Guercino's guardian angel—" my angel with me too ".
It is evident that the poet was puzzled by his own latent
uneasiness. Happily married to the woman he loved, what
was the reason for the sense of frustration that visited him,
disquieteningly, at times ? " With the deep joy in my heart
below . . . what *does* the head mean by its perversity ? " he
had once asked her. The question had never been answered ;
and here at Fano, unable to face the recurrence of it, Robert
Browning sought once more his own characteristic solution.

If this was ever granted, I would rest
  My head beneath thine, while thy healing hands
Close-covered both my eyes beside thy breast,
  Pressing the brain, which too much thought expands,
Back to its proper size again, and smoothing
Distortion down till every nerve had soothing,
  And all lay quiet, happy and suppressed.

3

At a quarter past two on the morning of March 9th, 1849,
Elizabeth Barrett Browning gave birth to a son. She had
borne the twenty-one hours' labour without a cry or a moan :
and now she refused to look at the child until Robert himself
could place it in her arms. Warm tears of joy dropped from
his face on to hers as he did so. Elizabeth was surprised at
his emotion ; for he had told her, repeatedly, that he had not
" the least touch in him of paternal instinct ", and only " two
days before, when I had caught cold and was not well and
made him more nervous than usual about me, he wished to
Heaven that the living creature would exhale and disappear
in some mystical way without doing me any harm ".[2] The

---

[1] February 24, 1847. Berg Collection. New York Public Library.
[2] April 30, 1849. Omitted letter. To Mrs. Jameson. Kenyon typescript.

new-born child was handed over to a wet-nurse, " a mighty woman that would cut up into twenty Bas "—where he fed placidly, undeterred by the cannons and *vivas* of the revolution just then taking place beneath Casa Guidi windows. " He slept and grew fat, Grand Duke or Guerazzi . . . and really a beautiful child too,—called a ' model for Micel Angelo ' by the accoucheur and ' an Jesu bambino ' by the monthly nurse, the wet-nurse being of the opinion that ' the Signora must have seen some very pretty people when she walked out in the streets '." [1] A small tuft of the fine, dark hair was clipped off for Robert to send to his mother. It was destined never to reach her. Even as he wrote and sealed the letter, the woman to whom it was addressed lay gravely ill in her home at New Cross. A week later, she was dead.

The first great sorrow of his life descended upon Robert Browning with catastrophic force. He had been, as Elizabeth once said, " spared, up to this time, the great natural afflictions, against which we are nearly all called, sooner or later, to struggle and wrestle " : in a life of " unscathed joy ", the only tears he had hitherto shed had been tears of happiness, or of sympathy with happiness. He was doubly unprepared, then, for the blow which fell upon him : and the " discord between the joy and the grief . . . the thought that we were rejoicing here just while his mother was dying ",[2] produced an almost intolerable anguish and confusion of mind. " It has been very painful altogether," wrote Elizabeth, " this drawing together of life and death." More painful, perhaps, than she realised : for, following so closely one upon the other, the birth at Casa Guidi and the death at New Cross appeared like complementary aspects of the same event : and if, visibly, the poet shrank from the sight of his new-born son, it was with something of the same emotion as a man might feel in the presence of a child whose birth has rendered his own hearth motherless : " the very thought of accepting this new affection for the old became a thing to recoil from ". Elizabeth, naturally enough, found it hard that her " Poor little babe, who was too much rejoiced over at *first* " should " fall away " from favour in this fashion. What she could not know was that the circumstances which had conspired simultaneously to

[1] April 30, 1849. Omitted letter. To Mrs. Jameson. Kenyon typescript.
[2] Ibid.

give Robert Browning a son and deprive him of a mother, were to qualify unconsciously the whole basis of the poet's attitude towards the child who, at the French Evangelical Protestant Church in Florence, was given, a few months later, the name Robert Wiedeman Barrett Browning.

After the first violence of his grief had subsided, Browning fell into a state of profound depression. Month after month went by, and still he could not eat or sleep ; pale and thin, he sat listless in a corner of the drawing-room at Casa Guidi ; and whenever, Elizabeth wrote, " I leave him alone a little and return to the room, I find him in tears ". She dreaded the arrival of letters from England. " If he has a letter from home," she told her sister, " he is unwell the whole day after it—he bursts into tears over it, and thinks it over and over for hours, till I am obliged to reproach him on my side." [1] Temporarily, the situation between husband and wife was reversed : for the first time since the loss of her brother, Elizabeth's face was turned fully towards life ; while for the first, and perhaps the only time in his life, Browning was wholly absorbed in the contemplation of death. To " live rightly ", Elizabeth urged, we " must press forward and not look back morbidly for the footsteps in the dust of those beloved ones who travelled with us but yesterday ". But Browning did not rally : it was his belief that he never would recover his old spirits : " never again ", he told her, could he " feel as he used to do ".[2] Elizabeth was puzzled by the deep sense of remorse that his attitude betrayed. " There is no root of bitterness in this grief that it should embitter life for ever," she wrote ; "—it is a flowering grief, and not poisonous. Up to this point, it has drawn him nearer to God . . and whatever does that, is not evil in its nature indeed. That Her God is his God, Her saviour his saviour, is the thought oftenest with him when he takes any comfort. If she had died years ago, twenty years ago, when he had his fit of scepticism . . how would he have borne it then ? he observed that to me himself. As it is, he has her faith to comfort him, losing her. . . ." [3]

But Browning was not comforted : " His mother's death," Elizabeth saw, " affected him not only acutely for the time but deeply and permanently " : and as the months dragged

[1] Florence 2-3-4-5- [1849]. Huxley typescript.   [2] Ibid.   [3] Ibid.

by, " bowed down in an extremity of sorrow ", he began to
look so " worn and altered " that she became alarmed, fearing
" that the end of it all . . . would be a nervous fever or
something similar ". Earnestly she begged him to take a
holiday : Browning remained apathetic : he " had no mind
for change or movement ", he said. Making the heat of
Florence a pretext, Elizabeth insisted that she, at least, needed
a change ; and forced him thus to accompany her on an
exploratory journey in search of lodgings for the summer.
What unwise impulse was it that directed their steps towards
Lerici ? They found no pleasure in the " unimaginable
beauty " of that land-locked bay. Something of the " intense
presentiment of coming evil " that, for Mary Shelley, had
darkened just such another June day twenty-seven years ago,
seemed to communicate itself to the travellers. Standing on
that rocky shore, faced with the waters in which the boat
Don Juan had foundered, Elizabeth realised with a shock that
she was re-visiting, under this guise, the scene of her own most
critical tragedy ; and since " the arrowhead of anguish was
broken too deeply into my life ever to be quite drawn out ",
the beauty of the scene caused a revulsion of feeling which she
was at pains to conceal from Robert. Unknown to her,
Robert however, had his own burden to bear. For him, too,
the air of Lerici was laden with echoes out of the past. On
the edge of the sea stood Casa Magni, the " white house, with
arches ", which Shelley had loved so much : it was there, as
Browning knew,[1] that a week before his death :—" Let us see
the truth, whatever that may be," the poet had written.
" The destiny of man can scarcely be so degraded, that he was
born only to die ; and if such should be the case, delusions,
especially the gross and preposterous ones of the existing
religion, can scarcely be supposed to exalt it." This was not
a message which, in his present condition, Browning felt himself able to bear : painfully his thoughts vacillated between
the wine-lit flames of a funeral pyre at Viareggio, and the
humble earth of a dissenter's grave in Nunhead cemetery,

[1] The letter was published in 1840. Every word that Shelley wrote impressed
itself clearly upon Browning's mind. When Buxton Forman's Library edition
appeared, he was able to detect, at a glance, a minute error in the poem *Similes*,
printed over forty years previously, " in the ' Athenaeum ' where I read it—to
remember it all my life ".

until the sight and associations of this " divine bay " became alike intolerable to him. It was with relief that husband and wife left Lerici behind them. They had come to the conclusion, Elizabeth wrote, that lodgings in that place were beyond their means.

The Brownings spent the rest of the summer at the Baths of Lucca ; " a wasp's nest of scandal and gaming " whose beauty held no painful associations for either of them. They took an apartment in " the highest house of the highest of the three villages . . . which lie at the heart of a hundred mountains sung to continually by a rushing mountain stream ". Beneath the green shade of the chestnut forests there was nothing to be heard but the sound of the river and the cicala : the silence, said Elizabeth, " is full of joy and consolation ". Browning did not appear to find it so. This place, he wrote to Sarianna, " or any other, would do me no good of itself, any more than Florence—for apart from the folly and wickedness of the feeling, I am wholly tired of opening my eyes on the world now ". Nor did the sight of his son, kicking like " a cupid in a fountain " in bathwater whitened with bran, " mend his spirits much ". Everybody, Browning wrote of the child, " seems to think him remarkably flourishing. All of which ought to be unmixed pleasure to me, but is very far from it." So far from it, indeed, that there were moments when Elizabeth felt that she shared with her babe this inexplicable disfavour. Knowing how Robert envied his sister, whose " comforts and memories ", he said, " are infinitely beyond mine ", she regretted bitterly that it should have been her fate to intervene between mother and son ; depriving him, not only of " the personal face-to-face shining out of her angelic nature for more than two years ", but of the consolation, as it must have been to him, of " her last words and kisses ".

It was, perhaps, upon witnessing the painful engrossment of her husband (" I have been thinking over nothing else, these last three months, than Mama and all about her, and catching at any little fancy of finding something which it would have pleased her I should do "), that Elizabeth suggested to him the possibility of enshrining that beloved memory in poetry.

To Browning the idea was peculiarly repellent. In " the two or three great sorrows of my life ", he later said, " it has been the last thing that occurred to me ". He was reluctant to compose as much as an epitaph for his mother's tombstone : and over grave number 1304, purchased for Sarah Anna Browning on March 26, 1849, the blankness of a headstone overgrown and sunken testifies still to the inability of the poet

> to find his love a language
> Fit and fair and simple and sufficient——

in which to perpetuate his own sense of loss. Nevertheless, an outcome to the situation, not death but love, was to be celebrated : for it may well have been on this very occasion, this " one evening at Lucca ", that there took place between husband and wife a discussion on the whole subject of " putting one's loves into verse ". The consequence of which, we know. The next morning, as Browning stood at the window, looking at " the tall mimosa in front, and little church-court to the right ", approaching him, Elizabeth " said hesitatingly, ' Do you know I once wrote some poems about *you* ? '—and then —' There they are, if you care to see them.' " It was that " strange, heavy crown ", the " wreath of sonnets ", afterwards to be known as the *Sonnets from the Portuguese*.[1]

During these months at Lucca, Elizabeth was busy preparing the new edition of her poems for Chapman and Hall. Browning did no writing at all. " I scold him about it in a most anti-conjugal manner," she said, " but, you know, his spirits and nerves have been shaken of late ; we must have patience." Elizabeth's health, on the other hand, was better than it had been " at any point of my life since I arrived at woman's estate ". She was able to walk with Robert for several hours at a time, to climb the hills and explore the chestnut forests. She even performed the feat of riding on donkey-back " deep into the mountains to an almost inaccessible volcanic ground not far from the stars " ; the Prato

[1] E. B. B. held that this episode took place in Florence, in 1850. R. B. told Gosse that it was at Pisa, in 1847, that the Sonnets were pushed " into the pocket of his coat "; and Furnivall that it was in " spying about " that he found the " tiny roll of paper ". Julia Wedgwood and 2 others were told that the event took place at Lucca in 1849 : Miss Swanwick, that the poets " had been wedded 2 years " before it happened ; and R. B.'s daughter-in-law, that he found " the roll . . . in the top bureau drawer that first winter of their marriage ".

Fiorito, to whose grassy slopes another couple, Shelley and Mary, had once preceded them, and where the smell of jonquils nearly caused Shelley to " faint with that delicious pain ". Here, they sat amongst the mountain goats and picnicked on chicken and ham ; while at a discreet distance, the balia—a stout rosy woman, with " a physique quite uninjured by intellectual cultivation—she doesn't know even the *names of the months* " [1]—suckled the baby, whose round face was, by now, burnt brick-red by exposure to the sun. " Wasn't it daring of us to take Baby ? " Elizabeth asked her sister. But the truth was that she could not bear to be separated from him. For she who had once written to Miss Mitford that " after all if I had to choose . . . I should choose the smile of my own father to that of my own child ",[2] had now caught up her " parental pleasures with a sort of passion ". Her delight in this child, born to her three days after her own forty-third birthday, is touching to witness ; and male editors have had to cut by the pageful long accounts not only of his intelligence and high moral qualities, but of his " round, delicately mottled, dimpled limbs ", his cloaks of " fine white merino trimmed with blue silk braiding ", his dislike of his daily pap, and his love of his daily bath in which, said his mother, he " kicks, plunges and splashes and blinds himself and chokes himself with the water in ecstasies of joy ". It is to be noted, too, that after neglecting all her life " the duties belonging to my femininity ", Elizabeth Barrett Browning had purchased in Florence, in order to sew " little hems for tiny habiliments "—the " first thimble I have possessed since my childhood ".[3]

On September 12, the Brownings celebrated their third wedding anniversary. In the morning, " Baby came in to me with a rose in his fist, stretching it out for me to take ; and then he took another to Robert. (That was dear Wilson's contriving.) His own cheeks were redder than his roses, and he smiled to give them away ;—only he wanted to have them back afterwards." Husband and wife spent the day quietly, for the skies were overcast, and it rained heavily in the afternoon. " Since our marriage ", Elizabeth wrote a few days

[1] April 30, 1849. To Miss Mitford. Kenyon typescript.
[2] April 15 [1848]. Ibid.   [3] December 16 [1848]. Ibid.

later to her sister, " we have lost some precious things . . he, the earthly presence of an adorable affection . . I, some faith in attachments I had counted on for tenderness and duration ; but you may thank God for us that we have lost none of the love, none of the belief in one another . . and that indeed we have consciously gained in both these things.[1] There is more love between us two at this moment than there ever has been—he is surer of me, I am surer of him : I am closer to him, and he to me. Ours is a true marriage, and not a conventional *match*. We live heart to heart all day long and everyday the same. Surely you may say thank God for us. God be praised."

4

Nearly five years were to elapse before the Brownings re-visited England. " One's heart is pulled at through different English ties and can't get the right rest," Elizabeth wrote in June, 1850, "and I think we shall move northwards—try France a little, after a time." It was not, however, until a year later that they set out : one reason being, perhaps, that although, at twenty months, little Wiedeman was sufficiently " learned in Tuscan art " to distinguish between Cimabue and Giottino, he was by no means ready to relinquish the services of his bounteous wet-nurse. At the beginning of July, 1851, with Wilson and Flush in attendance, the Brownings arrived in Paris ; where Elizabeth was able to admire " disreputable prints, and fascinating hats and caps, and brilliant restaurants, and M. le President in a cocked hat and with a train of cavalry, passing like a rocket along the boulevards to an occasional yell from the Red ". As to England—" oh England—how I dread to think of it ", she wrote. " I feel here *near enough* to England, that's the truth." To Henrietta she had already confided that if " it were not for Arabel, I would stay in Paris by myself, and beseech Robert to take Wiedeman with him to New Cross, leaving me for six weeks or two months. And *that* proves how I am feeling ".[2]

[1] September 19, 1849. Huxley typescript.   [2] March 4 [1851]. Ibid.

Robert, however, was almost as agitated and distressed as his wife. The thought of seeing his old home again, of envisaging at close quarters the scene and circumstances of his mother's death, was " enough quite to prostrate and unnerve him " : and observing this, Elizabeth suggested that instead of going direct to New Cross, as arranged, they should stay for a few days, first, in lodgings in town. I am certain, she said, " that if he could once safely go he would be infinitely happier afterwards. By the lodgings, you see, we escape the first shock. He had exaggerated to himself frightfully every possible incident of the arrival at New Cross . . how he was to stop with the train, walk up the little road, open the gate, and take his wife and child with him into his mother's place. Now, there's a change altogether, you see. He will go to see his father and sister by himself and get it all over and come back to me—and it will be broken—and if he finds he can't bear it, he needn't go to *stay* there at all." [1]

Apparently, Robert found that he could not " bear it ". Seven years before—

> Here's the garden she walked across,
> Arm in my arm, such a short while since

—he had celebrated his mother's garden, and her presence amongst the rose-bushes, in a poem, *The Flower's Name*, which has a certain affinity with Part II of Shelley's *The Sensitive Plant*. Now—(" it would break his heart ", he had told Elizabeth, " to see his mother's roses over the wall, and the place where she used to lay her scissors and gloves ")—in the desolation at New Cross he experienced something of the horror of Part III of that poem, where the death of the garden's owner has left rankness and corruption in its wake. " But after the first," Elizabeth wrote, " it will grow better to him, I dare say, and I *expect* to be able, after a week at 4 George Street, Portman Square, where Arabel has taken us rooms, to remove to New Cross for the rest of our English visit." [2] It did not grow better to him : and it was in lodgings in Devonshire Street that the Brownings passed the remainder of their stay in England. On two occasions only, it seems, did the second Mrs. Browning visit the little house at New Cross where, she said, " my hus-

---

[1] Paris—Sunday–Monday [July 21, 1851]. Ibid.   [2] Ibid.

band's father and sister have received me most affectionately. She is highly accomplished," Elizabeth added, " with a heart to suit the head." Nevertheless, for all the real goodwill between them, the impression emerges that the sisters-in-law did not discover, either now or later, a spontaneous sympathy one for the other. Can it be that Ba found Sarianna's " fine clear animal spirits " a trifle exhausting ? Or that the nervous susceptibilities of the poetess aroused in a forthright nature a faint, but inevitable sense of irritation ? (" When we came to Italy first," Elizabeth confided to her sister, " Robert wrote and said that his desire was that his family should never, under whatever provocation, make mine the subject of conversation anywhere, even by a word. To which, Sarianna answered briefly, that it was not her custom to interfere, even by a word, with other people's affairs . . . she is a high spirited person, and probably thought Robert's recommendation a superfluity on his part.") [1] Nothing, however, was allowed to mar the overt cordiality of the relationship : Sarianna was constantly in Devonshire Street : and on August 20th, Robert, Elizabeth, little Wiedeman and his aunt Arabel Barrett paid a visit in their turn to New Cross. " We dined and had coffee there, and walked in the fields, and Wiedeman behaved like an angel just alighted, and charmed his relations. He has taken a passion for his ' nonno ' as he calls him—and I thought vainly of the other grandpa who will never, perhaps, hold him in his arms and kiss him." [2]

A sense of bitterness permeated the whole of Elizabeth's stay in England. Sorrow lay in wait for her on the shore, and it claimed her as soon as she set foot on her native soil. Like " a retreating wave, going and coming again ", her old grief for the loss of Edward broke over her, reminding her, poignantly, that " death and separation have no power over such love ". Resuming an old habit, she began at once to cough : and coughed so incessantly that—" Husband, lover, nurse "—Browning became alarmed and considered the advisability of returning forthwith to Paris. This was not possible : taking her first holiday for five years, Wilson had gone to stay with her mother near Sheffield : leaving Wiedeman in a state

[1] Florence 2-3-4-5 [1849]. Huxley typescript.
[2] Thursday [August 21, 1851]. Ibid.

of " deplorable grief " and the conviction, which nothing could shake, that " the world is in a conspiracy against him to take ' mama ' away after having taken ' Lily ' and he is bound to resist it ".   Thus, even Wiedeman had his share of the sorrows and agitations that characterised for his parents this first visit to England.   Every day, as soon as Mr. Moulton-Barrett had left the house, Arabel sent her maid, Bonser, to bring the child back with her to Wimpole Street.   " Ah yes, Henrietta," Elizabeth wrote to her sister, exiled in Somerset, " you think me ' bold ' . . brazen-faced, now isn't the word better *so* ? . . to have dared to send Wiedeman every day, and to have gone myself several times to that house ?   Did Arabel tell you how once, lately, she kept me in her room while she dressed, and how I heard Papa come up stairs, go down again, talk and laugh . . I, in a sort of horror of fright and mixed feelings ? and how I walked home with Bonser while they were at dinner, past the dining-room door ?   But it made me very sad all the evening after, and Robert was not pleased, and called it ' imprudent to excess '." [1]

Browning, during this time, had heavy troubles of his own to contend with.   Nothing could have been further from the disciplined austerity of Mr. Moulton-Barrett than the self-effacing gentleness of Robert Browning, senior : and yet this gentleness, this tender-heartedness, was to provoke its own characteristic problems.   Was it, perhaps, on discovering at New Cross evidence of an entanglement with a woman, that the poet felt unable to spend as much as a night under his father's roof ?   For such an entanglement did, in fact, exist. Mrs. Von Müller lived with her parents in a house not far from Craven Cottage.   Twice widowed, she was an attractive middle-aged woman, with three children.   On his way to the Bank every morning, Mr. Browning passed her house : and there, in December, 1850, he was to be observed, it seems, " waving his hand and looking with great earnestness . . . until he had waved himself out of sight ".   A month or so later, meeting the lady in the street, Mr. Browning begged leave to accompany her home ; after which he made her a proposal of marriage.   Mrs. Von Müller was willing to marry for the third time : and by the time his son and daughter-in-

[1] Monday [October 6, 1851].   Ibid.

law arrived in England, Mr. Browning was writing impassioned letters to his " dearest Minny ", as she had now become : letters which were one day to be produced, with disastrous effect, in evidence against him. No affront to the memory of his mother could have been more painful to the poet ; and the distress he endured may well have helped to prolong, if it did not precipitate, the sharp attack of influenza which, during the latter part of his stay in London, kept him confined for so long to his uncomfortable lodgings in Devonshire Street.

Nor was this to be the only shock that the visit to London had in store for him. Earlier in the year, in May, 1851, Moxon, Browning's former publisher, had bought in the Wilks sale at Sotheby's twenty-three letters of Percy Bysshe Shelley. Unaware that of these letters two only were " genuine Shelley creations ", the rest being the work of that indefatigable forger and impostor, Major Byron, Moxon asked Browning to write an introductory essay to the letters he proposed to publish. One result of this commission being that, some time between the end of July when the Brownings arrived in London, and September 25th, when they departed again, Robert Browning made the acquaintance of Shelley's old friend, the bookseller and publisher, Thomas Hookham, junior. 1858 has hitherto been accepted as the date of this encounter ; but William Rossetti, in his Diary, records the fact (ascertained in conversation with Browning) that " a set of letters from Harriet, then in the hands of Hookham the publisher . . . were placed in Browning's hands at the time he was editing the forged letters ". 1851, then, was the year in which Browning met the man who had once seen Shelley very plain indeed. Founded in the middle of the eighteenth century, the " excellent, indeed unique circulating library " of Mr. Hookham was still in Old Bond Street ; and Thomas Hookham, junior, who had printed the first copies of *Queen Mab* for Shelley, was now a " hale and hearty " man in his late sixties. Here, in his " splendid old library, with its fine old gallery and underground rooms full of priceless books ", Hookham was able to produce some memorabilia of Shelley that disconcerted, exceedingly, one nourished on the more tender reminiscences of Leigh Hunt. There had been, many years ago, a latent resentment in Hookham's attitude towards Shelley (Shelley died owing him money), the burden of which, curiously enough, was now brought to bear upon Robert Browning. Hookham had disapproved strongly of the elopement with Mary Godwin ; and in order to emphasise how badly Shelley had behaved at the time, he pressed Harriet's letters into his visitor's hands— " offered them to me unreservedly on the only occasion of our interview ", Browning later said. It is instructive to compare this account of a conversation with Hookham, with an identical conversation which the publisher held on the subject with a Mr. J. Mitford ; [1] where, in an effort to vindicate Harriet at the expense of Shelley, the same letters were produced and, it seems, the same commentary. " Hookham says ", wrote Mitford, " there was nothing wrong in the character of the erstwhile Miss Westbrook, nor deficient ; (he [Shelley] had commenced teaching her Latin) but he was fascinated by the attraction of Miss Godwin. . . ." The bookseller showed him Harriet's account of the nocturnal attack in Wales, as well as several other letters : all of them, Mitford comments, " sensible, affectionate, & very well written ". Browning, in his turn, had the same comment to make : " all the letters ", he said, " were well written in every respect ". The final letter, betraying the greatest " surprise and bewilderment " at her husband's disappearance, was the most disconcerting of all to Browning, since it seemed to him to prove conclusively, as he later told Swinburne, that Shelley " *did* desert Harriet and their child, and the child with which she was then pregnant, without fair warning or fair provision ".

Nothing that he had hitherto read or heard had prepared Browning for this revelation. Leigh Hunt in 1828 had informed the reading public that Shelley's first wife " was not of a nature to appreciate his understanding " ; that the couple had " separated by mutual consent, after the birth of two children ". Galt in 1830 spoke of a rash, unhappy marriage, and of " a separation, by mutual consent " : while Medwin in 1847 emphasised once more that it was after " mature deliberation " that " a separation took place by mutual consent " between the poet and " an individual neither adapted to his condition in life, nor fitted for his companionship by

[1] Brit. Mus. Add. Mss. 32, 574, f. 19–21. Quoted by W. E. Peck. Appendix L.

accomplishments or manners ". In startling contradiction to this unanimity was the tone of Harriet's last letter to Hookham : and with the utmost reluctance, after studying it, Browning came to the conclusion that, for no other reason than that he was " fascinated by the attraction of Miss Godwin ", Shelley had indeed deserted his first wife. He was doubly smitten by this revelation. Already he had been forced to learn that eighteen months after the death of a beloved wife, a tender and devoted husband was ready to look elsewhere for consola- tion : now, to complete his disillusionment, he was to discover that the same fickleness, the same canker, as he felt it to be, disfigured the " pure face " of one whom he had always believed, in the words of Mary Shelley, to be " ' Gentle, brave, and generous ' . . . beyond any man I have ever known ".

Before leaving England once more, Elizabeth made a final effort to bring about a reconciliation between herself and her father. She wrote to Mr. Moulton-Barrett, therefore ; and Robert wrote, too—" a manly, true, straightforward letter ". In return, the poet received " a very violent and unsparing letter ", accompanied, to Elizabeth's despair, by " all the letters I had written to papa through these five years *sent back un- opened, the seals unbroken* ". The shock was a rude one. " I could never tell you, if I tried ", she wrote to her sister, " what I felt when those letters came back to me, nine or ten of them, all with their unbroken seals testifying to the sealed up heart which refused to be opened by me. Oh, if my child were cast out of society for the most hideous of possible crimes, could I keep my heart so sealed up towards *him*? Not while a pulse of life stirred in it. If God and man cried aloud to me not to open, I should yet open—I could not help it. Think of the black unbroken seals, Henrietta, and the black-edged paper. How did he know that I might not have been widowed and calling out to him in my desolation ?—But he let the letters lie on there, whatever they were. He fulfilled what he considered (he said, writing to Robert) ' his duty to himself, his family and society '." [1]

For Robert Browning, the winter of 1851–2 was to be in

[1] Monday [October 6, 1851]. Huxley typescript.

some ways a critical one. Superficially, as always, his life appeared both tranquil and fortunate. Upon their return to Paris, the Brownings had engaged for six months an apartment on the sunniest side of the Champs Elysées, which gave them not only spacious rooms and comfortable chairs, but a terrace whence they might contemplate, as from a *loge*, the life of the capital. Elizabeth's cough had vanished ; and she was well enough to go shopping and buy herself a bonnet trimmed with purple flowers, which won Robert's approval—(" he is so particularly critical of my bonnets "). She bought too, for Wiedeman, a white felt hat decked with feathers and blue satin ribbons ; but we are offered no clue as to Robert's reaction to that. In the apartment, Browning had two rooms of his own : a dressing-room and a writing-room : thereby affording him the privacy as essential, in his case, to one activity as to the other. " Now we are always together again, except when he writes about Shelley in the next room," Elizabeth told Arabel : [1] and in the same month, Browning himself wrote to Carlyle : " I have just done the little thing I told you of—a mere Preface to some new letters of Shelley ; not admitting of much workmanship of any kind, if I had it to give. . . . However it be done, it is what I was ' up to ' just now, and will soon be off my mind."

Not so soon, unfortunately ; for apart from the difficulties inherent in the task itself, he was interrupted, a few days later, by the arrival of visitors from London. The Brownings, wrote Elizabeth, " are an affectionate family and not easy when removed one from another ". On this occasion, however, Mr. Browning had reasons of his own for wishing to absent himself, temporarily, from the neighbourhood of New Cross. Things were not going smoothly between himself and Mrs. Von Müller. In particular, he had been perturbed by reports that Minny had married Captain Von Müller, an officer in the Austrian service, without waiting for conclusive evidence of the death, in the Spanish service, of a Mr. Meredith, his predecessor. Old Mr. Browning had good reason to know how painful the whole matter was to his son : and it was no doubt out of diffidence that he attempted to mitigate the history of

[1] [12–14 October, 1851.] Sotheby catalogue : Moulton-Barrett Papers. June, 1937.

his own infatuation ; representing himself, more creditably, as the reluctant victim of an unscrupulous woman. Without this version of the story, Browning would scarcely have volunteered to write to the widow taking the tone he now did : for on November 1, Mrs. Von Müller received a peremptory letter from the poet in which, as an opening gambit, he stated that " his father had informed him of the manner in which she had annoyed him, and of the persecution he had undergone for some time ". It can scarcely be said, however, that the poet's intervention in his father's affairs was a judicious one ; for it was while " under the influence of his son ", as it was later alleged, that Mr. Browning wrote the widow a letter saying that " his reason for breaking off the match " was " her misconduct from the time she was a girl " : a letter which later enabled Counsel to demand " large damages " not only for breach of promise, but for the " wanton and malicious " manner in which his client's character had been defamed.

It was the middle of November before the visitors finally departed, and the poet was able to resume his work on Shelley. Confronting him at such a moment, the task was calculated to arouse the deepest and most contradictory emotions : and by devoting almost half the essay, in which Shelley's name is not mentioned, to a comparison between the objective and subjective poet, Browning betrays a certain reluctance to come to grips with his subject. (What emerges, nevertheless, is Browning's opinion, self-condemnatory, of the objective poet, or " artificer ". Lacking the " self-sufficing central light " of a Shelley—or, more culpably, shunning the " pure white light " of his own inspiration—he is a mere " fashioner ", a maker of " chains of cherry-stones " ; not like Shelley, like the true poet, a prophet and a " seer ".) After the death of Sarah Anna, in *Christmas Eve and Easter Day*, Browning had made belated amends for the spirit of opposition which had driven him from the Independent chapel of his boyhood. That he attempted now, dutifully, to put into practice the conclusion arrived at in the *Christmas Eve* portion of the poem, we hear from Elizabeth herself. " Robert ", she wrote, " keeps steady to the little church of French Independents, where he ' quite loves ' that ' angelic M. Bridel, who has the face of Tennyson

and the apostle John ', he says, ' together '." [1]   To the influence of Shelley, his " delirious Queen Mab notes and the
like ", Browning attributed much of the pain that he had
inflicted on his mother : to the same source he could attribute,
too, the remorse which continued to embitter his grief.   That
he had injured his mother, however, without liberating himself, is proved by his eagerness to sponsor, after her death, the
very ideas which his own reason had earlier forced him to
reject : and what, by way of reparation, he now set out to do,
was forcibly in this essay to gather Shelley, too, into the shadow
of the Walworth Road congregation.   Ignoring the fact that
to the day of his death Shelley never modified his attitude to
" the existing religion ", that he died, not in adolescence, but
in his thirtieth year, Browning implored his readers not to
" persist in confounding any more than God confounds, with
genuine infidelity and an atheism of the heart, those passionate,
impatient struggles of a boy towards distant truth and love,
made in the dark, and ended by one sweep of the natural seas
before the full moral sunrise could shine out on him.   Crude
convictions of boyhood, conveyed in imperfect and inapt forms
of speech,—for such things all boys have been pardoned.
There are growing-pains, accompanied by temporary distortion, of the soul also."   It was not enough, however, to white-
wash Shelley's past misdemeanours : to insist that " in religion,
one earnest and unextorted assertion of belief should outweigh,
as a matter of testimony, many assertions of unbelief " :   his
future was also to be regulated :   his salvation assured, and
along orthodox lines.   " I shall say what I think," wrote the
Robert Browning of *Christmas Eve and Easter Day* ;   " had
Shelley lived he would have finally ranged himself with the
Christians " :   a hypothetical anticipation, remarks Dowden
dryly, which " is to be classed with the surmise of Cardinal
Wiseman . . . that Browning himself would one day be found
in the ranks of converts to Catholicism."   But Elizabeth had
already summed up the whole situation when, after the death
of Browning's mother, she wrote that " the thought oftenest
with him when he takes any comfort " is that " ' Her God is his
God, Her saviour his saviour'".   It was this identification,
the persistence, within the massive framework of Browning's

[1] April 1 [1852]. Huxley typescript.

163

poetic achievement, of the narrow ideals of Sarah Anna Browning, that was to disconcert, amongst others, the future author of *The Dynasts*. " The longer I live," wrote Thomas Hardy to Edmund Gosse, " the more does B[rowning]'s character seem *the* literary puzzle of the 19th Century. How could smug Christian optimism worthy of a dissenting grocer find a place inside a man who was so vast a seer and feeler when on neutral ground ? " [1]

" Robert has finished and is sending off his Shelley," wrote Elizabeth, " and I am about to prepare a third edition of my poems, which is likely to be called for soon. We don't mean to idle away our time in Paris. . . oh no." It was December 1st, 1851. That same night, while they slept, the agents of Louis Napoleon were stealthily placing into position the various pinions, military and political, of the engine which at dawn was to spring upon Paris the *coup d'état* of December 2. A few hours later, with Elizabeth at his side and his son held aloft in his arms, Browning stood at a second-floor window while in the Champs Elysées beneath the President rode " through a shout extending from the Carrousel to the Arc de l'Etoile ". Wiedeman was so excited by the martial music, the white horses, the glittering helmets, that he screamed aloud in his enthusiasm ; and indeed, said his mother, " all that ' pomp and circumstance ' might well move older children than our babe ". So it would seem. For Elizabeth, like Queen Victoria, found " something fascinating, melancholy and engaging " in the personality of Louis Napoleon : (" I felt —I do not know how to express it—safe with him," wrote Her Majesty in 1855). Fired, at once, with " artistical admiration for the consummate ability and courage " of the *coup d'état*, she declared that " no sight could be grander " : adding, fervently, of the " grand spectacle " she had witnessed, that she " would not have missed it, not for the Alps ".

There is no doubt that to Browning the sight of his wife's exaltation was as distasteful as the *coup d'état* itself. More painful still, in the days to come, he was to hear her describe

[1] March 3, 1899. Brit. Mus. Ashley 282. Extract quoted by Wilfred Partington : *Thomas J. Wise in the Original Cloth.* Robert Hale, 1946.

republican resistance as " a little popular scum, cleared off at
once by the troops " ; to find her, in her " immoral sympathy
with power ", accepting even the censorship of the press and
the deportations to Cayenne as a " necessity of the dictator-
ship ". " Robert and I ", she wrote, " are not as *one* as we
are accustomed to be on the subject, I must confess to you." [1]
And again : we " have had some domestic *émeutes*, because he
hates some imperial names ". So, it will be remembered, did
Shelley. " Buonaparte ", wrote the young man in 1812, " is
to me a hateful and despicable being . . . you could not have
mentioned any character but Buonaparte whom I contemn
and abhor more vehemently." When, therefore, we hear
Browning, in domestic *émeute*, profess his hatred of " all
Buonapartes, past, present, or to come ", we are reminded
of a characteristic which, surviving less indigenous impulses,
Browning had all his life in common with Shelley ; an
" irreconcilable enmity ", as the latter put it, to every form
of " domestic and political tyranny and imposture ". In
Browning's eyes, domestic tyranny was almost the larger sin.
A week before his marriage : " My own Ba, if I thought you
could fear me, I think *I* should have the courage to give you
up to-morrow ! " he wrote. Elizabeth, for her part, was more
willing to fear than to be feared. What she was reluctant,
at first, to do, was to accept her lover's invitation to impose
upon him the weight of her own " desires, and teaching, and
direction ". It was only gradually, testing herself out in the
intimacy of marriage and discovering herself the stronger, that
she had come to accept the responsibilities and privileges of
that position as her natural due. This was all the easier for
her in that, the first-born of a large family, she had early
acquired the attitude, solicitous and mildly domineering, of
the elder sister : six years older than her husband, the tempta-
tion seems to have been to treat him, at times, with the humor-
ous firmness applicable to a spirited but inexperienced younger
brother. The passage of the years reinforced perceptibly this
self-opinionated aspect of her character. " Gentle yet pertina-
cious in difference " is how H. F. Chorley describes her ;

[1] January 2, 1852. To Mrs. Martin. Omitted letter. Kenyon typescript.
On the same day, Browning, " in the next room ", wrote *Childe Roland to the
Dark Tower Came*.

". . . at once forbearing and dogmatic, willing to accept differences, resolute to admit no argument ". She was proud of her own independence in this respect. " I do see with my own eyes and feel with my own spirit, and not with other people's eyes and spirits, though they should happen to be the dearest," she wrote. Robert Browning could scarcely say the same—had he not once addressed her as " you whom I implicitly trust in to see for me " ? Five years ago : " I hope if you want to please me especially, Ba, you will always remember I have been accustomed, by pure choice, to have another will lead mine in the little daily matters of life." By pure choice, he had surrendered his independence in the little every-day matters of life, only to discover that in the major matters, too, the power of franchise had unaccountably been taken from him. Already it was plain enough, for instance, that he was to have no say in the upbringing of his son. When the baby was six months old, Elizabeth, who wished to make an Italian of him, complained that " Robert will persist in talking English to him, in spite of my disposition ". That it was her disposition and not his that prevailed, we may gather from Miss Mitford who, in the summer of 1851, was astonished to hear " the English father, English mother, and English nurse talk Italian " to the boy. An even greater bewilderment was aroused, in later years, by the child's appearance. Concentrating on his person all the extravagance she withheld from her own, his mother presented him to the world in such a glory of silks and satins, of feathers and laces and long burnished ringlets, that wherever they went the poet was molested by the curiosity of strangers who wished to know whether the child was a boy or a girl. Wiedeman's clothes, said his mother, " are much admired, I assure you. People stare at him, Wilson says, and turn round to stare again." Protest, expostulation, both were useless : and for twelve years, Browning had to endure the sight of a child overtly neither English nor Italian, neither masculine nor feminine ; a child beribboned and pampered ; feeding on his mother's kisses, his mother's adulation, as he fed, throughout her lifetime, on an indulgence as unrestricted as it was indiscriminating. For she would not allow Wiedeman, or, rather, Penini, as he now began to call himself, to be disciplined in any way. Anticipating some latter-day theories of child education, she ridiculed " the mythology of children being spoilt by too much love ; it's too pagan, such a creed ".[1]   Robert did not agree : and on one occasion, when Penini had misbehaved, he told him severely that he was " ' molto cattivo ' ".   " Upon which ", wrote Elizabeth, Penini's " lip began to quiver directly . . and I interfered and insisted on it that he meant to be ' very good ' on the contrary.   ' Go and kiss Papa,' said I—and off he ran, and kissed his coat ; as high up as he could reach.   The child is too susceptible—the least word overcomes him. . . .   I really don't know a fault in his temper and disposition . . . poor little precious darling ! " [2]

On December 1, according to Elizabeth, Robert had " finished . . . his Shelley " and was about to send it off to Moxon.   But the *coup d'état* intervened, and then, two days later, the " terrible Thursday ", December 4th, when the cannons of Louis Napoleon mowed down, in the streets of Paris, the last semblance of Republican opposition.   That night, listening to the distant firing from the boulevards, Elizabeth could not make up her mind to go to bed.   She put on a dressing-gown, wrapped herself in a shawl, and until nearly one o'clock sat beside the fire, while Robert " did some writing ".   What writing, we are curious to know, did Browning do under the circumstances ?   He has given us the answer : at the end of his essay on Shelley the poet added the words : *Paris, December 4th, 1851.*   Examining the essay in this light, the penultimate paragraph appears to have all the emphasis and roundness of a conclusion ; giving to the paragraph that follows it, the air of something written later, and under a separate impulse.   It was while listening to the sound of Louis Napoleon's cannons, and remembering all the while on which side of the barricades Shelley himself would have been found, that Browning chose openly to recall the " signal service it was the dream of my boyhood to render to his fame and memory ".   The dream had long since faded, or been suppressed : as had the generous passion with which a Camberwell schoolboy proclaimed himself " vowed to liberty ".   And here, in his fortieth year, his hair " already streaked with grey about the temples ",

[1] April 2 [1850].   Deleted passage.   Kenyon typescript.
[2] March 3, 1852.   Huxley typescript.

the disciple of Shelley sat mute and unprotesting, while in the streets of Paris yet another tyrant silenced in cannon-fire the voice of liberty.   Robert Browning, it is true, was not ready, like his wife, to " salve a tyrant o'er ".   Neither was he, as one of the unacknowledged legislators of the world, prepared to oppose himself to political tyranny : and in the days to come it was Victor Hugo's hand that " reached out of the shadows to tear the mask " from the crime of December 2 : it was the voice of Alfred Tennyson that demanded fiercely of his countrymen :

> What ! have we fought for freedom from our prime
> At last to dodge and palter with a public crime ?

Why did not Robert Browning speak ?   Why did he wait twenty years before, in *Prince Hohenstiel-Schwangau*, he offered the public his own characteristic apologia for compromise and failure ?   Perhaps because a certain essential dignity had been taken from a man who had to hear his own hatred of the tyrant belittled, by his wife, as yet another example of Robert's " self-willed, pettish way . . . of dismissing a subject he won't think about—and knowing very well that he doesn't think about it."   Five years ago, Robert Browning had impressed upon Elizabeth Barrett that what he desired, in marriage, was a prolongation of the conditions of his own childhood.   He could scarcely complain, then, when this was precisely what was meted out to him :   when he recognised, in his wife's attitude towards him, an echo of Sarah Anna's :   the same kindly and fundamentally complacent manner of silencing the contentions of a misguided schoolboy.   In other words, it seemed, he was back where he had started from.   Browning was bewildered.   How had it all happened ?   How and when was it that this *coup d'état* had taken place in his domestic life ?

A few weeks later, on January 2, 1852, *Childe Roland*, coming upon him " as a kind of dream ", revealed to him in a landscape fully as ominous as that of Dante's *Inferno* (all of which, Browning once wrote, I have " in my head and heart ") the retribution appropriate to his own sin :   the corruption and sterility that must claim one who has failed, like many another " poor traitor " before him, to deliver to mankind the full burden of the message with which he has been entrusted.

The second visit of the Brownings to London coincided with, and was very largely overshadowed by, the action for breach of promise which, on July 1, 1852, before Lord Campbell and a special jury, Mrs. Von Müller brought against the father of the poet. Up till that moment, Robert had accepted Mr. Browning's version of the affair : that he had been molested, against his will, by a persistent and unscrupulous woman. But when upward of fifty letters were read in court, all professing " the most intense love of the writer for the lady he was addressing ", letters beginning, many of them, " My dearest, dearest, dearest, dearest, dearest, dearest much-loved Minny ", it was with a rude shock that the poet was forced to envisage that which he was so often to return to, afterwards, in his own poetry : the ephemerality of even the deepest masculine devotion. The best that counsel could do under the circumstances was to suggest that the defendant was " a besotted old man ", a " poor old dotard in love " : the letters, he said, being merely " the encores of dotage ". A clerk in the Bank having stated that Mr. Browning's salary was " about £320 a year ", verdict was given for the plaintiff, who was awarded £800 damages. The following day, *The Times* carried a full report of the proceedings into the home of friend and foe alike : notably, to the breakfast table of number 50, Wimpole Street. Browning, who had not for a moment, said his wife, " apprehended the real character of the letters . . . felt it to the heart of his heart, and could scarcely raise his head after the blow of that dreadful newspaper ". But, she added, " he has been to see his father with his own noble promptitude and generous tenderness, and held the grey head on his shoulder and loved and pitied him . . as indeed the poor old man deserves ".[1]

Mr. Browning was either unable or unwilling to pay damages. In order to avoid doing so, it was arranged that he should leave the country without delay. To Robert fell the melancholy task of accompanying his father into this self-imposed exile. Leaving his wife and son in lodgings in Welbeck Street, he

[1] July 8, 1852. To Mrs. Jameson. Wellesley College Library.

set out once more for Paris, where, wrote Elizabeth, he " safely deposited the poor victim, and left him tolerably composed and comfortable. I do hope it may all end well. In any case the end can't be worse than the beginning. Robert's spirits are better, I think. But the vexation of it all is immense." [1] The vexation was not yet at an end ; as soon as Browning returned from Paris, he had to occupy himself with the manifold details of his father's affairs. In particular, a house recently bought or rented in Bayswater had now to be disposed of, and the furniture and fittings sold. With Sarianna, the poet was busy for days at a stretch over the negotiations involved ; so " vexed and worn " all the while by " this strange and calamitous visitation " (which, he said, " has grieved me as few things could ") that visibly, in three weeks, he lost weight and spirits alike. Letters from Paris added to the burden : separated from his family, from his books, from a life-long routine of tranquil and unexacting work, Mr. Browning became ill and depressed : and seeing her husband, in his turn, so " worn and teased " with anxiety over his father's condition, Elizabeth wished from the bottom of her heart that " we were rich enough to pay the money and bring him back to his own country ".[2]

All the while, left very much to her own devices, Elizabeth was spending a good deal of time in her old home in Wimpole Street. These stolen visits, which she could not resist, brought her as much pain as pleasure. Visibly, the passage of the intervening year had left its impression both on the house and its inhabitants. " It was sad and strange," she wrote after her first visit : seeing in her younger brothers an " unpicturesque tendency . . . to overstoutness " ; while Minny, the house-keeper and family friend, " was paler I thought, and moved heavily. Altogether it ' did me up ' (an expressive phrase which you must forgive for being slang) and I couldn't get to Carlyle's in the evening, which vexed Robert." [3] She returned, nevertheless, day after day, to lunch and gossip with Arabel and Minny, while the head of the house was away in

---

[1] Saturday, July 23, 1852. Huxley typescript. *In Three Days* may have been written on this occasion : the only one in their married life when husband and wife were separated for so long.

[2] Thursday [September 16, 1852]. Ibid.

[3] Saturday. July 23, 1852. Ibid.

the city. " For my own part, I do really sometimes, wonder how I bear to do it—but then I go again, just as if I didn't wonder at all. Horribly frightened, too, I get about six o'clock—and two days ago I all but met Papa who was coming up Wimpole Street as we were walking down, and only had time to turn abruptly round Hodgson's corner. Penini is frightened besides, seeing me so. His idea is that a ' Mitaine ' inhabits the house and comes out about dusk. He was trembling all over yesterday evening while Arabel tied on his hat. Minny is very angry with me for ' letting the child frighten himself about such nonsense '. But I say . . Better that he should be afraid of the ' mitaine ' than of the truth as it stands." [1]

It is scarcely surprising that for the rest of his life Pen Browning had a marked aversion to England as a place of residence. Once again, on this visit, it was to reveal itself to him as a source of pain and deprivation. For, as before, Wilson had disappeared : and although there was none of the " screaming and crying " of the previous year, with quivering lip the little boy followed his mother about the room asking, " Will mama go away and leave Penini all alone ? " To console him, Robert was sent to occupy Wilson's room, and Pen slept in his mother's bed where, she said, he " wakes me in the morning with a quantity of hugging and kissing—' O buona Mama ! ' and then he pulls open my eyes.' " [2] There were other consolations. While Wilson was away, Mam: could no longer go out to drive with Monckton Milnes or to dine with the Procters ; and had perforce, with Pen at her knee, to entertain her visitors in the little sitting-room in Welbeck Street. Through the eyes of a friend, we are offered a glimpse of mother and son as they appeared in that same year : the frail woman, " all eyes and hair " who, " from illness, I suppose, held her head on one side " ; and the child with his golden ringlets and white embroidered drawers, clinging to his mother as, lovingly, she ran her fingers through the heavy locks and demanded, " Has he not got beautiful hair ? " Penini at this time had taken to drawing ; and when " Mr. Millais the Pre-Raffaelite " called, confidently, the young

---

[1] Saturday [September 25, 1852]. Ibid.
[2] Thursday [September 16, 1852]. Ibid.

artist presented him with some of his sketches ; as he did also Mr. Ruskin, who came to Welbeck Street bringing " his pretty natural sprightly wife with him . . ' whose single naughtiness,' said he, ' is the love of continental life and discontent with England ' ". (" Sundry affidavits ", added Elizabeth, " have been made to me that Mrs. Ruskin was victimised by the Graduate's continental tasks and had been breaking her heart at Venice while her husband was about the ' stones '. All of which is to be read exactly backwards. She teases me, he tells you, to buy a house at Venice. Pretty she is. And exquisitely dressed . . *that* struck me . . but extraordinary beauty she has none at all, neither of feature or expression. . . . She loves art, she says.") [1] So did Fanny Haworth who, in verse, had once addressed Miss Barrett as " gifted lady " and as " Sweet Maiden Poet ", and who wished, now, to adorn the next edition of Mrs. Browning's poems with " pretty and graceful illustrative outlines ". Another visitor, Dante Gabriel Rossetti, had not only made Browning's poem *The Laboratory* the subject of his first water-colour, but had traced in *Pauline* the concealed source of *Sordello*. To the house in Welbeck Street Mazzini, too, came, " with that pale spiritual face of his, and those intense eyes full of melancholy illusions ". He was escorted by Mrs. Carlyle, whose eyes no illusions could be said to obscure. Bearing before him a basket full of ripe peaches, William Johnson Fox arrived, to enliven, for Browning, " the black element " he was beset with during this London visit of his. Full of admiration for Penini, who seemed to him " a perfect little seraph ", Fox was no less susceptible to the charms of Elizabeth—(" more fascinated with her—more than ever ")—and this despite the zeal with which she " silver-electro-typed " the man whom Carlyle liked to call the " Copper Captain ". (" I never talk politics with her," wrote Mrs. Grote in 1852, " considering her fine intellect demented, as you say in Scotland, on that point.") Fox had by this time abandoned the pulpit for politics ; as the member for Oldham, being the first to introduce into the House a Bill for national secular education. In his sixty-seventh year, he was a squat white-haired man who moved sluggishly and suffered from

---

[1] Tuesday [September, 1852]. To Miss Mitford. Deleted passage. Kenyon typescript.

heart trouble. Now in comfortable circumstances, he had a large house in Regent's Park ; and there, rubicund and velvet-coated, he liked, on occasion, to display his fine voice in the Shakespearian readings which had been such a feature of the old days at Dalston and at Bayswater. After the death of Eliza Flower in December, 1846, a reconciliation had taken place between Fox and his wife : and Eliza's name, as a visitor observed, was " not now mentioned " between them. Nor was it mentioned between Fox and Robert Browning. For, delighted as Robert might be to " re-knit the old bonds ", there was all the while, in the memory of a woman whom both men had loved, and both relegated to silence, a source of constraint whose presence Elizabeth Barrett Browning could not be expected to detect.

6

" Overjoyed I was to feel myself *at home* again ! " declared Elizabeth. After an absence of more than seventeen months, after the tension, moral and physical, of life in London and Paris, it was a delight to see Florence " looking exactly as if we had left it yesterday " : it was a delight to take possession of " the old nest, still warm, of Casa Guidi, to sit on our own chairs and sleep in our own beds ". In Elizabeth's case, the relief was profound. Indeed, she said, what with " the lovely climate, and the lovely associations, and the sense of repose, I could turn myself on my pillow and sleep on here to the end of my life ". Her husband was not prepared to share her slumbers. " Fresh from the palpitating life of the Parisian boulevards ", he was appalled by the " dying stillness " of Florence ; and complained, " most strongly ", that there was " no life, no variety " : the whole place, he said, was " dead, and dull, and flat ".

The mood did not last. Before many weeks had passed, Casa Guidi had reasserted its spell ; and once more, evening after evening, Browning was content to sit at the fireside with no other company than his wife in the armchair opposite,

Reading by firelight, that great brow
And the spirit-small hand propping it,
Mutely, my heart knows how.

" You can't think ", wrote Elizabeth in her turn, " how we
have caught up our ancient traditions just where we left them,
and relapsed into our former soundless, stirless hermit life."
One of the ancient traditions now resumed was that identity
of aim and purpose, marred, temporarily, by the stress of life
in London and Paris. " Robert has not passed an evening
from home since we came—just as if we had never known
Paris," Elizabeth wrote : in unwitting confirmation of which—
" We live wholly alone here ; I have not left the house one
evening since our return," Browning told his friend Joseph
Milsand. Significant, too, in view of this resumption of
intimacy, is the letter which a few months later Elizabeth
wrote to her new friend Fanny Haworth. Speaking of mar-
riages in which illusion is lost : " Tell me if your friend
recovers her dreams again," she wrote: " I can conceive of
a strong attachment recovering from the shock of unexpected
points of difference, and of two souls growing together after
all." [1]

The winter that followed was one of the happiest in Elizabeth's life. " I have been well," she wrote, " and we have
been quiet and occupied ; reading books, doing work, playing
with Wiedeman ; and with nothing from without to vex us
much." It was a winter, for husband and wife alike, of sustained creative effort. Elizabeth had begun work on the long-
premeditated *Aurora Leigh*, while Browning—" a first step
towards popularity "—was writing some of those " lyrics with
more music and painting than before " which, assembled, were
to compose the two green-bound volumes of *Men and Women*.
Elizabeth held very strongly the theory that " thinking, dreaming, creating people . . . have two lives to bear instead of
one, and therefore ought to sleep more than others " : accordingly, the " vital energy " squandered, latterly, in the salons
of London or Paris, was canalised now within the banks of a
sober and productive routine. Browning got up at seven,
because " he is longer dressing than I am " ; and after Wilson

[1] April 4, 1853. Omitted letter. Kenyon typescript.

had dressed, first Penini and then his mother, the family breakfasted together at nine o'clock sharp : thereby leaving to the poets " whole ribbands of long bright morning time " in which to work. After dinner, Elizabeth dozed on the sofa, while Browning went for his usual afternoon walk through the streets of Florence and out onto the surrounding hills. On his return, Penini, tambourine in hand, was ready to entertain his parents by singing and dancing for them : in peremptory mood, he would break in on their discussions with a " Don't *peat* (speak) Papa and Mama ! You saying nossing at all." Evening, after this " absolute Caesar " had been put to bed, restored the hours of intimacy, when, heaping up the olive-wood in the grate, husband and wife sat " dreaming over the fire, reading heaps of books, from M. Proudhon to Emanuel Swedenborg inclusively. . . . Robert marvels at me (at the degree of transition I mean) when I put down Alexandre Dumas to take up Emanuel Swedenborg—but I like holding the world by two handles. As for him he is as fond of digging at Vasari as I am at the Mystics, and goes to and from him as constantly, making him a betwixt and between to other writers." [1] The fidelity to Vasari is not surprising ; for it was in " digging " at *Le Vite de' Pittori*, that, anticipating the method applied to *The Ring and The Book*, Browning uncovered the raw material for *Fra Lippo Lippi* ; for *Old Pictures in Florence* ; for the most beautiful of all his monologues : the " twilight piece ", *Andrea del Sarto*. With regard to the latter, we have only to examine Vasari's opening remarks on that " eccellentissimo Pittore Fiorentino ", to discover what chord it was whose attendant echoes gained upon the imagination of the poet as he sat musing one evening, book in hand, over an olive-wood fire in Casa Guidi. " Had this master possessed a somewhat bolder and more elevated mind ; had he been as much distinguished for higher qualifications as he was for genius and depth of judgment in the art he practised, he would beyond all doubt, have been without an equal. But there was a certain timidity of mind, a sort of diffidence and want of force in his nature . . . nor did he at any time display one particle of that elevation which, if it could have been added to the advantages wherewith he was endowed, would have rendered him a truly

[1] April 13, 1853. To Mrs. Martin. Omitted letter. Ibid.

divine painter." It was a deficiency which, in the poem of that name, Andrea del Sarto chose without rancour to attribute to the influence of his wife—(" Why do I need you ? What wife had Rafael, or has Agnolo ? ")—the beautiful golden-haired Lucrezia whose presence in his life—" So free we seem, so fettered fast we are "—had served to suppress and hold in abeyance the deepest creative forces of his own being.

In the middle of March, surprising Florence with the sudden brilliance of its sunshine, spring put an end to the months of hibernation. Regretfully, Elizabeth relinquished a winter with had brought her so much happiness. " We have had so much repose, and at the same time so much interest in life, also I have been so well, that I shall be sorry when we go out of harbour again with the spring breezes." It was not, however, until July that the family left Casa Guidi in order, once more, to spend the summer months at the Baths of Lucca. They took with them Wilson and a new manservant, Ferdinando, who " makes soups and creams and iced puddings and pastry to our uttermost satisfaction," wrote Elizabeth ; but who is disconcerted, she added, by the amount of responsibility laid upon him, since his former mistress " was constantly in the kitchen, giving directions, he says, and that's by no means a way of mine, you know ".[1] Flush, too, accompanied the Brownings on what was to be the last summer excursion of his career ; the agile young puppy who had first greeted Miss Barrett in a sick-room at Torquay being now, in his thirteenth year, a ponderous old dog, slow, fat and almost hairless. The ménage installed itself in a comfortable two-storied house in Alla Villa—" We have a row of plane trees before the door in which the cicale sing all day, and the beautiful mountains stand close around, keeping us fresh with shadows "—and here, promising one another " to be industrious à faire frémir ", the two poets settled down " with a stiff resolve of not calling nor being called upon ". Not even Penini was suffered to be wholly idle ; and for a quarter of an hour each day read in his spelling book about ' lame pigs " and " warm muffs " ; but when, " absolutely wild with the sight of the mountains

[1] July 26 [1853]. Huxley typescript.

and the liberty of the garden, he shut his eyes and kicked his legs indolently, as he sate on my knee, and said ' I not lite mine lesson a bit ' ",[1] the hard-hearted Robert shut him in a room by himself, thereby punishing him for precisely those " crimes of inattention " which sixteen years later, in the opinion of Benjamin Jowett, were to disqualify him for a scholastic career at Balliol. During these tutorial sessions, Elizabeth tucked *Aurora Leigh* under a cushion : but when Pen was finally released to play with Flush or to fish with a net in the river, assembling her quill pens, her " half-pint " sheets of paper, she settled down with resolution to do a long morning's work on her novel-poem. Browning, allotted " a little blue-room " of his own to write in, was busy on his playlet, *In a Balcony* : a resumption of the dramatic form inspired, perhaps, by Helen Faucit's recent performance, in London, of *Colombe's Birthday. By the Fireside*, its scenery rather than its emotional inspiration, derives also from this time.[2] Husband and wife never worked in the same room. Nor did they show their work to one another until completed. " An artist must, I fancy, either find or *make* a solitude to work in, if it is to be good work at all," Elizabeth wrote. For the Brownings were becoming increasingly conscious that in this sense at least, it was an undeniable disadvantage to two poets, to have but " one soul between them " ; a condition that, enmeshed as they were in a common sensibility, they sought vainly at times to escape. " Surely," wrote Elizabeth before her marriage, " we feel alike in many, many things—the convolvuluses grow together ; twisted together " : a process which threatened to become a stranglehold upon the independent vision of each. Of the two, it was Browning who was in the greater danger ; he who in his Wimpole Street days, after submitting his unpublished poetry to her inspection, had eagerly adopted " every one " of her suggested emendations : who had assured her that

[1] August 30, 1853. Ibid.
[2] It is possible to identify, in the letters of W. W. Story who spent the summer at Lucca, many of the details which appear in the poem. Thus, the sculptor's " little old church " near the Prato Fiorito is the " ruined chapel " of the poem : his " wondrous *fungi*, some as red as coral ", the poet's " Yon sudden coral nipple ", etc. After Story left, Browning set himself " to make a sketch or two (in emulation of your pencil) " of the autumnal landscape they had explored together.

he needed her letters to " *train* " his, to " guide me and half put into my mouth what I ought to say ". Now, in marriage, he was to find " the personality of my wife . . . so strong and peculiar ", that for many years he was unable successfully to assert himself in the face of it. But if Elizabeth's was the stronger character, hers was the lesser genius ; and in this connection it is possible to compare both the affinity and the disparity between husband and wife in two poems published, one in 1844, and the other a year later : the first part of Browning's *Saul*, and Elizabeth Barrett's *A Rhapsody of Life's Progress*. Here is the relevant extract from each.

Elizabeth Barrett :

Then we leap on the earth with the armour of youth . . .
And we run with the stag, and we leap with the horse,
And we swim with the fish through the broad water-course,
And we strike with the falcon, and hunt with the hound,
And the joy which is in us flies out by a wound.
And we shout so aloud ' We exult, we rejoice ',
That we lose the low moan of our brothers around ;
And we shout so adeep down creation's profound,
　　We are deaf to God's voice.

Robert Browning :

　　And the wild joys of living ! The leaping
　　　　From rock up to rock—
　　The rending their boughs from the palm-trees—
　　　　The cool silver shock
　　Of a plunge in the pool's living water—
　　　　The hunt of the bear,
　　And the sultriness showing the lion
　　　　Is couched in his lair :
　　And the meal—the rich dates—yellowed over
　　　　With gold dust divine,
　　And the locust's-flesh steeped in the pitcher—
　　　　The full draught of wine,
　　And the sleep in the dried river channel
　　　　Where tall rushes tell
　　The water was wont to go warbling
　　　　So softly and well,—

178

How good is man's life here, mere living !
　How fit to employ
The heart and the soul and the senses
　For ever in joy !

Irresistibly, one is reminded of something that Robert Browning wrote in August, 1846. " What man of genius," he asked, " would not associate with people of no talent at all, rather than the possessors of *mere* talent, who keep sufficiently near him, as they walk together, to give him annoyance at every step ? " It is unfair, admittedly, to quote this remark in such a context ; for Browning had all his life the greatest admiration for the " divine " poetic powers of his wife. During her lifetime, Mrs. Browning's poetry went into edition after edition ; while her husband's languished, unsaleable and unsought after, on the hands of his various publishers. Taste changes : and today, while we recognise a certain genius latent alike in the poetry and the personality of Elizabeth Barrett, it is hard to share even Rilke's reverence for " the forty-four wonderful ' Sonnets from the Portuguese ' " which in 1907 he translated into German. Indeed, it is not so much in Elizabeth Barrett's poetry as in her prose, in the sensibility, wit and justice of the best of her letters, that we find the most convincing evidence of the " inexhaustible affluence and power " which continued to inspire in her husband such open admiration for " that wonderful mind of hers ".

Despite Elizabeth's reluctance to " tumble out of my nest again ", the Brownings left Florence at the end of November in order to spend the next six months in Rome. After " a most exquisite journey of eight days ", they entered Rome in the highest spirits, " Robert and Penini singing actually " ; and were gratified to find the lamps lit and the fires crackling in their apartment in the Via Bocca di Leone : a hospitable gesture on the part of William Story and his wife, who, with their children Edith and Joe, had spent the preceding summer with the poets at the Bagni di Lucca. After which propitious circumstances, it is surprising to hear that the following morning, Browning was " in a fit of bilious irritability " so vehement that in a gesture of " suicidal impatience " he " shaved away his whole beard, whiskers and all ". Barely had Elizabeth recovered from the shock of this transfiguration, before, pale and stricken, Edith Story arrived in the care of a manservant with the news that little Joe was seriously ill with gastric fever. Hurrying to the assistance of their friends, the Brownings spent the whole day at the child's bedside ; and in the evening watched him die.

Rome, thereafter, was blackened for Elizabeth. She had seen Penini's former playmate laid " close to Shelley's heart " in the fresh gravel-clay of the English cemetery ; and it was as much as she could do not to drop from the seat of the carriage in which the bereaved mother sat so calmly beside her. " I am horribly weak about such things. I can't look on the earth-side of death ; I flinch from corpses and graves. . . . When I look deathwards I look *over* death, and upwards, or I can't look that way at all." Spiritualism provided the bridge, affording her " *scientific* proof", that " *no part of us* will ever lie in a grave ". Borne across the Atlantic by American carriers, the virus of Spiritualism had already formed potent foci of infection in the various capitals of Europe. In Rome in 1854, spirits were rapping, tables were rising into the air, pencils were prophesying, ladies' maids were addressing their employers in Hebrew and in Greek. " Nothing interests me so much—I shall not have rest till I know what there is to be known on it," Elizabeth wrote to Mrs. Jameson. " I expect from the solution that it will be a breaking up of some of the deepest and dumbest mysteries of our double Being." [1] There was in this eagerness something more than intellectual curiosity. Despite the excellent quality of Elizabeth Barrett Browning's mind, certain beliefs, illusions even, were on her own admission essential to her. She was incapable, for instance, of a stoic resignation before the idea of the soul's extinction in death. " My whole nature would cry aloud against that most pitiful result of the struggle here —a wrestling only for the dust, and not for the crown. What a resistless melancholy would fall on me if I had such thoughts ! —and what a dreadful indifference." Spiritualism offered an alternative to melancholy : an assurance, reinforcing

[1] August 23, 1853. Omitted letter. Kenyon typescript.

faith, that she had not, after all, slain her own brother. In Rome, therefore, where the testimony was " various and strong ", evenings on the third floor at the Via Bocca di Leone were devoted almost exclusively to the entertainment of spiritual visitors. By candle-light, in the little drawing-room, the latest apparitions were discussed ; messages were written under dictation from the unseen ; a heavy table, on one occasion, struggled manfully to answer, in alphabetical code, the questions addressed to it. " The panting and shivering of that dead dumb wood, the human emotion con-veyed through it—by what ? had to me a greater significance than the St. Peter's of this Rome," wrote Elizabeth reverently : a reverence which survived the curiously " impious and dis-cordant " nature of some of the messages received at times from the spiritual world.

> Do we indeed desire the dead
> Should still be near us at our side ?

Tennyson had enquired in *In Memoriam*. Robert Browning, for one, did not desire it : and it is scarcely surprising to find that in Rome this winter the man who was reputed " never to have spent an evening away from home " throughout his married life, was ready to accept with alacrity the invitation of friends whose hospitality was to be in terms of flesh and blood only. Fortunately, Roman society, in 1854, catered for worldly as well as other-worldly tastes : and a letter of Elizabeth's offers us a pleasant glimpse of a musical soirée at Mrs. Sartoris's at which, characteristically, Elizabeth " stayed by the fire . . . and talked spiritualism " to a believer, while her husband spent his time " standing in the doorway of the quadrille-room, admiring the pretty women, and protesting that his own venerable age would prevent his dancing again. . . ." [1]

" ' What is to be said for a woman ', says my husband, ' who believes in Louis Napoleon and the rapping spirits ? ' " The tone is a light one. It was necessary, her husband knew, to make allowances for a woman who, until her fortieth year, had led a life of almost total seclusion. Slowly, however, the amused tolerance of the first years in Florence was giving

[1] January 11, 1854. To George Barrett. Illinois University Library.

way to something grimmer. Much of Robert Browning's
early love for Elizabeth Barrett was bound up with admiration
for " that wonderful mind of hers ", on whose discernment
he felt that he could with impunity altogether rely.

> Oh I must feel your brain prompt mine,
>   Your heart anticipate my heart,
> You must be just before, in fine,
>   See and make me see, for your part,
> New depths of the divine !

" Consider," he had written to her in 1846, " how much of
my happiness would be disturbed by allying myself to a
woman to whose intellect, as well as goodness, I could *not*
look up. . . . It is pleasanter to lie back on the cushions
inside the carriage and let another drive—but if you suspect
he cannot drive ? " The suspicion was gradually becoming
a certainty. In her manner of bringing up Pen, in her passion
for Louis Napoleon, in her obsession with spiritualism, Elizabeth's driving was becoming more and more wilful and
unpredictable. Snatch the reins, then ? But it was he
himself who had resigned them—nay, pressed them—into her
hand. Nor, indeed, could she be expected to relinquish them
now. There is no doubt that Browning was deeply troubled
by the dilemma that confronted him : a dilemma that was
rooted in his very affection and concern for his wife. Loving
her less, there would have been no problem : loving, however,
he must obey : and obey, (it had happened once before in his
life) where he could no longer respect.

" The pleasantest days in Rome ", wrote Elizabeth in May,
1854, " we have spent with the Kembles—the two sisters—
who are charming and excellent, both of them, in different
ways ; and certainly they have given us some exquisite hours
on the Campagna, upon picnic excursions, they and certain
of their friends. . . ." On one such occasion, fortified by
mayonnaise and champagne, the guests suggested taking a
walk together to some distant spot. Elizabeth was too languid
to join them, and at once Browning offered to remain behind
to keep her company ; thereby eliciting from Mrs. Kemble the
exclamation that " he was the only man she had ever known
who behaved like a Christian to his wife ". Laughing and

chattering, the picnic guests departed, leaving two in the Campagna to contemplate in silence the " champaign with its endless fleece of feathery grasses everywhere ". Solitude, however, could no longer bring the old intimacy ; hands were linked, but spirits remained separate ; and aware of this hiatus, Browning was filled with a desperate longing for the unimpaired communion of happier days.

> I would that you were all to me,
>   You that are just so much, no more.
> Nor yours nor mine, nor slave nor free !
>   Where does the fault lie ? What the core
> O' the wound, since wound must be ?
>
> I would I could adopt your will,
>   See with your eyes, and set my heart
> Beating by yours, and drink my fill
>   At your soul's springs,—your part my part
> In life, for good and ill.

But this—he admitted it, perhaps for the first time—was no longer possible for him ; and as, under the stress of new emotion, he felt his soul detach itself from its chosen harbour, a sense of loss and anxiety followed upon this new, this wholly unwished-for liberation.

> Must I go
> Still like the thistle-ball, no bar,
>   Onward, whenever light winds blow,
> Fixed by no friendly star ?

Was Elizabeth aware of this mood which darkened, unaccountably, a " morn of Rome and May " ? Nine months later, back once more beside her beloved chimney piece at Casa Guidi, she wrote to Mrs. Jameson : " I did not like Rome, I think I confessed to you. . . . I lost several letters in Rome, besides a good deal of illusion."

7

On their way to England in the summer of 1855, the Brownings paused long enough in Paris to see Wilson married to their manservant, Ferdinando Romagnoli : a necessity similar to that which caused the Shelleys to hasten the marriage of their servant Paolo to Elise, the children's nurse they had brought out with them from England. The ceremony took place on July 11th : Wilson, we learn, expected to be confined at the end of October. After a " hideous rolling, heaving passage of two hours ", the travellers arrived in London at three o'clock in the morning, to creep exhausted into the unfamiliar beds that awaited them there. The next morning, watching, from the window, a steady drizzle descend upon Dorset Street, Ferdinando exclaimed compassionately : " Povera gente, che deve vivere in questo posto ! " A few days more of " heavy London air ", and Pen's ringlets hung limp about his face, while his mother spent herself, vehemently, in " hating and detesting this London which hangs weights on my very soul and sinks me to the bottom of things ". Nevertheless, when her old friend Mrs. Martin invited her to stay in Herefordshire, near Hope End, Elizabeth declined with a shudder : " I never *could* go into that neighbourhood except to die, which I think sometimes I should like."

Looking " quite brilliant " in a Parisian bonnet, Arabel called regularly to take Penini to Wimpole Street ; and despite her earlier resolve not to be seen " creeping and sliding behind the doors of what was my own home as if I had stolen the tea pot ", Elizabeth soon followed suit. " Yesterday," she wrote, " Arabel deceived me into going when Papa was in the house, I understanding that he was going out : and under such circumstances of course I was in a continual state of nervous alarm. Think of Penini being absolutely caught the other day. George was playing in the hall with him and he was in fits of laughter. Papa came out of the dining-room and stood *looking* for two or three minutes. Then he called George, and went back. ' Whose child is that, George ? ' ' Ba's child,' said George. ' And what is he doing here, pray ? ' Then, without waiting for an answer he changed the subject. To hear of it thrilled me to the roots of my heart. . . ." [1]

There was one other topic capable of evoking an equally vivid reaction. " As to Hume, [*sic*] " Elizabeth wrote to her

[1] Friday [July 17, 1855]. Huxley typescript.

sister in Somersetshire, " we shall see *him*, and I will tell you. He's the most interesting person to me in England, out of *Wilton*, Taunton, and 50 Wimpole Street." Ten days later, by special invitation, the Brownings drove out to Ealing and there, in the house of a solicitor called Rymer, they were introduced to the celebrated medium, Daniel Dunglas Home. Mr. Home was not unprepared for the visit of two poets, having previously gathered clematis from the garden, and with the assistance of young Miss Rymer, also a medium, fashioned the flowers into a wreath. " The wreath ", wrote Home, " was afterwards put on the table at which we were sitting, but whether naturally or by spirit hands, I do not remember." A hand, however, did appear ; " Clothed in white samite, mystic, wonderful "—or, as Browning more prosaically describes it, " clothed in white loose folds, like muslin ", and proceeded to crawl, " up Mr. Home's shoulder, and . . . put the wreath on my wife, *how*, I was unable to see ".[1] For, contrary to the assertion of Home, Browning did not leave his place in order to stand behind his wife's chair as the wreath approached her. He made no investigations of any kind ; unwilling, as a guest, to embarrass his host by an overt expression of incredulity. Masking his own feelings he behaved throughout the evening with the greatest restraint ; and was honest enough, in retrospect, to admit that there were certain phenomena, such as the lifting into the air of a heavy table, which he was totally unable to account for. What placed the greatest tax upon his equanimity, however, was not so much the " humbuggery " of Home, the spiritual messages—(" Dear Papa,—is not God *good*, isn't he *lovely* ? ") [2] —but the whole personality of the young man, which aroused in the poet an instant and enduring antipathy. " Home," Browning wrote, " affects the manners, endearments and other peculiarities of a very little child indeed—speaking of Mr. and Mrs. Rymer as his ' Papa and Mama ' [partly erased] and kissing the family abundantly—he professes timorousness, ' a love of love '—and is unpleasant enough in it all—being a well-grown young man, over the average height, and I should say, of quite the ordinary bodily strength. . . ." [3]

[1] July 25, 1855. To Mrs. Kinney. W. L. Phelps. Robert Browning on Spiritualism, *The Yale Review*, Autumn, 1933.   [2] Ibid.   [3] Ibid.

Distasteful, certainly : all the more so, perhaps, in that the situation contained a reflection, aggrandised into caricature, of another over-valued son, also of quite the ordinary bodily strength, who, readily embracing both Mama and Papa, as he " never broke the habit " of calling them, avowed himself incapable, to the day of his marriage, of packing his own carpet-bag, or of walking " into a shop " to " buy his own gloves ". But if there was, thus, an element of self-recognition in Browning's recoil from Home, his sustained hostility sprang from a more complex source. At one level there is a certain affinity between the rôle of the medium and that of the poet.

> Who will, may hear Sordello's story told.
> His story ? Who believes me shall behold
> The man . . .
> Only believe me. Ye believe ?
>   Appears
> Verona . . .

It is the confidence trick of the poet who, " Catching the dead, if fate denies the quick ", by a faculty denied to other men, can summon back from the past " Many a lighted face Foul with no vestige of the grave's disgrace ". Like the poet, the medium attempts, through the resources of his own craft, his own magic, " to bring the invisible full into play ". Both claim to discern, beyond the natural frontiers of life, those " mysteries of things " which, without their intercession, would remain unavailable to the great mass of mankind. But the gift of second sight, of inspiration, call it what you will, brings with it, so Browning always believed, obligations which the artist ignores at his peril. " A poet's affair is with God, to whom he is accountable, and of whom is his reward : look elsewhere, and you find misery enough," he wrote a few months later to John Ruskin. Now a poet who, looking elsewhere, has falsified, or even modified the burden of the message with which he is entrusted, is as culpable as a medium who simulates an experience which he knows to be beyond his own range : a guilt, a fall from grace, which over and over again in his poetry Robert Browning has chosen to analyse and defend. (" Moral character and action," he once told Moncure Conway, " depend so much on circumstances that

it is almost impossible for men to judge each other fairly.")
It is in order to satisfy the demands of other people, we learn,
that, debarred in early life from " laughing free, speaking
plain ", Sludge the Medium consents to speak only that which
is expected of him : " enjoined be sweet And comely and
superior ", submits himself, deliberately, to a career of " Hug-
gings and humbug ". And it is here, in the supposed resentment of the Medium at the loss of his own integrity, that there
is a sudden vehemence in which we hear plainly, for a moment,
the voice of his creator.

> It's too bad, I say,
> Ruining a soul so !

" It has been ", Elizabeth wrote sadly, " a most uncomfortable and unprofitable visit to England." For everything
seemed to go wrong with her plans that summer. Henrietta,
who was expecting her second child, was unable to leave
Taunton : and Elizabeth, on her side, was prevented from
undertaking so expensive a journey because " that dear
Mr. Kenyon has *again forgotten our fifty pounds* ". Nor was she
permitted to see Arabel for long : summarily, in August,
Mr. Barrett despatched his entire household to Eastbourne,
while he remained behind to preside over the re-carpeting
and furnishing of Wimpole Street. (" It is supposed, however," wrote Elizabeth enigmatically, " that the real reason
of the delay is, a reluctance to leave the *mesmerizer*, who arrives
regularly every morning, and engrosses a mysterious hour or
so with fast-locked doors ").[1] Penini was coaxed into going
to Eastbourne with Arabel and his Uncle Occy : during
which time, Wilson, whose behaviour had " shocked and
pained " Mrs. Browning, left to await her confinement in the
bosom of her own family. Despite the shrimp-nets and
donkeys, however, Pen was not happy at Eastbourne.
" Whenever he was tired, poor darling, he cried out for his
' own friends '—and woke Arabel one night by screaming in
his sleep. . . . ' Oh untle Otty, untle Otty, I must do to
mama ! ' "[2] Even if she had wished to do so, Elizabeth
could not have joined the family party at Eastbourne, " —be-

---

[1] Monday [August 27, 1855]. Huxley typescript.
[2] Wednesday [October 3, 1855]. Ibid.

cause although Robert might let me, he assuredly would not
like it. Also, I should do worse than spend money in doing
so. I should choose to be away from Robert just when I am
of most use to him every day in the proof-sheets. No—it
would not be possible." [1] Pen was brought back to Dorset
Street, therefore ; where, contentedly, he sat on the floor
reading Miss Edgeworth in Italian translation, while at the
table above his parents corrected in partnership the proof-
sheets of *Men and Women*. Elizabeth, who had not added a
line to *Aurora Leigh* since she left Italy, devoted her whole
energy and attention to this task : a labour of love indeed ;
her admiration for the poetry of Robert Browning having
preceded by many years her introduction to the poet. " You
have in your vision two worlds," she wrote to him on
January 15, 1845, " or to use the language of the schools of the
day, you are both subjective and objective in the habits of your
mind. You can deal both with abstract thought and with
human passion in the most passionate sense. Thus, you have
an immense grasp in Art ; and no one at all accustomed to
consider the usual forms of it, could help regarding with
reverence and gladness the gradual expansion of your powers."
Whatever modification the years may have produced in her
personal relationship with Robert Browning, this reverence
remained unimpaired ; and it was with an eager and discriminating humility, ten years later, that she assisted at the
task of correcting, in proof form, poems which, she said, " for
variety, vitality and intensity " seem to me " as fine as anything
he has done ". This is, of course, an objective judgment on
her husband's work. What, one would also like to know, did
Elizabeth think of the fact, curious enough in all conscience,
that of the fifteen poems in *Men and Women* whose inspiration
may be attributed to the married life of the poets, twelve at
least portray love frustrated or incomplete ? For even *The
Guardian Angel* has its sediment of dissatisfaction ; and as for
the remarkable *Love Among the Ruins* (written in Paris the day
after *Childe Roland*), it is only on a vast substructure of pride
and ambition overthrown that unity in love is therein achieved.
Alone amongst these poems, *By the Fireside* offers us a glimpse
of that tranquil and impassioned harmony which might seem

[1] Thursday [September 13, 1855]. Huxley typescript.

to be the inevitable sequel to the love letters : and it may have been a wish to redress, belatedly, the balance of so unexpected a reckoning that caused Robert Browning, a bare ten days before the books were finally printed, to add the laboured poem *One Word More* which appears there as epilogue and dedication to E. B. B.

At the end of October, the Brownings returned to Paris, leaving behind them in England Wilson and her newborn son, Orestes. A young girl was engaged to perform, in Wilson's absence, the duties of lady's maid and nurse, while Ferdinando, grass-widowed, continued disconsolately to cook and shop for the household. Through the indiscretion of a friend, the family was committed to a cramped and draughty little flat in the rue de Grenelle, a situation which pleased no one but Pen, who gained thereby the privilege of sleeping on the floor of his parents' bedroom, where his dreams were punctuated nightly by the harsh spasmodic sound of his mother's coughing. In these circumstances, " lying *perdus* in our hole ", and with nothing to do but " smoulder over the fire and read George Sand's memoirs ", husband and wife awaited from day to day the publication of *Men and Women*. Elizabeth was " ready to die at the stake " for her faith in the book : and as for Browning, while he had, on his own admission, made therein a deliberate bid for popularity, he was at the same time aware that to the production of these poems he had devoted ten of the most vital and significant years of his life. It was with alternating equanimity and apprehension, therefore, that the Brownings awaited the verdict of critical opinion on the book, hoping that with its appearance the neglect of two decades would be erased, and the full stature of the poet revealed to all.

Men and Women was published by Chapman and Hall on November 17, 1855. On the day of publication, a review appeared in the *Athenaeum*. " These volumes ", wrote the reviewer, " contain some fifty poems, which will make the least imaginative man think, and the least thoughtful man grieve. Who will not grieve over energy wasted and power misspent,—over fancies chaste and noble, so overhung by the 'seven veils' of obscurity, that we can often-times be only sure that fancies exist?" During the next few months, haunting Galignani's reading room and searching there a table covered with journals and newspapers of all kinds, Browning was to read many other notices which made it plain to him that once again contemporary opinion had chosen to ignore or deride the work of a major poet. The target of obtuse reviewers, Robert Browning was familiar with every degree of neglect and contempt. His disappointment on this occasion was none the less acute : the more so, perhaps, in that today, when the critics refused " to praise me for my poems ", he could no longer, as in days of old, " go very lighthearted back to a garden-full of rose-trees, and a soul-full of comforts ". Denied this resource, a new bitterness makes itself felt in his references to his detractors. " Meanwhile," he wrote to Edward Chapman, " don't take to heart the zoological utterances I have stopped my ears against at Galignani's of late. ' Whoo-oo-oo-oo ' mouths the big monkey—' whee-ee-ee-ee ' squeaks the little monkey and such a dig with the end of my umbrella as I should give the brutes if I couldn't keep my temper, and consider how they miss their nut[s] and gingerbread."

By the time that letter was written, rectifying the mistake of their friend, the Brownings had moved into a larger and more congenial apartment in the rue du Colysée. Promptly once more Pen claimed a corner of the parental bedroom. (" He was so pathetic about it," his mother wrote, " that we would not lose him." We ?) Elizabeth's cough subsided ; and she was able to resume, each morning, the task of teaching her son to read and write. " Penini works an hour and a half," she wrote to Henrietta, " but then he loses half that time with talking and kissing. He does all his lessons except the writing sitting on my knee—and my hair is out of curl and my cheeks hot with kissing before I have done." [1] Re-established, generally, in health, (" there has been no return of the spitting of blood ") Elizabeth set to work again on *Aurora Leigh*. She hoped to deliver the completed manuscript to the printer on her return to England in the early summer : and with this end in view, she gave herself up wholly

[1] Tuesday, March 4 [1856]. Huxley typescript.

to the task of composition ; working hour after hour in " a sort of *furia* ", which left her no time to read even the daily newspaper. One thing alone disturbed her : her husband at this period was doing no writing whatsoever. Daily, on his return from a moody perusal of the journals at Galignani's, hours of idleness confronted him, and the sense of this barren-ness weighed upon Elizabeth, slackening, in sympathy, the impetus of her own pen. As much for her sake as for his, she cast about for a means of harnessing, profitably, that unem-ployed energy ; and found it in reverting to a suggestion she had already put before him in 1845. Sordello, she then said, " is like a noble picture with its face to the wall just now—or at least, in the shadow. . . . And such a work as it might become if you chose . . if you put your will to it ! . . . it wants drawing together and fortifying in the connections and associations. . . ." Browning had agreed with her : " When we are together one day—the days I believe in—I mean to set about that reconsidering," he wrote : and now, ten years later, at the renewed insistence of his wife, he gave himself to the long deferred task of creating " the new avatar of *Sordello* " which she had desired to see. For a few weeks, the old har-mony of concerted work re-established itself between husband and wife ; and then abruptly, the poet abandoned what he saw to be a wearisome and wholly unrewarding task. (" I will strike, for the future, on the glowing, malleable metal ; afterwards, *filing* is quite another process from hammering, and a more difficult one.") And why, in any case—as at this time he had himself written to Ruskin in an impassioned defence of his own poetic method— " expect that a Druid stone-circle will be traced for you with as few breaks to the eye as the North Crescent and South Crescent that go together so cleverly in many a suburb ? "

The breakdown in Browning's scheme of industry was a disaster which, this time, Elizabeth saw no immediate prospect of rectifying. Unexpectedly, her father-in-law came to the rescue. Soon after his arrival in Paris, Mr. Browning had applied for permission to draw at the Louvre : at this occupa-tion his son now joined him, " and after thirteen days applica-tion ", Elizabeth wrote with delight, " he has produced some quite startling copies of heads. I am very glad. He can't rest from serious work in light literature, as I can ; it wearies him, and there are hours which are on his hands, which is bad both for them and for him. The secret of life is in full occupation, isn't it ? This world is not tenable on other terms."

It was a conviction which Pen could not be expected to share. Already, his aversion to work was equalled only by his " decided vocation for kissing and hugging ". " Perhaps his fault presently will be some excess of sentimentalism," wrote his mother. " What if he runs away with a third love, at sixteen. I said the other day . . . ' Well, Penini, I hope, whatever you do, you'll always live with Mama.' ' Oh yes, dear mama, I will ; if I tan, you know,'—' How do you mean . . *if you can* ' ? ' Why, if I don't *die*.' ' Oh, Peni ! I hope it is more likely for mama to die than for you to die.' ' Ah—but if *you* died, dearest mama, it would be worse for *me* than if *I* died ! ' " [1]

It was Mr. Kenyon's wish that when the Brownings visited England in the summer of 1856 they should occupy his house in Devonshire Place. The " princely " Kenyon, " poet and the friend of poets ", who had presided so discreetly over the long maturation of Browning's courtship, was now, in his seventy-third year, failing rapidly in health. Under a doctor's care in the Isle of Wight, he was unable to welcome his visitors when they arrived in London : but the servants who remained in the big silent house were instructed to attend to their comfort throughout their stay. If therefore the Brownings felt at times " rather afraid of moving our elbows for fear of breaking something ", they were compensated by dining in a room which Thackeray considered the prettiest in London, where graceful pillars supported a bay overlooking the green lawns of Regent's park. Straight from the warm airless rooms of their Paris apartment, Elizabeth, however, shivered every time a door was opened. Swathed in cashmere, she huddled in a corner of the sofa, scribbling feverishly at *Aurora Leigh* ; which Browning, a few days later, was to read in its entirety for the first time. With unmistakable emotion (" I wish, in

[1] Thursday and Friday [April 11, 1856]. Huxley typescript.

one sense, that I had written, and she had read it, so ") he recorded the fact. " Read this Book, this divine Book, Wednesday night, July 9th, 1856.—R. B., 39, Devonshire Place," he wrote on a page of his wife's manuscript. On the same day, July 9th, with " hands almost incapacitated from cold ", Elizabeth managed to scribble a letter to her sister in Taunton, apologising for not having written to her sooner. " One thing which has put me out of sorts since I came," she wrote, " has been a mistake or worse fault of the chymist here, (Twinberrow), through which my indispensable morphine was weaker than usual. So that I have had the feeling, people have in dreams, of being forced to *run*, for some great motive or other, and of not being able to move their legs. Now, however, Bell, my old man, (who told Robert he thought I was dead long ago) has sent me the right proportions, and I am myself and comfortable. Really quite well." [1]

Well enough, at all events, to breakfast two days later at Upper Brook Street with Monckton Milnes ; where Nathaniel Hawthorne, her neighbour at the celebrated round table, found her " more youthful and comely than I supposed ". Hawthorne, who had taken the precaution of fortifying himself in advance with coffee and cold beef, ate only " some delicate chicken, and a very small cutlet " ; Mrs. Browning, he concluded, was a vegetarian, since she, for her part, ate " nothing but an egg ". Afterwards, in the library, Robert Browning introduced himself to the American : and Hawthorne found him no less " appreciative and responsive " than his wife. A " younger man than I expected to see," he wrote, " handsome, with dark hair, a very little frosted. He is very simple and agreeable in manner, gently impulsive, talking as if his heart were uppermost." (This affability of the poet's is frequently commented upon ; and it is difficult to reconcile with his lifelong " habit of calling people ' fools ' with as little reverence as could be " ; with his desire to " find out " people, and the pleasure he took in " the power " that such knowledge gave him. " Tenderness," wrote Browning in 1851, " is not always a characteristic of very sincere natures " : a remark which may shed a certain light on the

[1] July 9 [1856]. Ibid.

question.)[1]   Thomas · Woolner, who was occupied at this time in making a bronze medallion of the poet, found his sitter a " first rate man and most delightful companion " : but the medallion, when it was finished, drew from William Bell Scott the puzzled comment that " the connection between Browning's face and his work seems to me as little understandable as well can be. Of course his conversation would connect the two immediately, but his head is I think the most unprepossessing poet's head it is well possible to imagine."

Meanwhile, the presence of the Brownings in Devonshire Place had not passed unnoticed. Mr. Moulton-Barrett responded, with characteristic peremptoriness, by despatching his whole family to Ventnor in the Isle of Wight.   " It was hard, Henrietta," Elizabeth said, " his resolving to send his family away, the very day on which he knew I was near— hard ; —almost inhuman. But I won't talk of it here. Let Arabel offend him, and he would turn her out at a moment's notice—which she is so prepared for, that she was considering in London, whether, in that case, she would go out as a companion, or apply herself among the wood-engravers—poor darling ! " [2] A single alternative remained, and the Brownings availed themselves of it without hesitation : at a day's notice, they packed up and accompanied Arabel and her brothers into exile at Ventnor. Here, under the threat, always imminent, of Mr. Moulton-Barrett's sudden arrival amongst them, they spent a " happy sorrowful " fortnight : after which husband and wife went north to visit Mr. Kenyon in his home at West Cowes. It was soon apparent to them that their old friend was very ill indeed.   " The face lights up with the warm, generous heart ; then the fire drops, and you see the embers. The breath is very difficult—it is hard to live. He leans on the table, saying softly and pathetically : ' My

---

[1] Mrs. Angeli has pointed out a discrepancy between the eulogistic terms in which Browning thanked D. G. Rossetti for his " masterly " *Poems*, and the denigratory way in which, almost simultaneously, he spoke of them to Isa Blagden. Jane Welsh Carlyle, visiting Mrs. Montagu, wrote : " Browning came while I was there, and dropt on one knee and kissed her hand, with a fervor ! And I have heard Browning speak slightingly of Mrs. Montagu." Thomas Powell (who at one time knew Browning better than Browning later cared to acknowledge), recognised a " contradiction in his nature ", which " probably proceeds from that false courtesy which is, perhaps, his solitary blemish ".

[2] Thursday [September 8, 1856]. Huxley typescript.

God ! my God ! ' '' Henrietta, during this time, was writing affectionate letters imploring her sister to come and stay with her in Somerset ; and with some hesitation, Elizabeth finally agreed to do so. " Shan't we ruin you ? Break up your comfort ? In that case, put us in a farmhouse, as I prayed. We shall require a bedroom for ourselves, and some little closet for Robert to dress in. . . ." [1] Travelling from Southampton through Yeovil, the Brownings arrived in Taunton in the last week of September : and Elizabeth was overjoyed to find the sister she had not seen for four years so felicitously established, as she said, " in that nest of love, with the three babies round you, and the laburnum tree looking in at the window ". No premonition that this was to be their last meeting marred the happiness of the two sisters : and it was with the pleasantest of memories that, after a fortnight at Taunton, the Brownings took their departure and returned, in a second-class carriage " full of professed wits ", to Devonshire Place. Here, Ferdinando awaited them ; and here too Wilson introduced them, proudly, to Orestes : " A pretty, interesting baby of just a year, with great black Italian eyes." [2] London was shrouded, already, in autumnal fog ; and, since the proofs of *Aurora Leigh* were coming in thick and fast from the printer's, Elizabeth worked all day, and coughed with " house-rending " force all night. Penini, meanwhile, wrote a letter to his cousin in Somerset :

MY DEAREST ALTHAM,

I hope you are going to enjoy yourself sweeping up the grass, as you say Hutchings was mowing it, and I wish I was there to help you. Now the rain is pouring down here, and I can't go out ; but I have had a pleasure today in getting your letter and in reading it too. I go out in the streets almost every day with my sword and my gun and frighten all the people. And now my story's begun. And now my story's done.

Goodbye !
Your affectionate,
PENINI. [3]

---

[1] Ibid. [2] Wednesday [October 1, 1856]. Ibid.
[3] Saturday [October 11, 1856]. Ibid.

8

Returning to Florence, after two summers and a winter spent alternately in London and Paris, was like dropping " suddenly down a wall out of the world ".

Elizabeth at least was not sorry to resign herself, in the shadow of the wall, to the curative effects of solitude and monotony : and despite the fact that the mountains all round were white with snow, her cough dwindled and her strength increased. In London, she had yearned continually " for the quiet of my Florence, where somehow it always has gone best with my life " ; and now restored to her own chair, her own especial corner at the fireside, she rediscovered with pleasure the serene domestic intimacy which prospered nowhere so well as at Casa Guidi, wherein lay its root. By the time the first tramontana swept the corner of the Via Maggio, logs of olive-wood and pinewood had been stacked in the cellar ; chairs and sofas drawn up to the hearth ; and with windows closely locked and fires ablaze Casa Guidi settled down once more to a season of hibernation. Advance payment on *Aurora Leigh* permitted one or two minor innovations : Pen had a new bed, which was placed, at his earnest insistence, in a corner of his parents' bedroom : the empty stone-flagged room which Browning used as a dressing-room, was furnished and carpeted, in order that it might serve him, henceforward as dressing-room and work-room combined. Fortified, thus, against the climate and opinions of the outside world, husband and wife awaited in joint expectancy the publication of *Aurora Leigh*.

The reception accorded to this " poetic art-novel " astonished everyone, not least the author of it, who had fully expected " to be put in the stocks . . . as a disorderly woman and free-thinking poet ". Within a fortnight of publication, the first edition was exhausted ; a second was called for, and then a third : in the lending libraries, the demand was so great, that a limit of two days was placed on the loan of a book which, Elizabeth was told, " ' the mamas of England ' in a body refuse to let their daughters read ". In America, a publisher " shed tears over the proofs " : " half drunk " with

its beauty, Landor spoke of " the wild imagination of Shakespeare " : while John Ruskin, who, a year ago, had seen little
to admire and much to criticise in *Men and Women*, described
Aurora Leigh as " the greatest *poem* in the English language,
unsurpassed by anything but Shakespeare—*not* surpassed by
Shakespeare's *Sonnets*, and therefore the greatest poem in the
language." Despite the " longing to be abused a little " of
which Browning playfully accused her, Elizabeth was naturally
delighted at this unqualified success of a major work : and as
for " that golden-hearted Robert ", she said, he is ' in ecstasies
about it—far more than if it all related to a book of his own ".
There can be no doubt whatsoever of the warmth and sincerity
of Browning's delight in his wife's triumph. Confirming his
own exalted opinion of her powers, was not this success something he had anticipated and looked for from the first ?
" Dearest friend," he had assured her a few months after their
first meeting, " *I* intend to write more, and very likely be
praised more, now I care less than ever for it, but still more do
I look to have you ever before me, in your place, and with
more poetry and more praise still, and my own heartfelt praise
on the top, like a flower on the water."

It was, nevertheless, what Elizabeth would have called
an epigram of destiny, that a room had been furnished and
set apart for Browning to write in, at a moment when it
seemed plain to him that he would write no more. Slighted
by the critics and ignored by the public, all that was left to
him, he felt, was the privilege of guarding and fostering the
success of his wife. Many years ago, in *Pauline*, he had avowed
himself capable, in " contented lowness ", of feeding another's
fame " from my heart's best blood " : in some such service,
now, he scrutinised proofs, supervised alterations to the text,
prodded and coaxed the dilatory Chapman into renewed
activity on behalf of *Aurora Leigh*. Thus, on December 2nd,
1856, Browning wrote a long letter to the publisher, urging
him to proceed as quickly as possible with the printing of
the second edition, in order, he said, " not to keep people
waiting a moment for further notice from us." (" *Us* ", he
added ; " —I am the church-organ-bellows' blower that
talked about *our* playing, but you know what I do in the
looking after commas and dots to i's.") It was an uprush of

bitterness from some hitherto unrevealed source : nor is it at all surprising that after the failure of *Men and Women*, an increasing resentment and irascibility should inform Browning's references to critics who refused so stubbornly to acknowledge his true poetic stature. " I saw the *Athenaeum*, *Globe*, and *Daily News*, that's all, hearing of eulogy from the *Lit. Gaz.* and blackguardism from the Press ", he wrote in this same letter : " All like those nightmen who are always emptying their cart at my door, and welcome when I remember that after all they don't touch our bread with their beastly hands, as they used to do. Don't you mind them, and leave me to rub their noses in their own filth some fine day."

Aurora Leigh was dedicated to John Kenyon. On December 3rd, a few weeks after its publication, this " dearest cousin and friend " died ; and Elizabeth's pleasure in the success of the book was darkened by the fact that he had not lived to see what would have given him so much pleasure. With tears falling on a " lock of the poor white hair . . . cut off for us . . . just after he had passed from the body ",[1] she reflected bitterly that he had been to her " much what my father might have been ", and that now the place was empty twice over. Letters from England, a few weeks later, brought news that under the terms of Kenyon's will, Browning was to receive £6,500 and his wife £4,500 : thereby " marking delicately " Elizabeth said, " a sense of trust for which I am especially grateful ". Although a year was to elapse before that sum became available to them, the economic pressure under which the Brownings had lived since their marriage was eased in anticipation : and some months later, Browning, it seems, was able to invest a sum of money " in the Tuscan funds ". " We shall have ", Elizabeth wrote to her sister, " five hundred and fifty a year from that source alone. Add a hundred and seventy-five from the English funds, and there is above seven hundred a year, besides the money from books which is an increasing income. . . . Altogether, we want nothing, observe—and, as we shall not change our way of life at all, and two servants, a man and maid, are sufficient for us, and as we don't need to *save* anything for Penini who will be well off, we shall be more able to give ourselves little indul-

[1] January 10 [1857]. Huxley typescript.

gences than we have yet been. . . ." [1] In Browning's case, the legacy produced one fundamental change. For the first time in his life, he had money of his own : for the first time since his marriage he was dependent neither on his wife's income, nor on his wife's earnings. In certain ways, this was a relief to both of them : easing between them a latent, if unacknowledged strain. " Robert," wrote Ba with satisfaction, " has taken to riding which he is passionately fond of and has never hitherto allowed himself to think of—and this is a luxury for me too, as you may suppose." [2]

The rest of the winter passed very quietly. " A few wandering pilgrims come to us in the evening, Isa Blagden generally twice a week—but we are in a state of dead calm for the most part," Elizabeth said. Since no poetry was to be written there, Browning turned his work-room into a studio, and sent to Chapman for a copy of *Instructions in the Art of Figure Drawing*, by Weigall. He took over the supervision of Pen's lessons, hearing him recite French verbs every morning before breakfast : one evening, father and son went together to see Stenterello, the jester ; an entertainment which Pen found superior even to the opera of the monkeys. Punctually, at the same hour every Sunday, Browning made his way to the Protestant church in Florence in order to hear Mr. Hanna preach—" the very dullest, slowest preacher I ever listened to " Elizabeth once called him. " Three words every five minutes—' entoned ' . . . in a high Scotch accent." [3] Disciplined in early life by the prolixity of the Rev. George Clayton, Browning endured two hours of Mr. Hanna without flagging : and when, late in this same year, the minister died, the poet was one of the chief mourners at his funeral. Fanny Haworth arrived in Florence : crouched over the fire at Casa Guidi, she confided her indeterminate love affairs to Elizabeth, and preached homeopathy to Browning, whose scepticism was so far undermined that he actually provided himself " with two bottles and an homeopathical treatise from Vanni's." " Decidedly," wrote Elizabeth, " the medicine agrees with him. . . . I am delighted for my part. Under the benignant influence of Camsamilla, even the vicinity of Hume

[1] June 2, 1857. Ibid.　　　　[2] November 6, 1854. Ibid.
[3] November 6, 1854. Ibid.

can be supported." [1] The poet, however, no longer spent every evening by the fireside ; nor was it expected, it seems, that he should continue to do so. Isa Blagden, a " bright delicate, electric woman ", whose black eyes and olive complexion suggested, to Henry James, a " hint of East-Indian blood ", had long been an intimate friend of both husband and wife. Four years younger than Browning, whom she loved and quarrelled with, there existed between them a brother-sisterly relationship, half irritable and wholly affectionate, which survived so successfully the vicissitudes of intimacy, that a year after the death of his wife, Browning was able to write to her, " . . . you are my—nearly one, certainly best, woman friend." She lived in a large airy villa on the slopes of Bellosguardo, where, amid the olive trees and bright flowering herbs, she wrote " the inevitable nice novel or two of the wandering English spinster " ; nursed ailing friends ; and attached to herself all the lame dogs, human and otherwise, of Tuscany. Amongst the expatriates and *litterateurs* of the day, the Villa Bricchieri was a centre of social life ; and it is interesting to speculate how many of these had come to Italy to escape the shadow of more eminent relatives : thus, in Isa's circle alone, we find at this time Alfred Tennyson's elder brother, Frederick ; Anthony Trollope's brother, Thomas Adolphus ; Bulwer Lytton's son, Robert ; and Caroline Norton's son, a young man " full of poetical sentiment, wearing sky-blue silk cravats, in delicate health, dreaming dreams, and wearing a gold cross under his waistcoat ", who, having married an illiterate peasant girl, refused to dine out, because he " liked to see Maria cook his soup and maccaroni ".[2] Elizabeth's eminence, in this circle, was plain enough : but there was little suspicion amongst these minor poets and artists that Browning's stature in any way exceeded their own. A " man of infinite learning, jest and bonhommie ", he was, however, very popular with all of them ; and no gathering was complete without the sight of Robert Browning, on the sofa, surrounded all the evening with a circle of smiling and attentive women. It became an understood thing that on these occasions Elizabeth could not always be expected to accompany her husband. " Robert ",

---

[1] March 18, 1857. To Miss Haworth. Omitted letter. Kenyon typescript.
[2] July 19 [1854]. Huxley typescript.

she wrote to Sarianna Browning, " is up at the villa three or four evenings of the week, and then I go to bed with a book, as usual." [1]

A heavy blow fell on Elizabeth at the end of April. A letter arrived from Wimpole Street to inform her of the death of her father, Edward Moulton-Barrett. For weeks she lay on the sofa, unwilling to move or speak ; and Browning had to endure as best he could the sight of that fixed and self-devouring grief. It was long before she could read or write a single line. " I take up books—but my heart goes walking up and down constantly through that house of Wimpole Street, till it ,is tired, tired." That her father would die, unforgiving, was a fear she had carried about with her from the first. " The summer before last," she wrote to her sister, " I made up my mind that there was *no hope* of any outward sign of forgiveness on this earth. I knew then that this which we have suffered was before us to suffer. Yet when it came, it seemed insuffer- able as if unforeseen." In the inevitable recoil against herself, one thing alone comforted her. " In that world ", she went on, " spirits learn and grow faster. It has been a great help to me that of late years I have apprehended more of the ways of life in that world." [2]

For the third and last time, the Brownings spent a summer at the Baths of Lucca. " On our arrival here at half-past ten at night, tell my dear Arabel, we were so reminded of her goodness to us by seeing the table spread ready for us—tea —a pigeon pie and a tart, bottles of lemonade kept in ice—all Mrs. Stisted's welcome to us ! . . . Just now Peni says— ' oh—I *do* like the Bagni di Lucca. It is so nice to smell the breeze, and to watch the lizards, and to hear every moment the little hoofs of donkeys.' " [3] Browning was perhaps less enchanted with a place whose people and scenery were by now so familiar to him ; and sensing this restlessness : " I am half sorry to have come," Elizabeth wrote, " because of Robert, who will certainly find it dull, and who leaves behind quantities

---

[1] [February, 1857]. Kenyon typescript.
[2] May 13, 1857. Huxley typescript.
[3] Saturday, August 4, 1857. Ibid.

of interest in various ways." The worst is, she went on, that he " has no models for his drawing, and no studio. Well—now poetry must have its turn, and I shall not be sorry for that. He has taken a passion for drawing, and through the facilities of Florence, devotes himself to it too much—perhaps, neglecting his own art." The neglect continued : no poetry of any kind was written at Lucca that summer. In the house with its closely curtained terrace, its garden overlooked by oleander and chestnut trees, a common lethargy gained upon the whole household : Elizabeth did nothing but dream for hours on end over novels brought out from Florence : Wilson, expecting her second child, sat fanning herself in an easy chair ; while an exacerbation of indolence inspired Ferdinando in his turn privately to farm out to a little peasant girl called Pistolina the most onerous of his own domestic duties.

The arrival of visitors from Florence provided both a diversion and a momentary stimulus. Isa Blagden brought with her Annette Bracken, a young girl then living with her at the Villa Bricchieri, and Robert Lytton, an early friend of the Brownings. The future Viceroy, a " delicate and excitable " young man in his early twenties, was beautiful, blue-eyed and almost beardless.[1] His grace had already inspired in Isa and Ba alike, an attachment, half sentimental and half maternal : and finding him now, languid and a little feverish after the journey out from Florence, they hastened to install him solicitously in his room at the hotel. To the consternation of all, he became exceedingly unwell ; and gastric fever setting in, for six weeks Isa and Browning had to take it in turn to nurse an invalid " inclined to talk of divine things, of the state of his soul and God's love, and to hold this life but slackly ". It has been, wrote Elizabeth, " a summer full of blots, vexations, anxieties ". Worse, however, was to follow : barely had Isa carried the acquiescent Lytton back to recuperate at the Villa Bricchieri, before Pen sickened with the

---

[1] He had a deep admiration for Browning, which expressed itself in a poem wherein, acclaiming him as " Our leader and king of us all ", he implored the poet to

Take the love which we languish to give ;
Give the love without which we must fall.

Ten years later, Browning heard that Lytton had " told somebody ' he had the love of a woman for me ' ".

same fever.   Wilson, too, became ill : and then her successor,
Annunziata, " performed her little piece of feverishness, till
we had enough of it " Browning wrote : and husband and
wife decided to pack up and return as early as possible to the
safe haven of Casa Guidi.

Before leaving the Bagni di Lucca, Browning paid a farewell visit to " The Cottage ", a small house on the banks
of the Lima, owned by Mrs. Stisted, popularly known as
" The Queen of the Baths ".   She was a stout and eccentric
old lady, blue-eyed, with a large flushed face and heavy grey
curls, whose custom, whenever she visited her friends, was to
bring her own armchair along with her.   Enthroned, now, on
crimson upholstery, she showed the poet her collection of
literary curiosities : amongst them, the manuscript of a poem
given to her by Captain Daniel Roberts, Trelawny's friend,
and the man who built the *Don Juan* for Shelley.   The name
of the poem, Browning saw with emotion, was *The Indian
Serenade*.   Thirty years ago, reading this " divine little poem "
under the title *Lines to an Indian Air*, the youthful Browning had
covered the margins of Shelley's *Miscellaneous Poems* with the
exclamation marks of a fervent admiration : and it seemed,
now, at once strange and appropriate that it should fall to his
lot to rescue " three or four variations " in the reading of that
well-loved poem.   For, with Mrs. Stisted's approval, he set
himself religiously to decipher the import of Shelley's lines :
and although the large sloping handwriting had become so
faint as to be, in places, almost illegible, with the aid of a
powerful magnifying glass Robert Browning was able to
discern and transcribe what he felt to be a superior version
of the poem : thereby rectifying, for the benefit of future
scholars, the version printed by Mary Shelley both in the
Posthumous Poems and her later edition of the *Poetical Works*.

The coldest winter for more than ten years descended on
Florence a few months later.   Within the hothouse seclusion
of Casa Guidi, Elizabeth heard reports that the Arno was
frozen over : that every second person was laid low with the
grippe.   She did not succumb to the prevailing malady ; but,
she said, " the weight of the whole year . . . seems to have

stamped out of me the vital fluid " : and a prey to deep depression, she did nothing but brood, or drowse over the fire, drugged with French and German novels. It was many months since either husband or wife had written any poetry : a state of affairs in which, through the very intimacy of their relationship, each was sapped anew by the sterility of the other. To escape from this *impasse*, Browning threw himself with eagerness into various forms of artistic activity. He haunted the studio of Hiram Powers, watching the sculptor, in cap and slippers, at work amongst his Psyches and Proserpines : he attended Mr. Stuart's lectures on the influence of Italian on English poetry : twice a week, he went to the Via de' Ginori to see Mignaty, a local artist, " draw from the nude ". " Furthermore," wrote Elizabeth, " he has made a great purchase of a skeleton, and has discoursed upon it till he made me dizzy and sick . . enlarging on the beautiful gutta percha finishing of the joints, and the facility with which the head comes off and on—and how, two months ago, this was a Florentine of thirty-six, straying, at evenings perhaps, by Casa Guidi. Well—I have not seen it yet. I leave it to you. I keep on the ' outside '—saying, that if I tolerate Robert's bones in the house, he should my spirits. . . ." [1]

Gradually, the sharp cold waned, and warmth and sunlight returned to Florence. Elizabeth improved, if very slightly, in health and spirits. " I am well in my chest ; and not ill otherwise, . . . only weak more than ought to be, and suffering from an ' ebranlement de nerfs ', which gives every little thing power to shake me." [2] A few weeks later, calling at Casa Guidi with her two daughters, Mrs. Hawthorne was " afraid to stay long, or to have Mrs. Browning talk, because she looked so pale, and I perceived that the motion of R's fan distressed her. I do not understand," went on Mrs. Hawthorne compassionately, " how she can live long, or be at all restored while she does live." Nathaniel Hawthorne and his family had arrived in Florence at the beginning of June. During the course of that month, husband and wife paid several visits to Casa Guidi, and their combined, or rather their contrasted

---

[1] [February or March 1858]. To Miss Haworth. Omitted letter. Kenyon typescript.
[2] Saturday [April 28, 1858]. Huxley typescript.

impressions, afford us an interesting double exposure of this
ménage de poètes. The first stars were already shining out of a
dark sky on the evening of their visit, but Penini had not yet
been sent to bed : " gentle, tricksy and intellectual ", he led
the visitors through the dim drawing-room and out on to a
terrace fragrant with lemon and pomegranate trees, there to
witness a scene which, described subsequently by the Haw-
thornes in their journals, was also to be recalled, with minute
fidelity, by Robert Browning himself.

> I turned, to free myself and find the world,
> And stepped out on the narrow terrace, built
> Over the street and opposite the church,
> And paced its lozenge-brickwork sprinkled cool ;
> Because Felice-church-side stretched, a-glow
> Through each square window fringed for festival,
> Whence came the clear voice of the cloistered ones
> Chanting a chant made for midsummer nights—
> I know not what particular praise of God,
> It always came and went with June.

" The music, the stars, the flowers, Mr. Browning and his
child, all combined," said Mrs. Hawthorne, " to entrance my
wits " : happily the arrival, soon after, of another American
couple, " a certain Mr. and Mrs. E.", restored her, sharply
enough, to a sense of reality. Tea was served : " graceful as
Ganymede ", Pen offered cake and strawberries : while Mrs.
Eckley, in the character of intimate friend of the family,
insisted on telling Mrs. Hawthorne, at some length, " what an
angel " that dear Mrs. Browning was. All the while, conscious, no doubt, of the blank pages of the journals awaiting
them at the Casa del Bello, husband and wife observed,
attentively, their host and hostess : and comparing their
separate impressions, one is surprised to find that in each case
the unprofessional eye of Mrs. Hawthorne detected a reality
concealed from her novel-writing husband. Confronted with
Elizabeth, " a pale, small person, scarcely embodied at all ",
Hawthorne wrote sentimentally of an " elfin " woman ; a
" good and kind fairy . . . sweetly disposed towards the
human race, although only remotely akin to it ". Mrs. Hawthorne, on the other hand, was impressed by the " deep pain

furrowed into her face—such pain that the great happiness of her life cannot smooth it away. In moments of rest from speaking her countenance reminds one of those mountain-sides, ploughed deep with spent water-torrents, there are traces in it of so much grief, so much suffering." Mrs. Hawthorne, moreover, divined in Elizabeth Barrett Browning something apparent at that time to few : the reluctance to live. " Only ' a great love ' ", she wrote, " has kept her on earth a season longer." As to Robert Browning, he seemed to the taciturn Nathaniel Hawthorne, " to be in all parts of the room and in every group at the same moment ; a most vivid and quick-thoughted person, logical and common-sensible, as, I presume, poets generally are in their daily talk ". It was left again to Hawthorne's wife to detect the presence of " an anxious line " on the poet's brow. Plucking a pomegranate-bud, he gave it to her to press in her memorial-book, and as he stood beside her, talking rapidly, she sensed that he was " full of vivid life, like a rushing river ". " Nothing ", Mrs. Hawthorne felt, " could resist the powerful impetus of his mind and heart " ; and yet, she went on, " this effervescing, resplendent life—fresh every moment, like a waterfall or a river—seems to have a shadow over it, like a light cloud, as if he were perplexed in the disposal of his forces. . . ."

A week after that evening at Casa Guidi, the Brownings left Florence for Paris. Dr. Harding had prescribed sea-water for the invalid, and their aim was, accordingly, to spend the summer on the French coast. As usual, Elizabeth enjoyed the journey—" no possibility of unpleasant visitors ! No fear of horrible letters ! quite lifted above the plane of bad news, or of the expectation of bad news "—and she was sorry when, arriving at their destination, she was exposed once more to the assault of circumstances. For Havre, a " roaring commercial city ", was " *hideous* " as Browning said ; and their house, itself " in a hideous angle ", offered no view of the sea. Browning, who would have preferred the simpler and more picturesque conditions which he had seen at Étretat, made little effort to conceal his ill humour ; and as for Elizabeth, creeping painfully down to the nearest bench on a bleak sea shore, she felt, she said, like a " dislodged ghost ". " I long ", she sighed, " for my dear lower life in Florence, and feel coldly

in the upper world here ; . . . the atmosphere is not favourable—and I long for my dim Hades, to faint away into the
dim and be quiet and silent, hiding my face in those dewy
water-lilies of the Lethe river." [1]

Even the presence in Havre of her sister Arabel, of her
brothers George and Henry who had travelled from England
to meet her there, was not an unmixed joy : partly, perhaps,
because Mr. Browning and Sarianna occupied rooms in the
same house ; thereby hampering, unwittingly, the intimacy of
the two sisters. (In Paris, she consoled herself, " we shall be
more to ourselves ; as Robert's family will separate from us
and go to their own domicile, and the gossip-time will be
enlarged by so much margin ".) [2] Browning, on his side,
found little to entertain him in the conversation of his brothers-
in-law : and imprisoned in an atmosphere of small talk and
family reminiscence, rejoiced when Joseph Milsand arrived
from Dijon to spend ten " very precious days " at Havre.
The departure of his friend threw the poet back into a vacuum
of inactivity and frustration. " What is to say about such a
dull life as this daily one of ours ! " he wrote to Isa Blagden.
" I go mechanically out and in and get a day through—
whereof not ten minutes have been my own—so much for
your ' quantities of writing ' (in expectation)—I began pretty
zealously—but it's no use now : nor will the world very
greatly care."

9

Elizabeth Barrett Browning's health was now so frail that
it was no longer possible for her to endure the asperity of a
Florentine winter. Once more, therefore, the Brownings
turned south : and as they were to do for the next three
years, they spent the winter and the early spring in Rome.
Although it was to the third floor of " that fatal ' Bocca di
Leone ' " that they returned, the sombre associations of five
years ago had long been dispersed : newly painted and

---

[1] September 1, 1858. To Miss Haworth. Omitted letter, Kenyon typescript.
[2] August 30 [1858]. Huxley typescript.

carpeted, its rooms "swimming all day in sunshine", the apartment presented an aspect so gay and inviting that simultaneously, both husband and wife felt that they would have, here, "a happier time of it than before".

The presentiment was to be realised. Six months of seclusion, of a tranquil and restorative happiness lay before Elizabeth : while Browning, in a brief and well-earned reprieve from care, was thrown, by reaction, "into a striking course of prosperity, as to looks, spirits and appetite". In an access of renewed energy, he rose at six every morning to stride through Rome at the side of his friend Mr. Eckley : he ate, as he said, "vulpinely"—which means, his wife commented, "that a lark or two is no longer enough for dinner. At breakfast the loaf perishes by Gargantuan slices." This energy, which could no longer be confined to the domestic tête-à-tête or to the restrictive conditions of a small overheated flat, overflowed, spontaneously, into the larger channel of Rome's social life ; where, "caught from one hand to another like a ball", the poet often went out "every night for a fortnight together, and sometimes two or three times deep in a one night's engagements". Each time, the front door safely shut behind him and a sudden silence fallen on the flat, Elizabeth would retire to her bedroom, where Pen, propped on one elbow, lay reading *The Count of Monte Cristo* by the light of a candle. Settling herself on her pillows with her favourite copy of Swedenborg, Elizabeth was glad to think that Robert, on his side, was so well amused : and if she regretted anything it was simply that he found no time, in the midst of so much activity, to do any writing. Plenty of distraction, she sighed, but "no Men and Women. Men and women from without instead !" Browning, however, looked fit and well, and had begun to put on weight. "Dissipations decidedly agree with Robert, there's no denying that, though he's horribly hypocritical, and ' prefers an evening with me at home ' which has grown to be a kind of dissipation also."

Once more, the ambiguous shadow of Louis Napoleon falling across Europe, darkened, indirectly, the hearth at the Via Bocca di Leone. Two obsessions, in the spring of 1859, coalesced in the mind and heart of Elizabeth : her faith in the probity of the Emperor, and her passion for Italian emancipation. It is not too much to say, with Henry James, that these two obsessions combined to work in her " as a malady and a doom ". And indeed, reading henceforward page upon page in exalted defence of " my Emperor ", coupled with " impotent rage " against his " selfish, inhuman, wicked enemies ", one cannot but recognise " a possession, by the subject, riding her to death ", that prompts us, in wonder and exasperation alike, " to ask wherein it so greatly concerned her ". Elizabeth herself was unable to recognise the emotional basis of her own preoccupation. " I dreamed lately that I followed a mystic woman down a long suite of palatial rooms. She was in white, with a white mask, on her head the likeness of a crown. I knew she was Italy, but I couldn't see through the mask." Nor, at this distance, may we presume to do so : but in view of her attitude to Louis Napoleon, her close identification with the cause of Italy, it is not surprising to find that the " personal calamity ", as she called it, of Villa-franca, coming like a " blow on the *heart* ", caused her to collapse with the worst illness she had ever known in Italy, an attack combined, for the first time, with symptoms akin to those of *angina pectoris*. With that unstinted tenderness which was so marked a trait of his character, Robert Browning nursed his wife day and night for three weeks ; during which time, " ground to death with cough ", raving of " inscrutable articles of peace and eternal provisional governments ", the invalid scattered, involuntarily, all possibility of repose for herself and for her devoted companion. When she was sufficiently re-stored to endure the journey, Browning took her to Siena for the summer, where, " a dark shadow ", he lifted her from the carriage and bore her into the house. Here, in the silence of a large, airy, sparsely furnished villa, she slowly and painfully recovered a measure of strength. " It was the *peace*, I think," she wrote to Fanny Haworth, "—I had lived too long in a state of exultation, and was struck with despair—could do nothing but weep and talk in impotent rages. . . . Any way I have nearly made my farewell to this world, and feel shaken in the standing ground I have recovered." [1] Aware of this, Browning would allow her neither to teach Pen his lessons, nor to expend herself in political discussion of any kind. (" He

[1] July, 1859. Omitted letter. Kenyon typescript.

had rather a fright, you see, and I have grown precious, accordingly, far above my just value.") [1] Wisely, he isolated her from her friends, and applied, to good effect, the emollient element of silence. Meanwhile, he himself was, as he said, " uninterruptedly busy " : for, besides instructing the ten-year-old Pen in grammar and arithmetic, he had also undertaken the tutelage of the octogenarian Walter Savage Landor. " Robert always said ", wrote Elizabeth, " that he owed more as a writer to Landor than to any contemporary "—an influence that, close on twenty years ago, she herself had detected in Browning's poetry. (" Did it strike you ", she wrote of *Pippa Passes*, " that there was an occasional *manner*, in the portions most strictly dramatic, like Landor's, in Landor's dramas, when Landor writes best ? . . .") [2] Poor Landor, she now told her sister, " having been treated in a monstrous way by his family (to whose arms he returned after thirty years absence) eloped from them to us at Casa Guidi one morning, swearing that he never would return. This was before I was ill. Robert did what he could, went up with Mr. Kirkup to the Fiesole villa, and used all his eloquence towards a peace. In vain. Mrs. Landor indeed came down to our door and was announced. ' Let her come in,' cried her attached husband, ' and I throw myself out of the window.' ' The best thing he could do,' rejoined the tender wife when she heard of it. His daughter told Robert that ' to save her father's life, she couldn't give him a glass of water '. The sons are savage uneducated men—to whom he has given up his villa and English property, on whom therefore he is dependant, and who treat him thus at eighty-five. Poor old man . . he wept as he spoke of it. Robert wrote to Mr. Forster. He applied to Landor's brothers and niece—who have generously and kindly made an allowance to him of two hundred a year, which Robert is to dispense—for Mr. Landor is like Peni, as to matters of money, and was prepared, in fact, to give one hundred pounds to Garibaldi, as soon as he received two. The plan is, to settle him under Wilson's care, who is to take an apartment and furnish it, and live there with her children, she having the full charge of Mr. Landor ; even undertaking the cooking and

---

[1] September 13 [1859]. Huxley typescript.
[2] To Miss Mitford. July 15, 1841. Wellesley College Library.

general attendance. She has a maid of her own ; so that she won't be overworked and will be very well paid. It will be an excellent thing for her. He is irritable and full of fancies —but Robert has much influence with him and he likes Wilson's gentle voice, and I dare say it will answer well." [1]

" The older one grows the faster time passes. Do you observe that ? You catch the wind of the wheels in your face, it seems, as you get nearer the end." For once more winter had come, and the Brownings were back in Rome. It was a very different Rome, however, to which they now returned : a city mute with political tension ; empty, for the most part, of English and American visitors. Denied the routs and dinner-parties of the previous year, Browning was thrown back, forcibly, on his own resources, with the result, that for the first time in many months he gave himself, once more, to the composition of poetry. " Robert deserves no reproaches," said Elizabeth, " for he has been writing a good deal this winter —working at a long poem which I have not seen a line of, and producing short lyrics which I *have* seen, and may declare worthy of him." Of the shorter lyrics, *Youth and Art*, at least, is to be attributed to a brief friendship with Val Prinsep, who, with an unnamed French artist, introduced the poet that winter to the more unconventional aspects of Rome's artistic colony. As to the " long poem ", this refers not to *Prince Hohenstiel-Schwangau*, of which only a " few lines of the rough draft " were written in the Via del Tritone, but to *Mr. Sludge*, ' *The Medium* '. Browning's hatred of Home, ignited at Ealing in 1855, had smouldered irregularly ever since the fateful séance, in which, as Browning afterwards liked to assert, he had caught the medium in the act of cheating. (There is no evidence, by the way, that the poet did anything of the kind.) Despite the fact that he had exerted his whole " soul's strength " in an effort to awaken her to the duplicity of Home, Elizabeth continued to believe in the good faith of the medium : and now, five years later, Browning was to stand by and see his wife duped all over again by a woman whose integrity he had suspected from the first. By this time, however, the com-

[1] September 13 [1859]. Huxley typescript.

plicated diffidence which had prevented him, in the early years
of marriage, from enforcing his own point of view, had given
place to a certain half-resentful obstinacy : he lost no opportunity, now, in making plain to his wife his own very decided
opinion of Sophia Eckley. To no purpose. Elizabeth persisted in her belief that Mrs. Eckley was " a poetical, pure,
lovely creature ", who, she said, " covers the earth with her own
white garments, and walks clean-footed over dirty places ".[1]
(As for " *seeing* the truth ", Browning wrote in despair, " it
seems to me such angelic natures don't.") For, by exploit-
ing alike the purity of her intentions and the strength of
her mediumistic powers, Mrs. Eckley succeeded in keeping
Elizabeth under a double thrall which Browning, for all his
efforts, was unable to break up. Brusquely, however, in that
winter of 1859–60, a rupture was effected. Elizabeth, we are
told, found " that she had been duped by a friend in whom
she had blind faith ". The shock of that discovery was two-
fold : not only was friendship betrayed, but her belief in the
authenticity of " spiritual manifestations " was rudely shaken.
" Mediums cheat certainly," she wrote ruefully. " So do
people who are not mediums. . . . I begin by seeing the
beautiful in people, and then comes the disillusion."
Alas, my bubbles, my bubbles ! " For, " taken somehow by
flattery ", she had failed to see that Sophia's " vanity was
monstrous enough to present a large foundation for an extraordinary falseness of character. She is truly false—her life is
one ' *maniere de poses* ' "[2] It was as an intimate witness to this
drama of vanity, duplicity and disillusionment, as of its outcome in Rome this same winter, that Robert Browning sat
down to work with sudden impetus at the " long poem " which
Elizabeth was not to see a line of, and which began :

> Now don't sir ! Don't expose me ! Just this once !
> This was the first and only time, I'll swear,—
> Look at me,—see, I kneel,—the only time,
> I swear, I ever cheated. . . .

---

[1] September 1, 1858. To Miss Haworth. Omitted letter. Kenyon typescript.
[2] August 25, 1860. Ibid.

Elizabeth Barrett Browning

Robert Browning senior, Paris, 1861

Sarianna Browning

Pen Browning

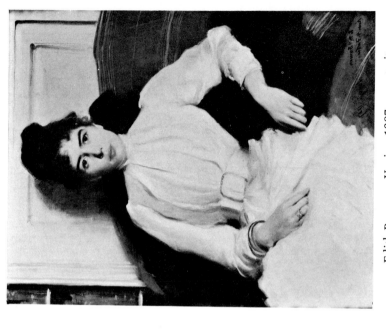

Edith Bronson, Venice, 1887, a portrait
by Charles S. Forbes

Robert Browning, 1876, a
caricature by Pellegrini

At the end of the year, after a summer spent once more at Siena, the Brownings returned for the last time to Rome. They arrived in their new apartment, the bitterly named Via Felice, in time to receive there the news, conveyed in letters from England, of the death of Elizabeth's married sister, Henrietta. Browning always believed that this blow hastened the death of his wife : there is no doubt that it weakened, conclusively, perhaps, her hold upon life. " How the spiritual world gets thronged to us with familiar faces," she wrote : " till at last, perhaps, the world here will seem the vague and strange world, even while we remain." Nevertheless, she struggled hard, that winter, to live on ; and although, as she said, life goes heavily with me, " it goes ; it has rolled into the ruts again and goes. . . ."

The contrast in appearance between husband and wife in the winter of 1860-1 was a striking one. In her fifty-sixth year, Elizabeth's hair was darker, still, than Robert's ; but the small face between its pall of incongruously girlish ringlets was wizened and deeply scored with pain. So drawn and desiccated was she, that the dark face had about it a look almost of mummification : the slight figure and ingenuously bent head, on the other hand, gave her the air of a very aged child. Comparing herself at this time with Robert, she could not but see that, despite the whitening of beard and side-whiskers, in his fiftieth year, her husband looked, now, " remarkably well and young ". A photograph taken in Rome in 1861 reveals a plump, bearded man, posed, with an air of tolerant solemnity, against a backcloth representing the ruins of the Colosseum. (Sarianna, on receiving it, complained that the cut of her brother's hair made him look like an épicier : Elizabeth was offended, forgetting that she herself had once condemned an engraving of the poet on much the same grounds.) " He is not thin or worn, as I am—no indeed—" she said, " and the women adore him everywhere far too much for decency. In my own opinion he is infinitely handsomer and more attractive than when I saw him first, sixteen years ago. . . ." She was, perhaps, peculiarly sensitive to the undiminished vitality of her husband at a moment when her friend Mr. Page, the artist, had married successfully for the third time ; when, in reply to Browning's letter of condolence on the death of his wife,

Joseph Arnould, an original member of " the Set " at Camberwell, wrote to say that he had taken another wife—" young and
pretty ". (" But, Isa," Elizabeth wrote to Miss Blagden at
this time, " I am afraid you don't sufficiently realise to yourself
the physical tendencies of the sexes. Oh—you may laugh.
But I do verily believe that you who are not spiritualist by
profession are too spiritual in your way of apprehending the
economy of sexual love. . . . Certainly the more I know of
the world the grosser it looks to me, and the less I wonder
that pure and high souls should have fallen into the mistake of
asceticism.") [1]

Browning, meanwhile, was much in demand this season,
when the dinner parties and balls were, if anything, more
numerous and splendid than before. " In the evening,"
Elizabeth said, " he generally goes out as a bachelor " : free
from " responsibility of crinoline ", he did not return, very
often, until four o'clock in the morning. In bed by eight,
Elizabeth found her own happiness in the tranquil bedroom
where Pen, who at twelve years of age, slept still in " mama's
room ", murmured contentedly " Goodnight, darling ", as she
put the candle out. The next day, Browning entertained them
both with accounts of the elaborate dinners he had eaten, of
the great ball at Mrs. Hooker's where " princes and cardinals
were present, and where the old Roman custom of attending
the princes of the church up and down the grand staircase
with flaming torches was observed ". Elizabeth, for her part,
was only " too happy to have him a little amused " ; painfully
conscious, as she now was, of her own inability to direct or to
deal with that " enormous superfluity of vital energy ", which,
unemployed, struck " its fangs into him ". For nearly a year,
now, since the previous winter, indeed, Robert Browning had
written no poetry. Despite the fact that a sitting-room with
three bright windows had been consecrated to his use, that his
wife lost no opportunity of reminding him that Tennyson
worked regularly at the same hour each day, he continued to
evade the duty, as he had previously felt it to be, of composition. Although he pleaded lack of inspiration as an excuse
for this prolonged abstinence, Elizabeth could not but see how
much the continued neglect of his contemporaries had begun

[1] Monday [November–December, 1860]. Kenyon typescript.

to affect him : a neglect emphasised, distressingly, she felt, by
the sustained success of her own poetry—*Aurora Leigh* being
then in its fifth edition. (Comparing himself with his wife, at
this time, Browning remarked : " She has genius ; I am only
a painstaking fellow. . . . The true creative power is hers,
not mine.") This sense of failure, of sterility, he deadened
effectively enough, perhaps, by " polking all night ", and
spending the better part of the day modelling in his friend
Story's studio. It was not wise, Elizabeth knew, " to dis-
hearten him about his modelling ". " For," she said, " an
active occupation is salvation to him with his irritable nerves,
saves him from ruminating bitter cud, and from the process
which I call beating his dear head against the wall till it is
bruised, simply because he sees a fly there, magnified by
his own two eyes almost indefinitely into some Saurian
monster. . . . And I know that whatever takes him out of
a certain circle (where habits of introvision and analysis of
fly-legs are morbidly exercised), is life and joy to him."

Three years had now elapsed since the holiday at Havre ;
and Browning was increasingly anxious to see his father and
sister once more. It was decided, therefore, that this summer
the two families were to meet, if not at the seaside, at least in
the vicinity of Paris : Fontainebleau, Elizabeth suggested, who,
all the while, contemplated with " positive terror " not only
the prospect of the journey, but the thought " of having to
speak and look at people ". The whole winter, shunning
" the workday world, daylight, open air and all ", she had
lain listless on the sofa, reluctant to walk " two paces out of
the room " : and now that there was a duty upon her to
emerge once more—" You would pity me," she confessed, " if
you could see how I dread it." At the same time, she did her
best to conceal this dread from Robert, protesting again and
again in face of his troubled enquiries, that she was perfectly
fit and willing to undertake the journey. " I feel myself, every
now and then . . . like a weight round his neck," she had
written after a bout of illness in 1852. Robert Browning did
everything in his power to conceal, not only from his wife but
from himself, the increasing gravity of that weight. Unavail-
ingly, however—since " the peculiarity of our relation is, that
even when he's displeased with me, he thinks aloud with me and

can't stop himself ". Elizabeth, therefore—" I who am in the inside of him and hear him breathe "—heard from time to time the unuttered wishes, the suppressed impulses which after her death were to find their way into words. (Ten years later : " You are independent," Browning wrote to Isa Blagden. " It is just what I never was in my life, with every desire to be so. In all my journeyings in Italy, I could never venture to leave the straight line of obligation . . . thus I never saw (after fourteen years' intention to see) . . . points of great interest to me,—Ba could not go, I could not leave her.") Once more, now, in Rome this spring, after consultation with his wife's doctor, Browning decided that the journey to France presented grave risks, and must be abandoned. On learning of the decision, Elizabeth became greatly agitated and distressed. There is no doubt that she would have preferred, under the circumstances, to court every risk than to be, once again, a source of disappointment or frustration : and her persistence in this attitude was so vehement, that, she said, it " touched the line of vexing " her husband. For Elizabeth no longer attempted to withhold from herself what was now all too evident : the fact that, for many years, not only had she obstructed Robert's freedom, but she had taxed, with heavier and heavier burdens, the substance of his love for her. " As for me," she wrote bitterly to Sarianna, " I know my place ; I am only good for a drag chain."

Florence was almost deserted when the Brownings returned there in the first week of June. Few visitors mounted the stairs to knock on the door at Casa Guidi ; and the silence of the big dark rooms was broken only by the sound of Pen practising Chopin at the piano. Elizabeth was too weak to dress : prostrated by the heat, by the news of the death of Cavour, which had greeted their return to Florence, she sat day after day in her own corner of the drawing-room, listlessly glancing through the newspapers or sipping, without zest, the asses' milk which Dr. Wilson had prescribed for her. There was nothing in her condition to suggest that the end was near : indeed, as Story said, " we had become so accustomed to thinking of her as different from all others in the matters of health that we began to think that she might even outlast us ". When, therefore, after a slight chill, bronchial complications set in, Elizabeth herself said : " This is only one of my old attacks. I know all about it and shall get better." Even Browning, nursing her, as was his custom, day and night, did not suspect that she was dying, all the while, beneath his eyes. For throughout this final illness of hers, Elizabeth was curiously light-hearted, gay almost. She smiled at her husband as he bathed her feet—" Well, you do make an exaggerated case of it ! " she said. Later in the night, she put her arms about him, kissed him passionately and murmured over and over again, " God bless you." Robert did not believe that his wife was, as he said, " aware of our parting's approach " ; but Annunziata, the maid, saw clearly enough that her mistress was happy in the certainty of her coming release. For Elizabeth knew, now, that nothing was lost : all that she valued was safe. Had she gone on living, dragging through the " sad dark days " to come, love itself might have died : now that she was to die, love would live : and knowing what it was that she regained, Elizabeth Barrett Browning went to her rest—" smilingly, happily, and with a face like a girl's ".

" The general impression of the past," wrote Robert Browning a few years later, " is as if it had been pain. I would not live it over again, not one day of it. Yet all that seems my real *life*,—and before and after, nothing at all : I look back on all my life, when I look *there* : and life is painful. I always think of this when I read the Odyssey—Homer makes the surviving Greeks, whenever they refer to Troy, just say of it ' At Troy, where the Greeks suffered so.' Yet all their life was in that ten years at Troy."

4

Third House from the Bridge

"I want my new life", wrote Robert Browning, "to resemble the last fifteen years as little as possible." The new life may be said to have begun when, after a painful hiatus and on the anniversary, almost, of the death at Casa Guidi, Browning moved with his son into

> that new stuccoed third house from the bridge,
> Fresh-painted, rather smart than otherwise !

The stuccoed house, whose position Browning had so accurately forecast in his poem *How It Strikes A Contemporary*, was number 19, Warwick Crescent : the bridge, the early weigh bridge to which Byron " once dragged a reluctant John Murray, to show him the spot where a publisher had drowned himself ". The spot thus dubiously celebrated has, even today, a singular picturesqueness : for here two canals meet, and the confluence of waters forms an artificial lake, upon the south bank of which Warwick Crescent stands, white-painted above its small front-gardens. In Browning's day, a curved balustrade, a row of plane trees overlooked the trodden tow-path ; while in the centre of the lake, as an early print reveals, a small humped island was closely planted with trees. Warwick Crescent has survived, thus far, the vengeance weapons of our contemporary civilisation ; it has not, however, survived the blight of civic indifference ; and, eroded by multiple tenancy, the tall narrow house faces the road with an air of resigned neglect ; a neglect which is not dispelled by " one of those graceful and unobtrusive roundels " of encaustic ware which erroneously informs the passer-by that Robert Browning, poet, lived here from 1861–87.[1]

In fact, it was not until June, 1862, that the poet left his lodgings in Chichester Road and moved into the house that was to be his home for the next quarter of a century. As soon as he signed the lease, he sent for his furniture and books from Florence : but when, at the beginning of July, they arrived in England, and a few days later, de-crated, were carried over the narrow threshold of his new home : " I hardly know," he said, " —or care to think—whether I like the things

---

[1] The borough of Marylebone, on the other hand, in July, 1937, picturesquely honoured Browning's Muse by giving his name to Browning Mews.

best here, or there, or at the bottom of the sea." Gradually, nevertheless, these relics of a now obsolete pattern were adjusted to the component angles and necessities of the new life : to the drawing-room on the first floor went the carved chairs and the sofas covered in faded green velvet ; in his small study overlooking the garden, the poet found a place for Elizabeth's work table, her favourite chair ; while on the walls of his bedroom he hung all the portraits of her, from the crop-haired vivacious child of Hope End days, to the sad pain-furrowed woman of the last months in Rome. With the assistance of Arabel, a housekeeper was engaged : down in the basement, the larder was re-stocked, the oven was lighted : above, meals were served ; beds were slept in ; and slowly the wheels of life began to revolve once more with a coherent motion lacking in the existence of Robert Browning since the early hours of June 29, 1861.

There was no coherency of any sort in the life of Pen. Few children can have been subjected to a change of circumstance as drastic as that imposed upon Robert Wiedeman Barrett Browning after the death of his mother. The metamorphosis began with the ceremonious shearing of the long ringlets of which Elizabeth had been so inordinately proud. Four days after the death of his wife : " Pen," wrote Browning, " the golden curls and fantastic dress, is gone just as Ba is gone : he has short hair, worn boy-wise, long trousers, is a common boy all at once. . . ." A common boy, indeed, is what he seems to have become overnight. Uprooted from his native climate—the presence of an indulgent mother, the soil and language of Italy, Pen suffers as a personality an almost total eclipse : re-emerging, at Warwick Crescent, as the colourless, undemonstrative youth who, in the years to come, was to tax to the utmost the patience and the understanding of a stubbornly conscientious father. (It was a situation, incidentally, which Elizabeth had anticipated with great accuracy in her description of the life and circumstances of the bereaved child Aurora Leigh, on her arrival in England after the death of an indulgent parent in Italy). " You know," wrote Browning of his wife, " I have her dearest wish to attend to at once—her child to care for, educate, establish properly . . . all just as she would require were she here."

The sincerity of the intention is evident : what is less acceptable, in effect, is the manner of carrying out Elizabeth's
expressed desires.   For, like his mother, Pen had always identi-
fied himself with Italy ; like her, he felt himself, indeed he
proclaimed himself to be, not English but Italian.   And what
Browning now set out to do was systematically to eradicate
this attitude ; an attitude which he had to tolerate, of necessity, in his wife, but which he was not prepared to envisage
anew in his son.   " I distrust all hybrid and ambiguous
natures and nationalities and want to make something decided
of him," he wrote, a little tactlessly perhaps, to his expatriate
friend, the sculptor Story.   There was no time to lose, for
with every day that passed he ran the risk of missing " the
critical time when the English stamp (in all that it is good
for) is taken or missed ".   Progressively, therefore, the " curls
and the cuddlings " were clipped, the " chatter of Tuscan "
silenced ; a tutor was engaged " sound to the core in gram-
matical niceties " and the process of re-education began in
earnest.

It is difficult to believe that Browning was not conscious
of the heavy strain placed upon an immature and bewildered
child.   And yet this would appear to be the case.   For
twelve years, he had stood by, disregarded, while with an
increasing wilfulness, Elizabeth had indulged and adorned her
only son.   It is natural enough that Browning should wish,
however tardily, to rectify her mistakes of judgment, and one is
surprised only that this " subtle-souled psychologist " should
carry out the process so inflexibly, and with so little real
sympathy for the subject of the experiment.   During the years
to come, Browning was to devote himself with an indefatigable
zeal to the welfare of his son : he was ready to go to any
lengths, even, as he said, to black people's boots for them,
" in the prospect of possible advancement to Pen ".   At the
same time, there is not the slightest indication that he detected
the emotional *impasse* into which the boy had been driven by
his change of environment ; or that he sympathised, adequately, with the predicament that he was to inherit : the
predicament, that is to say, of the over-publicised child of
celebrated parents who, self-consciously, beneath a borrowed
limelight, " imitates and emulates " that which he knows

all the while to be beyond his own wholly commonplace powers.[1]

The sustained neglect of Browning's poetry which had characterised and coloured the whole span of his married life, proved, as we have seen, a source of serious chagrin to husband and wife alike. Curiously enough, this neglect showed signs of dispersing almost as soon as the poet settled in England. Within a year of his return—" I who could never muster English readers enough to pay for salt and bread ! "—Browning was offered the editorship of the *Cornhill* Magazine : Chapman proposed to publish a new three-volume edition of his works ; while John Forster and Barry Cornwall already had in the press a joint volume of Selections, in the preface to which Robert Browning was acclaimed as one of " the few great poets of the century ". " Seriously," wrote Browning, " now that I care not one whit about what I never cared for too much, people are getting good-natured to my poems." At the same time, the long creative hiatus which had super-vened upon the failure of *Men and Women* in 1855, came to an end : resolved to " keep writing whether I like it or not ", by 1863 Browning had resumed the steady productive activity of his pre-marital days at Camberwell and at New Cross. " Yes—the years go," he wrote to Isa Blagden, " —we are in the *third* : at first . . . nothing seemed *doing*, nothing *growing*,—only the emptiness and weariness of it all : now, there seems really *use* in the process, and fruit." For despite his own assertion that he " could no more take root in life again, than learn some new dancing step ", by the second anniversary of Elizabeth's death, the poet was securely estab-

---

[1] The situation of Pen resembles, closely, that of another child of illustrious parents. Like Pen Browning, Percy Shelley was born in Florence : after a childhood spent in Italy, he, too, was brought to England, leaving in Italian soil the remains of a beloved parent. Mary Shelley was soon to discover that her son had " no ambition " : " Pen boats," Browning complained, " cares more for that than aught else, unless perhaps for shooting and breech-loaders ". In Percy, the blood-streams of Godwin, Wollstonecraft and Shelley conspired to produce a young man whose greatest interest in life was amateur theatricals and yachting. Each married a woman enamoured chiefly of the parental legend : each marriage was childless : and each ended his days, in happy mediocrity, collecting and presiding over the relics of his celebrated parents.

lished in the soil of his new environment. Nor had the process been a protracted one : there is no evidence, for instance, that the prolonged depression which followed upon the death of his mother claimed him again after the loss of his wife. " Well, for myself, I am certainly not unhappy, any more than I ever was. . . . In many ways, I can see with my human eyes why this has been right and good for me—as I never doubted it was for Her—and if we do but rejoin one day,—the break will be better than forgotten, remembered for its uses." The tone is a temperate one ; and we are not surprised to find that with his usual good sense the poet did not look for " communications " of any kind ; the difference between himself and " stupid people " in this respect being, he said, that " I don't confound the results of the natural working of what is in my mind, with vulgar external appearances ". His own communications with the past took a different form ; and we have the expression of some of them, at least, in his next volume of poems, *Dramatis Personae*. The first two summers after his return to England were spent at Sainte Marie, near Pornic, in Brittany. Lacking the golden patina of the poetry written in Italy, *James Lee* is grey with the austerity of sea and cliff ; bleak with a spiritual solitude under the rigours of which, like the wind-bitten vines in the fields outside, " my heart shrivels up and my spirit shrinks curled ". It was here, in the unsettled summer of 1863, and identifying himself, as he so frequently did, with the feminine point of view, that Browning composed these variations upon the theme of " people newly-married, trying to realise a dream of being sufficient to each other, in a foreign land (where you can try such an experiment) and finding it break up—the man being tired *first*, and tired precisely of the love ". One of the component sections is called, like an earlier poem of Browning's, *By the Fireside* ; and it is startling to compare the uncompromising bitterness of this second poem with the beauty and serenity of the first. Once more, husband and wife sit by the hearth ; but what they contemplate now over their fire of shipwreck wood is the spectacle of some intimate and irremediable failure. No sailor, storm-tossed at sea, need envy the light of " the warm safe house "—

> For some ships; safe in port indeed,
>> Rot and rust,
>> Run to dust,
> All through the worms i' the wood, which crept,
> Gnawed our hearts out while we slept :
>> That is worse.[1]

By the Fireside is reminiscent in mood of the embittered frustration of Browning's stay at Havre. On the other hand, the final stanzas of *Under the Cliff* belong, recognisably, to Sainte Marie ; to the circumstances of recent loss and separation. More than a quarter of a century ago, Browning had published in the *Monthly Repository* a poem beginning " Still ailing, Wind ? Wilt be appeased or no ? " Now, under the spell once more of " the wind with its wants and its infinite wail ", he added another ten stanzas to this : matching, with the tempered resignation of maturity, the grandiloquent despair of youth. " Nothing endures : the wind moans saying so " ; and under the autumnal skies of Brittany (described at this time in a letter to Isa Blagden) the poet found himself contemplating not only the ephemerality of human passion, but, more bitter, this, the ephemerality of human sorrow itself.

> Nothing can be as it has been before ;
>> Better, so call it, only not the same.
> To draw one beauty into our heart's core,
>> And keep it changeless ! such our claim ;
> So answered,—Never more !

Throughout the winter of 1863, Robert Browning was often to be seen mounting, top-hatted, the graceful flight of steps leading to the front door of Number 1, Cumberland Place, in Regent's Park. The house belonged to Hensleigh Wedgwood, the philologist, whose wife is described by Madame Sismondi as having " beneath that refreshing quiet . . . a lava of living fire that has made her give battle to all the governments in

---

[1] In manner and matter, *James Lee* recalls at times *Modern Love*. Meredith presented a copy to Browning, and Browning " expressed himself ' astounded at the originality, delighted with the naturalness and beauty ' ". [June 9, 1862].

Europe under the banner of Mazzini ". The poet, more mildly, described her as " a very charming and accomplished lady ". Charm, on the other hand, is not a quality so readily associated with the eldest daughter of the family, Frances Julia, known as " Snow " Wedgwood. On examining a portrait, in which the wide lips gape somewhat and the brown hair is drawn severely back behind a large, insensitive ear, one is reminded of Edith in Browning's poem *Too Late*.

> I liked the way you had with your curls
>   Wound to a ball in a net behind :
> Your cheek was chaste as a quaker-girl's,
>   And your mouth—there was never, to my mind,
>   Such a funny mouth, for it would not shut. . . .

More forcibly still, one is reminded of Susannah Wedgwood's son, Charles Darwin : the blunt retroussé nose and over-hanging eyebrow are characteristic of uncle and niece alike. No one, it may be thought, could look less like the fragile, be-ringleted invalid of Wimpole Street. And yet something of the same quality which he had discerned in Elizabeth Barrett was to draw Robert Browning into an emotional relationship with this severe and curiously graceless young blue-stocking.[1] " My wife ", he assured her, " never had any woman-friend so entirely fit for her as you would have been." Like Elizabeth, Julia was the eldest of a large family : as in Elizabeth's case, it was the death of a beloved brother—also " Bro "—that provided the basis of intimacy. (On June 30th, 1864, after lunching with him at Warwick Crescent, Browning parted from William Allingham at Bishop's Road Station : " I am going," he said, " to a house where the eldest son is dead.") Like Elizabeth, Julia lived with her family in a large, well-staffed house in Regent's Park : and in making his way there from Paddington, by the new Underground Railway which, said an observer, " feels very safe and quiet ", the poet must often have been reminded of the days, long past, when in May or June, as now, he used to walk rose-laden all the way from New Cross to Mr. Moulton-Barrett's house in Wimpole Street.

---

[1] It is surprising, having studied the austerity of Julia's profile, as of her letters, to hear that E. M. Forster, who knew her in her latter days, found her " decidedly gay ".

Today, a widower in his fifties, time had grizzled his hair and halted the impetuosity of his step ; it had imparted, too, that air of sober and well-regulated prosperity which caused people to confound, increasingly, the poet with the successful man of business. Julia Wedgwood, born in the same year as " that unlucky *Pauline* ", was one of the few women, younger than himself, with whom Browning had been able to form an intimate friendship. There was nothing diffident or deferential, however, in her attitude towards her new friend. Like Harriet Martineau, Julia suffered from a congenital deafness ; and something of the same forthright candour, the same lack of coquetry, enabled her not only to take " the initiative in a friendship with a man ", but to confess to Browning just how much that friendship meant to her. " They say I am not feminine," she wrote to him : whereupon, " I am ' feminine ', if you are not," the poet retorted : and indeed in resolution and force of character, if nothing else, her masculine qualities exceeded his own. Browning was not alienated by the power he sensed in her. On the contrary : " From the beginning of my acquaintance with you, I was aware, in proportion to my knowledge of you, that it might greatly interest and advantage me," he wrote to her. For, like Elizabeth Barrett, Julia Wedgwood was a highly intelligent woman, whose critical commentary on the *Origin of Species* aroused the admiration of Darwin himself. Like Elizabeth, she was at once widely read and deeply religious. In her preoccupation with death, with certain superstitious fears (she was obsessed, for instance, with the idea that Pen was doomed to an early death) she might also be said to resemble her : but one has only to read her letters, if not her books and essays, to see that she lacked, wholly, the finesse and brilliance of the woman whom she admired so deeply. Her limitations must have been apparent enough to Browning—a touch of earthenware where he had long known only porcelain—but there was something in the general design of the personality that responded to an old and still-persisting need of his own : and since, under certain circumstances, " a poplar does as well for a vine-prop as a palm-tree ", three years after the death of Elizabeth Barrett, Browning was writing to Julia Wedgwood : " You shall take me in hand and teach me—if you don't get tired."

Robert Browning, 1882, a portrait by his son

Robert Browning and Pen Browning, Venice, 1889

Asolo, on the left, Mrs Bronson's house;
on the extreme right, Browning's lodgings

During the course of their friendship, the poet wrote thirty letters to Miss Wedgwood, and she wrote him forty-two. In reading these, it is curious to see how closely they echo at times the manner and phraseology of the Love Letters. There is the same emphasis on the term " Dear Friend ", and " dearest friend " : the same recondite literary and social gossip, alternating, in moments of tension, with prolonged and searching self-analysis. No less than with Elizabeth, a persistent desire for death, had, in Julia, " bent all my inward life like an unseen magnet ". If the poet needed her, however, she was no less prepared than her predecessor to " yield the grave " for his sake ; and there is a certain clumsy pathos in the letter in which she confesses as much. " Is it possible," she asked, " that I do not still pull against that chain ? and that it is only because a fellow-creature—not spotlessly perfect, by any means—tells me that my absence makes a hole in his life, that I am willing, oh more than willing, to keep my foothold here, while he cares to have me ? " Browning was moved by this into an admission, hitherto withheld, of his own sentiments. " And now," he wrote, " doing you this homage, let my own turn come, nor let mistake be feared, when I tell the pure truth, that you are most dear to me, and will be ever so." At the same time, aware of the claims of the past, as of a twenty years disparity in age, conscientiously, he sought to warn her not to " cut, in that royal way, your palm-tree to the heart, that the poor traveller you delight to honour may have a draught of palm wine, ' after which ', says Xenophon, ' the whole tree withers '. A better than I, God knows, should have the whole palm tree in its season. . . . Meantime, grow and be happy, and let me sit under the branches to my day's end, come what will."

But the refreshment yielded by this oasis was not always acceptable to a mature palate. Nor was the rest of Browning's life quite the desert that sentimental opinion insisted it must be. Of all the poet's friends, Carlyle alone was able to foresee this fact : he who, on learning of the death of Elizabeth, had sent Browning the following message : " Tell him from me to gird himself together out of these sore wrecks of the past (as indeed I see he is manfully doing), and that I expect *a new epoch for him* in regard to his own work in this world, now that he is coming back to England at last ; and that, in my poor opinion, which I have never changed, a noble victory lies ahead for him, if he stand by it while time yet is." [1] That new epoch in the life of Robert Browning had already begun. For the first time in his experience, a book of his had gone into a second edition : for the first time, too, since his marriage, he was sought out for his own sake, and not simply as " Browning, the husband ", title and summary of all his Italian years. Losing Elizabeth, he escaped also from her shadow ; and now, emerging from that long eclipse, he had recovered, spontaneously, the light of his own identity. This experience precipitated or coincided with a new, and, it will be thought, singularly belated growth of self-reliance, whose presence in himself he had not yet discovered when, habit-bound, he sought the friendship and guidance of Julia Wedgwood. The young Robert Browning had desired ardently to perfect himself under the authority of a woman more high-minded and more resolute than himself. Fate had offered him that experience : and it was a fixed emotional habit rather than a real necessity that drove him to seek a resumption of it in the drawing-rooms at Cumberland Place. But by now, having discovered the perils as well as the privileges of that condition in which soul is mixed with soul, Browning was less anxious than before to feel another " brain prompt mine ", another " heart anticipate my heart ". He had learnt, too, that " if you wish another spirit to keep close by you while you go up higher, offences must come, and the wings get in the way of each other ". Out of his own crisis of love and grief, he had won back solitude : and solitude was not again to be jeopardised. Such flights as still awaited him were to be undertaken on his own : on the lower levels of life, meanwhile, he was content, still, to grasp a firm and companionable hand.

" Goodbye, dearest friend," wrote Browning on August 2, 1864, " I go tomorrow, stay, as I very likely have told you, some two months, and see you prominently on the white cliffs as a landmark for return." A fortnight later, with his father and sister and Pen, he was at Cambo, fifteen miles from

---

[1] August 17, 1861. " Carlyle and John Forster : an Unpublished Correspondence." *Quarterly Reviews*, April, 1937.

Bayonne, in the Pyrenees. At first, bilious and sleepy, he foresaw the possibility of being bored in this remote little village : " it's a transparency I have no candle to put behind : it ' lights up ', I daresay, to the luckier sort," he wrote to Julia. It was to " light up " effectively enough to the poet himself, however, when a few days later, contemplating the mountain pass known as the *Pas de Roland*, spontaneously, the whole plan of *The Ring and the Book* presented itself with a detailed clarity to his mind : " the same transaction seen from a number of differing points of view, or glimpses in a mirror ", as he afterwards described it to William Rossetti. He did no work at Cambo, however : for the Southern atmosphere, the " mountains like those about Florence and Siena ", the little river " not unlike the Lima at Lucca ", all conspired to remind him of the past ; with the result that he complained of a constant feeling of being " somehow walled-about and overlooked . . . though the obstructions are purely spiritual in this case, the influences in the air—for nine times out of ten, I don't meet a soul ". Was he thinking, perhaps, of Elizabeth's distaste for the story told in the " square old yellow Book " he had picked up for a lira on a stall in Florence on another summer's day, four years ago ? His wife, he knew, had never shared his passion for the " curious depth below depth of depravity " which he found " in this chance lump taken as a sample of the soil " of human nature. On the contrary : " She never took the least interest in the story, so much as to wish to inspect the papers." Her distaste seems to have acted as a ban : for four years, Browning kept the book by him and made no use of it. And then the moment arrived, which he has described.

> The Book ! I turn its medicinable leaves
> In London now till, as in Florence erst,
> A spirit laughs and leaps through every limb,
> And lights my eye, and lifts me by the hair,
> Letting me have my will again with these.

It is interesting to compare the circumstances which inspired Shelley's tragedy *The Cenci* with those which attended the composition of Browning's major work, *The Ring and the Book*. In both cases, it was from a manuscript source that

231

the poets drew their material : and by a pleasing coincidence, not only did Browning's old yellow book contain a reference to Farinacci's defence of Beatrice Cenci, but a supplementary account of the Franceschini affair was copied for him in Rome from a volume which contains also an account of the trial of Beatrice Cenci. Despite his enthusiasm for the subject, Shelley, like Browning, did not at once set to work on the story : unready either to write or to relinquish it, like Browning, he too urged the story on others " as one fitted for a tragedy ". To the diffidence of those " others " we owe both *The Cenci* and *The Ring and the Book*. In a footnote to the former, Shelley speaks of the Papal Government's tragical " wickedness and weakness " : it is curious to see that Browning uses the same words in relation to his own story : " I was struck with the enormous wickedness and weakness of the main composition of the piece," he wrote to Julia Wedgwood, " and with the incidental evolution of good thereby. . . ." What, primarily, each discerned in his respective Roman murder story was a study in the problem of evil. " Such a story," wrote Shelley, " would be as a light to make apparent some of the most dark and secret caverns of the human heart " : and, as Browning was to do, he attempted " as nearly as possible to represent the characters as they probably were ", avoiding the error of " making them actuated by my own conceptions of right or wrong, false or true ". The central figure in each case is a " gentle and amiable " woman, of a marked " simplicity and dignity ", who, under extreme provocation is capable of a moment of violence : Pompilia attacks with his own sword the despicable Guido : Beatrice Cenci contrives the death of an evil father. Each story is further dominated by the personality of a Pope upon whose decision rests the fate of innocent and guilty alike : and here, by the most fortuitous of chances, each writer gets the Pope—if not that he deserves—best suited, at least, to his own purposes. Thus, Shelley found in Clement VIII a man more corrupt than his own most anti-clerical prejudice could well have devised : whereas in the liberal, humane and industrious Innocent XII, Browning was able to draw a Pope whose theology anticipated, conveniently, the broader conclusions of a nineteenth-century dissenter.

Browning had at all times the greatest admiration for Shelley's " superb achievement ", *The Cenci*.   He was delighted to be able to add a footnote to the story when, in 1876, he published his poem *Cenciaja* ; and ten years later, he was present at the Grand Theatre when Alma Murray took the part of Beatrice Cenci in a performance sponsored by the Shelley Society.   Despite the fact that, as he said of *Cenciaja*, he would be the first to " deprecate the notion " of " pressing into the company of his betters ", the suspicion that in *The Ring and The Book* Browning saw his own *Cenci* gains support from a letter that he wrote to George Smith before the poem was published.   " I have been thinking over the ' name ' of the Poem, as you desired,—but do not, nor apparently shall, come to anything better than ' The Franceschini ' ; *that* includes everybody in the piece, inasmuch as every one is for either Franceschini or his wife, a Franceschini also.   I think ' the Book & the Ring ' is too pretty-fairy-story-like.   Suppose you say ' The Franceschini ' therefore.   Good luck to it ! " [1]

In the middle of October, Browning returned to London. " I am glad to think of you at home again," wrote Julia Wedgwood, " —*home*, is a word, however, which you will hardly accept as being relevant here, I fear, or for the rest of your pilgrimage.   I can so well imagine how each return seems more purposeless than the last.   Oh, how long life is ! " One of the most trying things about Julia Wedgwood was her habit of putting into Browning's mouth the sentiments that, a notoriously bereaved man, he might be expected to entertain. While she was thus insisting on the melancholy and pointlessness of the poet's return to his home, Browning had arrived at Warwick Crescent with " the whole of that poem you enquire about, well in my head ", and the determination " to write the Twelve books of it in six months, and then take breath again ".   This pent-up energy is indication enough that there was at that moment no lack of zest or purposefulness in the life of the poet : and indeed, meeting him for the first time some months later, Benjamin Jowett was struck by his " great energy " and " his determination to make the most of

[1] July 30, 1868. Brit. Mus. Add. 43485.

the remainder of his life ". It was a determination which Julia, in a sense, refused to sanction. An impassioned admirer of the " beautiful soul " of Elizabeth Barrett, she had her own very emphatic notions of what was due in the way of homage to the memory of such a woman : and there were moments when, inexplicably, she felt, Browning failed to rise to the higher levels of so pious a sensibility. From the first, Julia had made it plain that her relationship with the poet was to be regarded, spiritually, as a *ménage à trois* : he was never allowed to forget this ghostly chaperonage, or to emerge, too freely, from the shadow of an exalted bereavement. " Some parts of our intercourse have been almost the best of life to me—specially when you have spoken of your wife— and these do not pass away. Oh, if she had been here when we met ! But I will not be so heartless as to bring in my wish into company with your grief which must move alone." Browning's grief was very deep and very real, as his love had been : but the moment had passed in which he was to be seen walking about the street in tears : he knew, now, not only the measure of his own loss, but the measure of his own gain ; and the adjustment could be appreciated by no one who was not familiar with all the circumstances of his married life. When he assured Isa Blagden that " no human being can give me one hand, with the feeling on my part that the other holds that of my Ba, as you can do ", it was because Isa, intimate friend of both husband and wife alike, knew exactly of what diverse ingredients this celebrated marriage was compounded. As long as she lived, she was his touch-stone with a reality whose proportions were so rapidly to become inflated by the breath of popular sentiment, that a year after the death of the poet, William Sharp, his first biographer, could write of the marriage in the following terms : (the passage deserves quoting in full) : " As for Browning's love towards his wife, nothing more tender or chivalrous has ever been told of ideal lovers in an ideal romance. It is so beautiful a story that one often prefers it to the sweetest or loftiest poem that came from the lips of either. That love knew no soilure in the passage of the years. Like the flame of oriental legend, it was perennially incandescent though fed not otherwise than by sunlight and moonshine. If it alone survive, it may resolve the poetic fame of either into one imperishable, luminous ray of white light : as the uttered song fused in the deathless passion of Sappho gleams star-like down the centuries from the high steep of Leucadoe."

Abruptly, on March 1, 1865, Julia Wedgwood wrote to Robert Browning asking him not to call on her again. " I have reason to know ", she said, " that my pleasure in your company has had an interpretation put upon it that I ought not to allow." She went on to write at once vaguely and portentously of the many " involved reasons " which lay behind this sudden decision of hers. Four years were to pass before she revealed to the poet the true motive which had prompted her to relinquish his friendship. It was, she said, " some refracted words of yours that made it possible to me to do as I did, (or what were represented as such). . . . My friendship with you was—is—the great blessing of my life, but it was impossible to me to carry on that outward indulgence of it after it had been implied to me ' He feels it a gêne.' " Did Browning ever discuss with others his relationship with Julia Wedgwood ? He denied emphatically that he had done so. On the contrary. Not having " the least notion of why that interruption must be ", he underwent, so he affirmed, " great pain from the sudden interruption of our intercourse ". There can be little doubt that the enforced cessation of his visits to Cumberland Place was, at the time, an appreciable deprivation : for, if he was less susceptible, now, to exhortations which called upon him to " live unfalteringly up to your highest ideal ", he still respected the acuteness of Julia's judgment, and admired the unassailable integrity of her character. It was without exaggeration, therefore, four years after the moment in which her company had so suddenly and inexplicably been denied to him, that Robert Browning could write to Julia Wedgwood : " I lost something peculiar in you which I shall not see replaced."

In the summer of 1865, Browning went for the third and last time to spend a holiday at Sainte Marie, near Pornic. As before, he occupied the Mayor's house ; a wealthy man, he wrote, who " out of pure preference for piggishness . . . sleeps in one room with his son and three daughters, the eldest being fifteen, and—the somewhat less ugly than usual maidservant of about nineteen or twenty,—who is lately taken into service, —four beds in a row—and the notion that such arrangement is queer will not enter a head in the village for the next fifty years ". The maid-servant reappears in characteristic posture in Browning's next letter to Isa Blagden. " Fancy the buxom servant girl," he wrote, " aged some 20, washing clothes before my window (on the pianterreno, dressed in a blue gown and nothing else, I can see, just covering the naked legs below the knees—and so kilted, turning her back to me and burying herself with linen she has to stoop for on the ground ! Primitive manners ! " That the primitive manners of the local peasant girls were not lost upon Pen Browning—a young man with " dreadfully incipient moustachios " who was dutifully reading Virgil under his father's supervision—the events of the coming years were materially to prove.

Sarianna Browning, who did not marry, was to spend a long, cheerful and active life in unfaltering devotion to the members of her own family. After her father's death in June, 1866, she came to live in Warwick Crescent, and from that date brother and sister were never separated, except for the briefest of intervals. Sarianna, at fifty-two, was a vigorous little woman with " quick, sharp, intelligent eyes, like her illustrious poet brother's, and an abundance of blue-black hair. . . . When she began to talk it was no use trying to interrupt her flow of words. . . . She generally stood up when she related anything, and as she was very short she would stand all the time on tiptoes." The description is Henriette Corkran's, who dwells not only on Sarianna's innocent snobbery (she did not like people to know that her father had been a clerk in the Bank of England, and used to tread reprovingly on his toe when he mentioned the fact) but also on her whole-hearted devotion to her family. " Her wonderful affection and admiration for a Browning was touching, nothing that any one of them said or did could be wrong, it was all perfection." With Sarianna once more under his roof, Browning was restored, it will be seen, to that uncritical family atmosphere from which marriage had temporarily subtracted him : a situation which, if it added manifestly to the ease and comfort of his life, robbed him at the same time of that ray of " foreign light ", whose effect is to defer the onset of complacency.

Sarianna brought with her from Paris not only her father's favourite chairs and pictures, but the entire library accumulated in fifty years' research by this impassioned bibliomane. The house in Warwick Crescent was all but submerged beneath this sudden influx of books : hastily, shelves were erected to dam the tide : bookcases buttressed all the rooms, obstructed every landing, and invaded even the primitive bathroom in which, at daybreak, the poet could be heard chanting Italian opera under the cascade of water released from an inverted tank above his head. In other respects, too, the arrival of Sarianna changed materially the character of the household. A home without a mistress, it had been hitherto little more than a museum of Casa Guidi relics ; an impression which drew from George Eliot, when she visited it in October, 1865, the comment that " she had seen nothing so interesting since Goethe's house ". Now, however, not only was the presence of Sarianna to tether the house more firmly to practical issues, but in the books and pictures she brought with her lay associations as imperative as those which derived from Casa Guidi itself. Belatedly, a fusion took place, in which books belonging to Hope End and the youth of Elizabeth Barrett shared the same shelf with those " wisest ancient books " which had nourished the roots of Browning's creative life in the far-off days at Hanover Cottage in Camberwell. He was to raise from that same soil a further crop of reflections and speculations: in 1887, two years before his death, appeared the *Parleyings with Certain People of Importance In Their Day*, in which all the characters interviewed, with the exception perhaps of Francis Furini, owe their reappearance to the poet's enduring interest in the very books which now had become his by inheritance.

Throughout the year, Browning was at work, " unintermittingly " on his Roman murder story. At the same time, he was busy supervising Pen's progress in Latin and Greek. " It is piteously comic ", wrote Michael Field, " to hear how the good dinners at which the poet ate all he liked and drank port wine from the beginning, told on the boy's Greek lesson next day. . . . The Old [Browning] was evidently intolerant of faults and forcing in his culture of virtues. He could write his poetry while Pen was practising, and run up to the room above to correct errors without breaking his inspiration. . . ." Browning had set his heart on Pen entering Balliol under Jowett ; and addressed himself so energetically to the fulfilment of this ambition, that Isa warned him of the danger of becoming a " monomaniac " on the subject of his son's education. " I am quite of your mind about college acquirements and fame," he replied, " and how little they prove the owner a person of soul's quality : but a race is a race, and whoever tries ought to win. . . ." Had he forgotten the days of his own youth, in which, rejecting all forms of scholastic and competitive discipline, he had chafed even under the moderate yoke of a few weekly classes at Gower Street ? It is here, while on the subject of discipline for the young, that one would give much to have overheard Browning's comments on his experience as a member of the Grand Jury at the Middlesex Sessions, Clerkenwell, on November 19th and 20th, 1866. Six prisoners were tried on the first day : amongst them, John Shoesmith, aged sixteen, accused of stealing lead, who was sentenced to six months' hard labour ; and James Pink, aged twelve, whose offence was that he had attempted to steal four herrings. The jury found Pink guilty of stealing one herring, and recommended him to mercy on account of his youth. He was sentenced to one day's imprisonment, and ten stripes of the birch. It is tempting, of course, to believe that it was the poet who, interrupting his work on the trial of Guidi Franceschini in order to attend that of James Pink and his contemporaries, insisted that justice be tempered with mercy in the case of the twelve-year-old boy. It may have been so : at the same time, there is nothing in Browning's attitude to crime in general and to children in particular which permits us to assume that he found anything in the least anomalous in the sentences imposed upon children in a Victorian court of law. The poet once affirmed that he " would rather submit to the worst of deaths, so far as pain goes, than have a single dog or cat tortured ". He was notoriously indifferent, on the other hand, to the appeal of

238

children ; and even his friend and admirer, Mrs. Orr, was obliged to comment on this aspect of his character : the helplessness of childhood, she wrote, roused in the poet " no special emotion ". Strong as was Browning's interest in crime, in " morbid cases of the soul ", his respect for the conventions of society was stronger still. " I am always strict upon *rights* in this world, and let generosity and all its derivative virtues and graces show themselves or keep quiet as they please—provided justice is done in the first place," he wrote. In illustration of which, it is possible to quote here yet another court case, in which Robert Browning himself was this time the defendant.

A POET'S LOST DAY

At Marylebone County Court a few days ago, Mr. Page, Italian warehouseman, of Westbourne Grove, sued Mr. Robert Browning, the poet, for 8 shillings, the value of two bottles of port wine. . . . Mr. Browning, in defence, said . . . he never drank port wine, nor did anyone else in the house. . . . Mr. Browning concluded an indignant speech by calling his housekeeper and page, both of whom deposed that they had never ordered or received port wine from plaintiff or anybody else for Mr. Browning's house. . . . Mr. Browning said he had lost the whole day in connexion with this paltry claim, but he resisted it on principle. He wished his costs to be appropriated to the poor box of the court, for which he was publicly thanked by the registrar.[1]

This was not the only day which was lost to the poet : the claims on his time were so incessant, and progress on his Roman murder story so much slower than he had anticipated, that throughout the winter, he was obliged to rise at five in order to get through his day's work. The responsibility, moral and educational, of his son was to become an increasing burden : added to this, the salvation of Wilson was belatedly laid at his door. After the death of Walter Savage Landor in 1864, Wilson had fallen on evil days. Browning offered, (reluctantly, in view of their known incompetence) to employ both Wilson

[1] Newspaper cutting, undated, source unspecified. Forster Collection, Victoria and Albert Museum. In the seventies, we are told, " Mr. Browning liked to drink port wine with his dinner and nothing else."

and Ferdinando at Warwick Crescent : Wilson, however, declined to enter his service, and one is left to wonder why. Torn between the rival attractions of a cigar shop and a pastry-cook's, she decided finally to open a lodging-house in Scarborough. The venture failed, as Browning foresaw that it would ; and the poet wrote to Wilson's sister, a milliner at East Retford, suggesting that it was now her duty to look after Wilson and perhaps take her into partnership with her in the millinery business. In return, Browning received " an impertinent, improper letter ", saying that " Wilson was quite able to take care of herself, and had been found so as long as she was of any use—' when worn out in the service she was to be thrown on other people ' and more of this sort of thing ". Browning resented the accusation deeply : all the more so, in that there was just sufficient justice in it to cause on his part an inevitable chafing of conscience. Resolutely, he chose to ignore this : he would not have done so, perhaps, but for the fact that his own preoccupations were grave enough, at the time, to obscure all other obligations. " How hard it is for people to get money ! " he wrote. " I don't wonder they grow misers. It is so terrible to have to leave all your soul's business and set about getting fifty pounds— even your sorrows you would have to give up." Again : " I have ten times the reason to lay up money, and do distasteful things . . . with a son who may want no end of money," he wrote in February, 1868. Pen was then within a few weeks of his nineteenth birthday. The previous summer, as the summer before, the Brownings had spent in Brittany : not this time at Sainte Marie, but at Le Croisic : a place, wrote the poet, where the people were " still Pagan a couple of hundred years ago, despite the priest's teaching and preaching, and the women used to dance round a phallic stone still upright there with obscene circumstances enough,—till the general civilisation got too strong for this ". There were still some impulses that the general civilisation had not succeeded in subduing. Pen Browning was seventeen on his first visit to this " wild and primitive " place : before he was nineteen, so Frances Winwar tells us, " he had two illegitimate daughters by different mothers, peasant girls of Brittany ".[1]

[1] *The Immortal Lovers*, p. 306. Hamish Hamilton, 1950.

On June 11, 1868, Arabel Barrett died. Although she had lived unobtrusively, occupied, to the exclusion of other interests, with her chapel and her charitable works, her presence at Delamere Terrace had been felt as a sustaining influence in the poet's life. Her death deprived him, he wrote, of " the ' one steadfast friend who never did my heart or life mis-know ' " : so keenly, at first, did it distress him to pass the tall austere house in which, like her sister before her, she had died in his arms, that he even contemplated, at one time, moving out of the neighbourhood altogether. " There has devolved upon me every sort of sad business that seemed duty, and I am as full as a sponge of vinegar and gall just now," he wrote to Isa. The beauty of June was darkened for him hereafter : within a few years of each other, his wife, his father and his sister-in-law had all died in that month.

Preceding the publication of *The Ring and the Book*, a six volume edition of the works of Robert Browning appeared in the spring of 1868. The only complete edition up to date, it included for the first time the hitherto unacknowledged *Pauline*. Only a few years before, Browning had spoken feelingly of his hatred of " clever, precocious immaturity " which, he said, " binds its author to many a crude, wrong and untrue profession of faith which seriously hampers him after and long after ". Why, then, did the poet consent to the reappearance of a work which he had done his best for five and thirty years to suppress ? It was to satisfy George Murray Smith that he consented, albeit with " extreme repugnance ", to the resuscitation of this " boyish work " : and there could be no greater proof of the goodwill that existed from the first between the poet and his new publisher than this unwonted acquiescence on Browning's part. " I will include *Pauline* as you desire," he wrote on December 10, 1867 ; and Smith can scarcely have known what it cost the poet to make such a concession. In the same letter (it is illuminating to compare the tone of it with that evoked by the " vile scatterbrain ways " of Frederick Chapman), Browning wrote : " You need no telling that your offer is a most liberal one which absolutely contents me,—but I need some reflecting on the probability that you understand business, and will not harm yourself by your generosity. All I can say is, that I hope you will be as satisfied with me, in our connection,—which will, I hope be a long one,—as I am with all your kindness and help from first to last." [1] The hope was to be realised : for more than twenty years, during which time the firm of Smith, Elder published all Robert Browning's work, the association between the poet and his publisher remained a happy and a successful one. George Smith was twelve years younger than Robert Browning ; it was not long, however, before he became not only the guardian of Browning's professional interests, but a necessary adjudicator in all the more prosaic difficulties of a poet's life. Since this poet, this seasoned man of the world who " looked more like a stock-broker than a bard " was notoriously unwilling to grapple single-handed with the practical intricacies of life, over and over again, in the years to come, he was to turn for the solution of his problems, major and minor alike, to the oracle at Waterloo Place. " My dear Smith, I have a French friend with me, here for the first time, who . . . wants, of all things, to see ' the Docks '—now, I am quite ignorant how he may be helped to this . . . do let me ask you if you can tell us how to proceed." [2] " My dear Smith, I only this moment hear that Pen's pictures will arrive tomorrow, Thursday, by the ' Baron Osy '. Can you procure their transport from St. Katherine's Dock to Queen's Gate Gardens ? " [3] " My dear Smith . . . I am going to ask you to kindly to [*sic*] cut out of any ' Times ' . . . the hours of departure of the Tidal train from Paris to London, via Boulogne—and to send it to me at the *Hôtel Suisse*, Turin . . . If in the envelope which is to enclose the advertisement you could tax your experience so far as to tell me whether I can send on straight to London from Turin my baggage, you would greatly oblige me. . . ." [4] " My dear Smith, I was fully intending . . . to call you to account for altogether omitting to set down the expenses to which you were put some two months ago in getting me the certificate of the death of my uncle Reuben Browning. Today, on presenting it at the Bank, I find that sagacious institution

---

[1] December 10, 1867 : in the possession of Sir John Murray.
[2] April 27, 1875. Ibid.   [3] December 29, 1880. Ibid.
[4] February 24, 1880. Ibid.

acknowledges no other proof of death than a Burial Certificate :
may I therefore ask of your kindness to get one of your
efficacious people to write for me to the Parish Clerk of
Shirley, Croydon, and obtain the document in question ? " [1]
" My dear Smith . . . The Frame of the Picture wants some
repairing, I believe. . . . I think you mentioned that you
knew and could recommend a Frame-Maker in your neighbourhood. If he would do all that is requisite in the case, I
should be greatly obliged." [2] " My dear Smith . . . You
may probably have received a note of mine, by this time,
soliciting your kind advice about a house I want to buy. . . .
If you could indulge me at any time on or after Monday morning by letting me call for you and giving a look at the property
in my company and that of the Proprietor, you would greatly
help my inexperience in such matters . . . yours—somewhat
helplessly but ever gratefully—Robert Browning." [3] And so
—somewhat helplessly but ever gratefully—it goes on. It is
the privilege of a poet to be unpractical in worldly matters :
but in Browning this prolonged naïveté was accompanied by
an almost hysterical irritation at a similar incompetence in
· others. Isa Blagden complained of his " ogre-fashion " of
snubbing her when she offended in this respect ; " the most
impatient man in the world ", was Julia Wedgwood's description of him : in later life, his " authoritative and disputatious "
manner caused many people, men in particular, to dislike and
avoid him. " There are so many fools in the world ! " This,
Henriette Corkran observed, was " a favourite expression of
the poet's ".

When, in the summer of 1868, Browning returned once more
to Brittany, his son did not accompany him. Pen remained
behind in England, under the care of a Tutor ; while dis-
embarrassed, temporarily, of responsibility, the poet and his
sister made their way to Audierne, niched, as he described it,
at the most westerly point of Brittany and the mainland of
Europe. " Is it not a good omen," he wrote to George Smith,
" that the first room I am shown into—of this little Inn where
I alight—in a place where the folks speak Breton, wear hair

[1] February 2, 1881. Ibid. [2] March 1, 1863. Ibid. [3] January 27, 1887. Ibid.

falling on their shoulders, and are dressed in the fashion of hundreds of years ago,—the first object that fronts me is a really capital print of Milton ? " [1] There, with " a brain which the journey ought to have swept clean of no end of cobwebs ", Browning set to work " tooth and nail " on the proofs of *The Ring and the Book* ; the first volume of which was ready for publication shortly after his return to Warwick Crescent. G. H. Lewes is reputed to have said that Browning was " morbidly sensitive to criticism, and eager for any kind of praise " : Leigh Hunt, he said, had told him that the poet " was so hungry for general approval, that he ' coveted that even of his own washerwoman ' ". After four years spent in the sustained solitude of poetic creation, it was natural enough that the poet should seek out recognition and reassurance : he turned for it now to one of the few women whose judgment he respected, and whose candour he knew that he could rely upon. Reopening a correspondence which some unexplained impulse on her part had sealed so abruptly more than three years ago, Browning sent Julia Wedgwood the first two volumes of his forthcoming work. A minor distinction was thereby conferred upon her. Other than the author and publisher of the poem, she was the first person in England to read *The Ring and the Book* in its entirety.

Her reaction to this " long, dark, complicated elaborate story of intrigue and crime " was primarily one of dismay. Characteristically, she did not fail to let him know this ; or that she had been disappointed in her hope that the poem was to be his " best gift to the world ". Do you remember, she wrote, " once saying to me that your Wife was quite wanting in . . . the scientific interest in evil ? . . . I feel as if that interest were in you unduly predominant." What most distressed her in the poem, she said, was that " I felt as if I were reading what you had lost in your wife. The sense of good seemed dimmed." And she went on to exhort the poet to give Elizabeth Barrett Browning " a monument more durable than that at Florence—give something that all who read may recognise as the utterance of one who has been taught supremely to believe in goodness by the close neighbourhood of a beautiful soul ".

[1] August 13, 1868 : in the possession of Sir John Murray.

A change is perceptible in Browning's manner at this point. The voice remains good-humoured, but he defends his own position with an increasing emphasis. " We differ apparently in our conception of what gross wickedness can be effected by cultivated minds—I believe the *grossest*—all the more, by way of reaction from the enforced habit of self-denial which is the condition of men's receiving culture," he wrote. It was the echo of an old controversy, an old conflict : he was addressing, not Julia Wedgwood, but the shade of Elizabeth Barrett : the Elizabeth who refused to admit the existence of evil in others : who " would not, or could not " recognise the falsity of Sophia Eckley, " and suffered miserably through her ignorance ". The worst is, he now wrote, " I think myself dreadfully in the right, all the while in everything. . . . I think this *is* the world as it is and will be—*here* at least." There was a double satisfaction in this assertion of his own point of view. Four years ago, Browning had discerned in Julia Wedgwood qualities which reminded him of his wife : when he sent her his poem, his desire had been to provoke, through her voice, an echo of Elizabeth's. The attempt was successful. " By the way," he wrote, " my wife would have subscribed to every one of your bad opinions of the book ; she never took the least interest in the story, so much as to wish to inspect the papers. It seems better so to me, but *is* it better ? So, the naturalists say that all female beauties are weaknesses and defects except to the male creature, and all real beauty is in *him*, if he could but see ! Only, he can't." The male creature, however, was no longer as blind to his own condition as may formerly have been the case. When, after reading *The Ring and the Book* in its entirety, Julia wrote : " I cannot sympathise in your choice of subject," and spoke of the possibility of his having spent " all these years on a mistake ", Browning's reply was laden with an emphasis whose significance cannot altogether have escaped her. " I have given four full years to this ' mistake '," he wrote, " but what did I do with my fourteen years in Italy ? "

" My son is at Ch[rist] Ch[urch] : my owl is still on his perch : my book is out : my intention is to hear Joachim play tonight : my friend is my friend. . . . ' What can I want beside ? ' as the psalm asks ! " For more than four years, two great enterprises had competed for Browning's energy and attention : the completion of his poem, and the education of his son. A constant preoccupation, the ambition to place Pen under the authority of Jowett at Balliol had proved also a constant source of disappointment : for despite the goodwill of Jowett and the efforts of his tutors, Pen failed, again and again, to reach the standard required. " He has been very industrious," wrote Jowett at last, " but he is not able to muster more than a certain amount of interest and attention." [1] At Christ Church, a few months later, Pen was more successful : he matriculated on January 15, 1869, in his twentieth year ; and after so many repeated set-backs and vicissitudes, Browning had at last the satisfaction of knowing that his son was now an undergraduate at Oxford. (" Yes," he wrote to Isa on February 19, " if I get a portrait of Pen in Academic costume, you shall certainly have it : but I fancy the youngsters think it *snobbish* to be so represented : they like to be reproduced in boating dress, shooting garb, etc.") This much achieved, Browning could sit back at Warwick Crescent in the company of Sarianna and his pet owl—a small bird, Oscar Browning wrote, rather like Shelley's aziola—and await the final verdict on *The Ring and The Book*. Nor was this to be long delayed : a few weeks later, the entire work was before the public. After the appearance of the first book, succeeding volumes had not won the unanimous approval of the critics who, like Julia Wedgwood, objected to the sordid nature of the subject, if not to the manner of its elaboration : but now, the poem completed and the remarkable strength and complexity of the design fully revealed, critical opinion accorded to Robert Browning a reception that, at its best, may well have exceeded his own most optimistic expectations. The *Fortnightly Review*, the *Quarterly*, the *London Quarterly* and the *Edinburgh Review* were unstinting in their praise. On March 13, 1869, a journal of a different kind, *The Court Circular*, printed the following statement : " Her Majesty on Thursday last had the pleasure of becoming personally acquainted with two of the most distinguished writers of the age—Mr. Carlyle and Mr. Browning.

[1] October 8, 1868. *Robert Browning and His Son,* by Gertrude Reese. P.M.L.A., vol. LXI.

These eminent men—who, so far as intellect is concerned, stand head and shoulders above their contemporaries—were invited to meet the Queen at the residence of the Dean of Westminster." A week later, the *Athenaeum*, which thirty-four years before had spoken briefly and slightingly of the same poet's *Paracelsus*, wrote : " We must record at once our conviction, not merely that *The Ring and the Book* is beyond all parallel the supremest poetical achievement of our time, but that it is the most precious and profound spiritual treasure that England has produced since the days of Shakespeare."

But if the early months of 1869 were to represent, thus, in the life of the poet, a period of exceptional tranquillity and satisfaction, the close of the same year found him in a state of pain and confusion unequalled, hitherto, in his own experience.   The first hint we have that Browning was no longer, in the opinion of his friends, " ' like my old self ' ", comes in a letter of July 27, 1869.   " I was unwell," the poet wrote to Mrs. Lehmann, "—having been so for some time—and felt the grasshopper a burden all day long in the house from which I never stirred."   What lay at the root of this unwonted state of depression ?   An entry in one of the notebooks of " handsome Dean Liddell ", of Christ Church, may supply a clue to the matter.   Under the heading *June 1869* the following comment appears in the Dean's notebook :   " Browning, L. P. & Gr. non S."   This formula—Latin prose and Greek Unsatisfactory—meant that, brief indeed as it had been, Pen's career at Oxford was already in jeopardy.   To Browning, the prospect of his son being sent down was nothing less than a major disaster.   It nullified, at a stroke, years of stubborn endeavour on his part ; knocking away all that he had hoped to build on " as a step to something else ".   Pen cannot be made to see, he wrote later, " that he should follow any other rule than that of living like the richest and idlest young man of his acquaintance, or that there is any use in being at the University than to do so. . . .   You see that all my plans were destroyed by this double evil—the utmost self-indulgence joined to the greatest contempt of work and its fruits." [1]

It is here that we must regret the omission or destruction of the July letter to Isa Blagden, which would have shed a

[1] To George Moulton-Barrett. June 17, 1870. Illinois University Library.

light, perhaps, on those " circumstances unforeseen and quite out of my control " which at this time caused Browning to cancel, so abruptly and inexplicably, his usual eight weeks' holiday in Brittany. Whatever the circumstances were (and the suspicion arises that yet another gallant exploit on the part of Pen had come home to roost at Warwick Crescent) they had the effect of accentuating the indisposition of the poet to such a degree that when he finally made up his mind to accept an invitation from Lady Ashburton to join her at Loch Luichart, in Scotland, " a stranger I met on the day of my departure confessed (afterwards) he thought me dying ". Sarianna and Pen travelled with him to Scotland ; accompanying them, guests also of Lady Ashburton, were William Story, his wife Emelyn, and their daughter Edith, Pen's old playfellow of Roman and Florentine days. The party arrived at Loch Luichart, only to find that with the " liberal oddity " which evoked in her friends " a kind of traditional charmed, amused patience ", the hostess had forgotten all about her invitation, and was many miles away from home at the date of the appointment. The disconsolate guests were forced to seek for accommodation in the neighbourhood : " flitting from bad place to worse ", they ended up in a " squalid " little inn near Garve, where, in inclement weather, they picnicked in the heather and awaited the return of more genial conditions. Towards the end of August, the errant hostess reappeared : and for Robert Browning, " bothered in the last three weeks past most folks' bearing ", her presence seemed spontaneously to put an end to the " hideous confusion " under which he had all the while been labouring. " The worst is over," he wrote to Isa, " and here, at an old friend's I am comfortable altogether." The sense of relief is obvious : at that moment, the mock-Gothic Loch Luichart Lodge was a haven, sheltering him from the forces of disorder that lay in wait without. " All goes well now in this beautiful place," he wrote. What if, succumbing to the beauty, protected thence-forward from anxiety and responsibility, he were to remain in this shelter for the rest of his life ? . . .

In his memoir of William Story, Henry James has bequeathed us a subtly-composed impression of Louisa, Lady Ashburton. Since, however, this impression is created, not by direct description of his subject, but " by dint of breathing and sighing all round and round it ", we must turn for more palpable information to the reaction of other friends : to the portrait by Landseer ; to the impression created, retrospectively, on Browning himself. The American sculptress Hatty Hosmer compared Lady Ashburton to the Ludovisi goddess : seventeen years after the visit to Loch Luichart, from the depths of an as yet unresolved humiliation, Browning was to remember, with a sort of terror, the " imperious stature, tall as some war-engine " ; the " Limb's war-tower tallness ". Miss Hosmer admired the " square-cut and grandiose features " of Lady Ashburton, her " keen dark eyes " and " exquisitely modulated voice ". What left an even deeper impression upon the poet was the dark mass of her hair :

> That black hair bristling solid-built from nape
> To crown its coils about . . .

(The women who played a rôle in the emotional life of the poet, Eliza Flower, Elizabeth Barrett, Louisa Ashburton, were all, like the members of his own family, dark-haired. It is the women who yield to illicit love, Porphyria ; Palma ; [1] Mildred ; Lucrezia ; the unnamed heroine of *In a Gondola*, who are conspicuous for their beautiful golden hair.) This physical opulence of Lady Ashburton's was matched by the splendour of her material circumstances : heir to an estate of nearly thirty thousand acres, she left a sum exceeding a quarter of a million at her death in 1903. Browning cannot have been altogether indifferent to the appeal of her dark-haired beauty : but the fact that he proposed marriage to her at this juncture, when the future of Pen had become so acute and menacing a problem, was simply another, and outstanding, example of that attitude which at all stages of his life had caused him to seek in the authority of others the solution of his own practical and moral difficulties. The proposal must have taken place between September 5 (when a jocular poem, written by Browning and signed by Lady Ashburton and her guests, gives no hint of tension to come) and September 19, 1869, when, having moved southward, Browning wrote to Isa from Naworth Castle :

[1] *Alias* Cunizza, who, Cary says, " is supposed to have cohabited " with Sordello " before her marriage ".

'' My ' worry ' is increased to pretty nearly the last degree, but there is no need to put it on paper yet,—or perhaps ever . . .'' What had happened, in the interval, to add to the poet's distress ? The second wife of Lord Ashburton, Louisa Mackenzie had once filled the place of a notable predecessor : five years widowed, she was not averse to repeating her former feat ; and all might have gone well on this momentous occasion but for the remarkably prosaic terms in which the poet chose, for the second time in his life, to make a proposal of marriage to a woman. No one, it is permissible to say, would have appreciated more the manner of this proposal than Elizabeth Barrett herself, who, throughout the love letters, had accepted with a tolerant tenderness her suitor's recurrent *gaffes* and infelicities of phrase (the headache, Browning once wrote to her, '' no sooner gone, in a degree, than a worse plague came. I sate thinking of you . . .'') : thirteen years of married life failed to mitigate this tendency, and in 1859 Elizabeth was to describe an occasion on which, characteristically, '' Robert stood up and attempted a compliment that failed tremendously as usual.'' Elizabeth would not have been in the least surprised to discover that Robert proposed marriage to a beautiful woman by informing her that his '' heart was buried in Florence, and the attractiveness of a marriage with her lay in its advantage to Pen ''. Nor can we be surprised, in our turn, that he '' failed tremendously '', to create thereby, the impression that he had anticipated : or that Louisa, Lady Ashburton rejected with scorn and with anger a proposal of marriage that, less bluntly and more picturesquely phrased, she had been ready, all the while, graciously to accept.

The immediate effect of this episode upon the poet was to shatter his peace of mind and seriously to undermine his health. The process which it set going, the long corrosion of remorse, was never wholly to burn itself out : to the end of his life, Browning reproached himself bitterly for this wanton and irreparable betrayal of a unique experience. By the time he returned to Warwick Crescent, the '' good old habit of soundly and expeditiously sleeping '' had deserted him : a few months later, he spoke of being '' very unwell and quite unable to write ''. If I tide over the next season, he wrote to Isa, '' I shall try and wash all away with divine salt-water, ' which cures all pollution ' says the ancient." The experience was not calculated to improve his relationship with Pen, " for whose sake ", he wrote to Isa, he had gone to Loch Luichart ; and when once again, in June, 1870, Pen failed to pass an examination at Christ Church and was asked to remove his name from the books, Browning's bitterness was open and unrestrained. " All I can do—except to give money—is *done* and done in vain," [1] he wrote. And again : " I am merely the manger at which he feeds, and nothing is more certain than that I could do him no greater good than by dying tonight and leaving him just enough to keep him from starving." [2]

At the beginning of August, ignoring the menace of the Franco-Prussian war, Browning and Sarianna went to St. Aubin, in Normandy, where they occupied for two months a primitive cottage on the sea-shore. " Exactly opposite this house," wrote Browning, "—just over the way of the water,— shines every night the lighthouse of Havre—a place I know well and love very moderately : but, it always gives me a thrill as I see, afar, *exactly* a particular spot which I was at, along with her. At this moment, I see the white streak of the phare in the sun from the window where I write and I *think*."

What he could not fail to recall, in that contemplation, was the fact that the holiday at Havre had represented in the history of his married life a sustained crisis in dissatisfaction and frustration. The impact of this memory accentuated, sharply, the sense of loss and betrayal which was the heritage of his recent experience at Loch Luichart. There had been, hitherto, no sense of guilt in Browning's attitude towards the dead. " I do not feel paroxysms of grief," he wrote the day after Elizabeth's death, "—but as if the very blessing, she died giving me . . had begun to work already." This equanimity, which contrasts so strongly with the depression which followed upon the death of his mother, was the natural legacy of a clear conscience. After the events of 1869, however, serenity was marred, irreparably ; henceforward, in the poetry of

[1] June 17, 1870. To George Barrett, Illinois University Library.
[2] July 17, 1870. Ibid.

Robert Browning, the image of the dead wife takes on a troubling and enigmatic aspect. We have only to compare the invocation to Elizabeth in *The Ring and the Book* with the first poem in the *Bad Dreams* series, to see the strange deterioration that was to take place, posthumously, as it were, in the relationship between husband and wife. The first expression of this is to be found in Browning's successor to his Roman murder story, *Balaustion's Adventure*, a " transcript " from Euripides, in which the emotion aroused by the memories of Havre—a vain regret at the thought of " my old peevish ways, which came from being too rich "—reinforce, recognisably, the contrition of Admetus, unworthy husband of a supremely worthy wife. Here, the speeches of Balaustion, an interpolation without counterpart in Euripides, all emphasise the inner predicament of Admetus : the tardy recognition of his own baseness, followed, after a passion of remorse, by spiritual regeneration. There is no indication in Euripides, for instance, that Heracles wished to test out Admetus ; or that he recognised, in the bereaved man's reluctance to accept a new wife, that Admetus

> Planted firm foot, now, on the loathly thing
> That was Admetos late! " would die ", he knew,
> Ere let the reptile raise its crest again.

It is the interpretation of Browning himself : and in this connection, the poet's omissions from the text of his " transcript " are as revealing as his additions. It is not altogether surprising, for instance, to find that Browning ignores the child's point of view. He omits, as inessential, what is perhaps the most touching of all scenes in Euripides : the lament of the small son of Alcestis for his dead mother. " I am so little, Father, and lonely and cold here without Mother. . . . Everything is spoiled when Mother is dead."

After the visit to Loch Luichart in 1869, " for two years together ", Browning said, he had been " resisting cajoleries and pathetic appeals ", on the part of Lady Ashburton that the friendship between them should be renewed. In spite of Browning's avowed reluctance, some measure of reconciliation does seem to have taken place. On March 31, 1871, the poet

sent Lady Ashburton's small daughter, a copy of *Morte dell'*
Uxoricida Guido Franceschini Decapitato with an affectionate letter
concluding " ' The gift is small, The love is all ' " : and on
August 8, the day *Balaustion's Adventure* was published, he wrote
to George Smith, asking him to send a presentation copy to
Louisa Lady Ashburton, at Loch Luichart. The book preceded his own arrival there : for, " after nine or ten month's
teasing with her invitations ", Lady Ashburton had succeeded
in getting Robert Browning " to promise to visit her for a day ".
The promise was kept. After leaving Glen Fincastle, in Perth-
shire, where he had been " perpetrating *Hohenstiel-Schwangau* at
the rate of so many lines a day ", Browning spent October 2,
1871, with Lady Ashburton at Loch Luichart.[1] He returned
to London a fortnight later. By the end of December, he told
Isa, he was " half way thro' another poem, of quite another
kind ". This poem was *Fifine at the Fair*.

That the sultry coruscations of *Fifine* were ignited by the
poet's recent visit to Loch Luichart seems, under the circumstances, likely enough. It was, however, to an earlier source
of experience that Browning owed the setting of a poem which
he described as " the most metaphysical and boldest he had
written since *Sordello* ". The original Fifine, Sarianna told
Alfred Domett, " was a fine fierce gipsy woman they had seen
at the fair at Pornic where they were staying ". But if Pornic,
as the poem indicates, had its fair of " Saint Gille ", Camberwell, during the youth of the poet, had its fair of Saint Giles :
when annually, in August, troops of gipsies mingled with the
local revellers on the noisy lamplit Green. For three days,
during which time " the residents were forced to witness dis-
gusting and demoralising scenes ", Camberwell Green was
encumbered " with its hordes of nomadic thieves ; its coarse
men and lewd women " : a " concentrated essence of vice,
folly and buffoonery ", which continued, until 1855, " to con-
taminate the youth of the district and annoy the more staid
and respectable residents ". The influence of Sarah Anna was

---

[1] This date does not tally with Browning's note on the manuscript at Balliol
where he says *Hohenstiel-Schwangau* was " finished at Milton House, Glen Fincastle, Perthsh., Oct. 7, '71 ". However, as the poet also wrote on the manuscript of *Balaustion* " Begun and ended in May, 1872 ", when it was published
almost a year *before* that date, no great reliance can be placed on his dating
of events.

not strong enough to keep her son away from the Green : forty years later, Browning was to describe to Isa, " Richardson the showman . . . at the Fair in my young days ", and Richardson's method of setting " the blue fire burning " in order to end " the scene with éclat ".[1] Not that the poet had to wait for St. Giles's Fair in order to see gipsies. Familiar since childhood, the sight of the " chimneyed house on wheels ", the brown figures camped in the glades of the Dulwich woods, inspired in 1842 *The Flight of the Duchess* : a poem which was to have consisted originally " of the Gipsy's description of the life the Lady was to lead with her future Gipsy lover—a *real* life, not an unreal one like that with the Duke ". It was this reality, the " free life, full liberty " of the vagrant, that caused the " God-fearing householder " to wonder if it was not the " Misguided ones who gave society the slip " who " held the corn, and left us only chaff " : to ask himself uneasily what inexplicable alchemy, in such a case

> Turns lawlessness to law, makes destitution—wealth,
> Vices—virtue, and diseases of soul and body—health ?

At another level, however, the conflict experienced by Don Juan between the attractions of " the fizgig called Fifine " and the " chaste, temperate, serene " wife, Elvire, is also the conflict between the moral standards of Sarah Anna and the exciting byways of speculative thought which all his life, denounce them as he might, held so strong an appeal for the enquiring casuistical mind of Robert Browning. Browning's Don Juan, Dowden pertinently remarks, " is more a seeker after knowledge than he is a lover ". It is not the " lithe memorable limbs " of Fifine that inflame this philanderer : it is the desire scientifically to " decompose " and assess the secret of her personality. What he hankers after is not forbidden pleasure but forbidden knowledge : he whores not after strange women but after strange ideas. In either case, he betrays a ghost : the pale, reproachful shade of the woman he loves : and it is this, the old conflict between Love and Knowledge which

---

[1] The *Observer*, August 19, 1832. " Camberwell Fair. The revels of this fair commenced yesterday . . . Richardson's theatre occupies a large space in the centre of the green, and is fitted up with a degree of splendour we would not have anticipated."

in *Fifine at the Fair* engages once more the poetic and metaphysical resources of a man who six years earlier had confided
to Isa Blagden that his only interest, now, in life lay in discovering " the proof of certain great principles, strewn in the
booths at a fair ".

Robert Browning was sixty years old when *Fifine at the Fair*
was published. For the next seventeen years he was to continue writing, rapidly, confidently, ebulliently : but it is at
this point, where the poet may be said to have taken leave of
his own poetic genius, that, regretfully, too, the poetry-lover
will relinquish the company of a man whose accents, the most
individual of his generation, Walter Savage Landor once compared with those of Chaucer himself. Only the biographer
could find satisfaction in *Red Cotton Nightcap Country* : a sordid
newspaper story which aroused Browning's interest at once
when he heard that the hero of it " had destroyed himself
from remorse at having behaved unfilially to his mother ".
(The sub-title, *Turf and Towers*, symbolises the divided nature
of a man torn between sacred and profane love, who, to expiate
his own sense of guilt after the death of a pious mother, thrusts
both hands into the fire and holds them there until they burn
down to the stump.) *Red Cotton Nightcap Country* was followed
by *Aristophanes' Apology* ; and then, in steady procession
throughout the seventies, *The Inn Album, Pachiarotto, The
Agamemnon of Aeschylus, La Saisiaz* and *Dramatic Idyls*. " But
I never have begun, even, what I hope I was born to begin
and end—' R.B. a poem ' . . . these scenes and song-scraps
are such mere and very escapes of my inner power, which lives
in me like the light in those crazy Mediterranean phares I
have watched at sea, wherein the light is ever revolving in a
dark gallery, bright and alive, and only after a weary interval
leaps out, for a moment, from the one narrow chink, and then
goes on with the blind wall between it and you. . . ." Robert
Browning was thirty-three when he wrote those words.
Throughout his boyhood, the blind wall had served to obstruct
the vision which he knew to be " bright and live " all the
while, within him. Alone amongst women, Elizabeth Barrett,
he had felt, offered him the prospect of release from this

impasse. But the years went by, the weary intervals grew longer ; the hidden light revolved, unseen in its dark gallery. Sarah Anna Browning died, and then Elizabeth Barrett Browning. What if, belatedly now, and in solitude, the poet were to succeed " in opening out a way whence the imprisoned splendour may dart forth ? " This, however, was not to be : and Browning himself, in a flash of bitter insight, had already anticipated and described the nature of his own defeat.

> Young,—you've a hope, an aim, a love : it's tossed
> And crossed and lost : you struggle on, some spark
> Shut in your heart against the puffs around,
> Through cold and pain ; these in due time subside,
> Now then for age's triumph, the hoarded light
> You mean to loose on the altered face of things,—
> Up with it on the tripod ! It's extinct.
> Spend your life's remnant asking, which was best,
> Light smothered up that never peeped forth once,
> Or the cold cresset with full leave to shine ?

5

The Court of Kate the Queen

"If Lord Houghton talked more than most people, he certainly was eclipsed by Mr. Browning, who spoke louder, and with greater persistency, than anyone I have ever come across in my life," wrote Lady St. Helier. " I think," added this Victorian hostess (she was a niece of Lady Ashburton's), " I think most people feared him rather than loved him—certainly men did ; but women adore poets, and they worshipped Mr. Browning."

In marked contrast to the early manhood of Robert Browning, to that " male prudery " which accompanied, so curiously, the sexual ardour of his own love poetry, were the last two decades of the poet's life in London. By that time, fame had brought with it the friendship and adulation of women ; in particular, of a small group of middle-aged women who, having attained, through widowhood, to a condition of emotional and financial independence, prided themselves on their spiritual intimacy with the master, and vied with each other in providing the setting and the amenities most congenial to the poetic temperament. With the greatest goodwill in the world Browning submitted himself to lionisation : a happy acquiescence which discovered him, on one occasion, drinking tea and eating muffins with female members of the Browning society at Newnham, who, having presented him with a wreath of roses, grouped themselves picturesquely at his feet, while the ageing poet sat " bland and ruddy, and slightly buttery from the muffins, with the crown of pink roses laid upon his white locks, and looking like a lamb decked for sacrifice ".

Through these latter years of his life, Robert Browning, we are told, " had more friends among noble-hearted women than fall to the share of many ". Noble-hearted as the women may have been, such friendships were not based on spiritual affinity alone : Browning was in his middle seventies, when his manner of taking her hand " with firm, secret pressure ", his " warm, fondling tender manner and watchful loving eyes " caused in Katherine Bradley, the florid-looking poetess, a longing to " put the clock back thirty years, and be loved by Robert Browning in his glorious manhood ". But this St. Martin's summer of new and sensuous intimacies was not to be enjoyed without pangs of conscience ; and the records of this secret travail is to be found in *Numpholeptos* : surely one of the most remarkable

259

of the autobiographical poems of Browning's later years. The poem appeared with the *Pachiarotto* collection, in 1876, when Browning, whose marriage to Elizabeth Barrett had lasted fifteen years, had been fifteen years a widower. For fifteen years, the woman who once dwelt with him in the flesh had dwelt with him in the spirit : for fifteen years, first her portrait, and then the sad-smiling, white-marbled bust by Story had gazed down on the man, " Your outcast, once your inmate," who, stained with " yellow license ", begs her in this poem, to grant, " not placid pardon now ", but love—" a mere drop from out the ocean erst He drank at ".

> As before, you show
> Scarce recognition, no approval, some
> Mistrust, more wonder at a man become
> Monstrous in garb, nay—flesh disguised as well,
> Through his adventure.

Questioned by Furnivall on behalf of the Browning society—" I had no particular woman in mind," the poet wrote. Despite this disclaimer, it is noticeable that the nymph is described in terms of the moon-imagery associated, particularly, with Elizabeth Barrett. In *One Word More* Browning compared himself to a " moonstruck mortal " bewitched by the " silent silver lights " of one who is " my moon of poets," : in *Numpholeptos*, the withdrawal of love, the " shrouding robe " that intercepts communion, leaves

> earth a mute waste only wandered o'er
> By that pale soft sweet disempassioned moon
> Which smiles me slow forgiveness !

The nymph, furthermore, is described as possessing a " quintessential whiteness ", while the man who loves her is stained with " every dye o' the bow Born of the storm-cloud ". (" You speak out, *you*," Browning wrote to Elizabeth Barrett, " I . . . give you truth broken into prismatic hues, and fear the pure white light . . .") *Numpholeptos*, wrote Browning, is " an allegory . . . of an impossible ideal object of love, accepted conventionally as such by a man who, all the while, cannot quite blind himself to the fact that the possessor of knowledge and purity obtained without the natural consequences of obtaining them by achievement—not inheritance—such a being is imaginary, not real, a nymph and no woman ". (" But NO, dearest Isa," wrote Browning, " the simple truth is that *she* was the poet, and I the clever person by comparison : remember her limited experience of all kinds. . . . *One* such intimate knowledge as I have had with many a person would have taught her,—had she been inclined to learn : though I doubt if she would have dirtied her hands for any scientific purpose.") There were times, however, when this detachment, this complacency, stung the lover to rebellion : and *Numpholeptos* contains a strange, belated flare-up of a resentment whose embers, long-smouldering, neither love nor grief has yet succeeded in extinguishing.

> O you—less hard
> And hateful than mistaken and obtuse
> Unreason of a she-intelligence !
> You very woman with the pert pretence
> To match the male achievement ! Like enough !
> Ay, you were easy victors, did the rough
> Straightway efface itself to smooth, the gruff
> Grind down and grow a whisper,—did man's truth
> Subdue, for sake of chivalry and ruth,
> Its rapier-edge to suit the bulrush-spear
> Womanly falsehood fights with ! O that ear
> All fact pricks rudely, that thrice-superfine
> Feminity of sense, with right divine
> To waive all process, take result stain-free
> From out the very muck wherein. . . .

The sentence remains unfinished. The " true slave " has had his " querulous outbreak " : once more, he resigns himself to slavery : goes forth on yet another sultry adventure, and returns, stained with " that tinct whereof the trace On garb and flesh repel you ", to find, as before :

> Calm above
> My passion, the old statuesque regard,
> The sad petrific smile.

Of Robert Browning's many friendships with women, there was one, the most valued of all, perhaps, which left behind it no residue of guilt or of self-dissatisfaction. Although they met in Florence during the lifetime of Elizabeth Barrett, the poet's acquaintance with Miss Egerton Smith had its roots in an earlier environment. The Egerton Smiths were close friends both of the Flower family, and of W. J. Fox and his wife : in the relationship, therefore, there lay the one remaining link with Browning's early life in the Fox-Flower circle at Dalston and Bayswater. A woman of wealth, " dearest Annie " was part proprietor of the *Liverpool Mercury*, which, during her lifetime, gave prominence to any article connected with the work of Robert Browning. She was reserved and diffident, a tall, earnest-looking woman who suffered continually from neuralgia : and although, " somewhat narrow, somewhat slow ", the scope and pace of their intercourse seemed at times to the poet, he found in the very restriction, which " Liberates the brain O'erloaded " (an echo here of *The Guardian Angel*), the " best of all restoratives ". He shared with her, as he had shared with no one but his mother, a deep love of music : regularly, throughout the season, Miss Egerton Smith would call in her carriage at Warwick Crescent to take Browning to concerts where

> night by night—ah, memory, how it haunts !—
> Music was poured by perfect ministrants,
> By Hallé, Schumann, Piatti, Joachim.

For twenty-five years, remote from the worldly occasions which claimed, in latter years, so much of the poet's time and of his energies, this relationship pursued its temperate course : and when, catastrophically, it was cut short by death, Browning became for a time a prey to the same depression which had visited him after the death of his mother nearly thirty years earlier.

There was no thought of calamity, however, when, in the summer of 1877, Robert Browning and Sarianna took possession, with their friend, of the chalet du Docteur Roussel, at Collonges sous Salève, in the Haute Savoie. The chalet, known locally and to readers of Browning's poetry as " La Saisiaz ", offered, from a third floor balcony where, Browning

wrote, " I sit aerially like Euripides ", a magnificent prospect :
" Geneva lying under us, with the lake and the whole plain
bounded by the Jura and our own Salève ", which latter, he
added, close as it seems to the house, " takes a hard hour and
a half to ascend ".   The poet spent his time reading ;   he
bathed twice a day in the live mountain stream, and went for
excursions in the neighbourhood with Miss Smith ;   glad, no
doubt, to escape at times from the company of Sarianna, whose
habit, in later life, of " repeating all things as on a rosary, as
if she did a sacred duty . . . used to make Robert impatient."
Despite the beauty of his surroundings, Browning was unusually
depressed, " and tried subsequently to account for this condition by the shadow which coming trouble sometimes casts
before it."   On the morning of September 14th, 1877, as the
party was preparing for an ascent of Mt. Salève, Anne Egerton
Smith, who had been " the evening before in exceptionally
good health and spirits ", was found dead on the floor of her
room.

In his poem *La Saisiaz*, completed some six weeks after her
funeral, Browning has left us a record of the effect produced
by the loss of " one of the most devoted friends I ever had in
my life."

> Dared and done : at last I stand upon the summit,
> > Dear and True !
> Singly dared and done ; [1] the climbing both of us
> > were bound to do.

The day before leaving Collonges, he had climbed to the
summit of Mt. Salève, and there contemplating in the plain
beneath a tiny cemetery set amongst the ripening vines, he
returned once more to the problem which, the evening before
her death, he had been discussing with his " old and precious
friend " : " Does the soul survive the body ?   Is there God's
self, no or yes ? "   Fifty years ago, a schoolboy newly primed
with the works of Voltaire and Shelley, he had given his
answer, and in the bosom of a pious household proclaimed
himself an atheist.   Today, curiously enough, when death
forced him to ask that question anew, it was in a setting
dedicated to the very minds which had inspired his own early

---

[1] An echo of Christopher Smart ? (" DETERMIN'D, DAR'D and DONE ").

rebellion. Yonder, " under that obscene red roof, arose, Like a fierce flying serpent from its egg, a soul—Rousseau's " : there, at Ferney, wrapped in his " robe-de-chambre of blue sattan and gold spots in it ", Voltaire had waged his war against superstition and intolerance ; there he had written those works which, discovered by the youthful Browning upon the bookshelves at Hanover Cottage, served to pave the way for an atheism confirmed and exalted by the Shelley of *Queen Mab*. Here, at Sécheron, Shelley himself had lived : there he had met Byron for the first time, and there, at the villa Diodati, evening after evening, the two poets sometimes " sat up in conversation till the morning light ". A week before, Browning himself had visited Diodati ; and, as Byron, in reverence, had once plucked " a sprig of *Gibbon's acacia* ", there, " for Byron's sake ", Browning in his turn plucked an ivy leaf. " Turn thence ! " Yonder " where the far snows blanch Mute Mont Blanc ", in an inn at Montanvert, Shelley had proclaimed himself " democrat, great lover of mankind, and atheist " : beside the lake which now lay sparkling in the autumnal sunshine, the young poet had written his noble *Hymn to Intellectual Beauty*. Sixty-one years later, a Victorian poet conceived amid the same surroundings a poem, *La Saisiaz* : in which unable, like his predecessor, for the sake of its intellectual beauty alone to honour life, he confessed that nothing less than a " second life " could compensate for the disappointments and deficiencies of his present existence. It was on this, then, on the promise of survival, of a second chance, that the whole of the poet's optimism was based : on this his moral equilibrium depended : and to the doubt that, after the death of his friend, grated raspingly upon the structure of that optimism, is due the uncharacteristic self-searching of *La Saisiaz*. Deprived of an essential support, thrown back upon his own resources :

> I must say,—or choke in silence—" howsoever came
> my fate,
> Sorrow did and joy did nowise,—life well weighed,—
> preponderate ".

In other words, the man who prided himself so boisterously that he " lived and liked, not poohed and pished ", who boasted that, unlike the " aimless, helpless, hopeless ", he did not " drivel ", did not turn his back, but, courageously, under all circumstances, " marched breast forward ", this man lacked the fortitude which permits a stoic nature to endure, un-remedied by compensation elsewhere, all the natural shocks to which the flesh is heir : a confession which surprises more than the hard-wrung admission that sorrow, and not joy, had all along preponderated, in this, " my life of wonders—absolute wonders ".

La Saisiaz, like *Pauline*, is a fragment of a confession. Like *Pauline*, it is incomplete. Germinating dangerously beneath the pressure of old associations, old conflicts, there was much that the poet strove, resolutely, to subdue.

> Life is stocked with germs of torpid life ; but
> may I never wake
> Those of mine whose resurrection could not be
> without earthquake !
> Rest all such, unraised forever ! Be this, sad yet
> sweet, the sole
> Memory evoked from slumber ! Least part this :
> then what the whole ?

2

Since his ignominious removal from Oxford in 1870, Pen Browning had been, as his father put it, " assiduously labouring in that occupation to which Providence apparently hath pleased to call him,—that is, in shooting, idling and diverting himself ". At the age of twenty-five, he decided to make art his career ; and on the advice of Felix Moscheles, was sent to Antwerp to study under Heyermans, who, a few months later, was able to report to the poet that his son was " making wonderful pro-gress : was very steady, and a ' bon enfant ' ". That Brown-ing, however, did not over-estimate this steadiness, we may gather from a cryptic entry in the diary of Michael Field, to the effect that " the story of the Belgian wife is the story of a fellow art-student grafted maliciously onto Pen ; and if the Old [Browning] behaved as they say he did, he certainly has

a deep blot on his scutcheon ". Pen had always hated lessons
" with the peculiar repulsion of a father-taught son " : now,
under Heyermans' tutelage, in the independence of his
butcher's-shop-lodging, he gave every appearance of being
" happier than he ever was in his life ". Before long, his
pictures began to arrive at Warwick Crescent : a hare lying
on a damask cloth : a " quaint old Flemish milk jug " ; an
old man contemplating a skull ; and Browning, overjoyed at
this palpable token of industry, if not of inspiration, was soon
canvassing his friends for approbation and support. This was
readily forthcoming. Millais pronounced Pen's drawing to be
" perfect " : Rudolf Lehmann offered a hundred and fifty
guineas for a study of a priest reading a book : displayed at
the Academy, a large canvas, *The Worker in Brass*, was sold on
the first day of the exhibition for a sum of three hundred
pounds. " One suspects ", wrote Browning's friend Alfred
Domett, " a little *practical flattery* to the poet in all this."
The suspicion was shared by the artist himself ; fully alive, from
the first, to the humiliation of his own success. Pen Browning
was unfortunate in that his outward appearance belied,
markedly, the sensibilities of his inner nature. Disconcerted
on first meeting him, " by the entry of a veritable curly ball,
most grotesquely ugly ", those two curious women, the aunt
and niece who wrote under the name of Michael Field, were
able in later years to discern that which was imprisoned all
the while beneath the " beef-red face, baldness and fawnish
smirk " with which he confronted the world. " Pen ", they
wrote, " is most touching in his sensitiveness and humility.
He says he is a failure, and yet he has the artist's temperament
and a delicacy that is finely touched. The amount of mis-
understanding he has met with and his own sorry sense of his
personal deficiencies has driven the poets' son deep within the
shell of Barrett common-placeness." At the same time, they
saw, he " is very proud and therefore suffers internally—every
blow is an unseen bruise," from which, (for " his high birth
from poets makes him nervous ") he escapes into " jocund
instinctive habits of life, like those of a squire ". This visit of
the Michael Fields to Pen's self-styled " Palazzo Pigstye " in
Asolo, took place a few years after the death of the poet. It
was evident to both women that despite the admitted " strain

in the relationship between himself and his father ", Pen, as they put it, " loves his father honestly ". A few days after the funeral : " My loss is irreparable," he wrote. His grief was simple and sincere. Six years later, visitors to Asolo were touched to observe that " when his father's name is mentioned, tears fill his eyes ".

Clara Jessup Bloomfield-Moore made no secret of the motive which inspired her to purchase some of the more unsaleable canvases of Robert Barrett Browning. She did so, she said, " in order to evince to the son my gratitude for the enjoyment and help I had found in his mother's poems ". Descending on London in 1879 with a letter of introduction to Robert Browning, this minor poetess, the fifty-five year-old widow of a wealthy Philadelphian archeologist, took Warwick Crescent by storm. For ten years, she was to devote to Robert Browning the resources alike of a transatlantic income, and of a generous, inconsequential and impulse-ridden nature. In her capacity of intimate friend, she accompanied the poet to Oxford in 1882 when the honorary degree of D.C.L. was conferred upon him : and the quality of her response is to be gauged in her description of the Arabian Nights' scene which followed, in which " groups of gayly dressed ladies with their attendant cavaliers " were regaled, on the lawns of Wadham, with " hot-house grapes, peaches and pineapples in lavish profusion ". In order that " we might live near each other to the end of our lives on earth ", she made her home in London : bringing over from America a daughter, mentally afflicted, who, with two attendants, was confined always to a part of the house inaccessible to visitors. It was not long before reports were current on both sides of the Atlantic that Mrs. Moore and Mr. Browning " were about to marry ". Mrs. Moore has described, in characteristic terms, the poet's contempt for the scribblings of all such penny-a-liners. " Like an eagle cleaving heaven's blue vault," she wrote, " this great poet soared beyond the reach of the earth-worms that attacked him " : for her own part, she was content secretly to cut out and preserve to the end of her days references which, it is clear, her own words had served to inspire. (" I recollect one afternoon, when visiting mutual friends," wrote Henriette Corkran, " a wealthy American widow rushed in, exclaiming, ' I thought till today that Mr. Browning only cared for me platonically, but such is not the case, I assure you.' ")

To quite a remarkable degree, this subject, the nature and value of Platonic love, seems mutually to have engaged the attention of a woman in her late fifties and a man in his early seventies. Mrs. Moore's poetry, privately printed and dedicated to Robert Browning, returns again and again to the question ; with portentous quotations from Platonic and mythological sources exalting the superiority of " Uranian " over " Pandemian " love. More disconcerting, perhaps, to Browning, was the fact that in this volume he found himself once more addressed in terms reminiscent of the *Sonnets from the Portuguese*.

> Thou wilt not turn away—thou wilt not say
> ' I care not for such sad, wild strains as these. . . .'
> A beggar might choose pebbles by the road,
> As well, to take unto a king whose crown
> Is set with gems. . . .

It was an experience that he recoiled from : as he did, before long, from her continual insistence on the superior, the " god-like " aspect of his character. Resolutely, Browning sought to make plain to her the earthy quality of his own nature : countering her plea for what she called " Soul-love " with a vigorous insistence on the needs of sense.

> Man I am and man would be, Love—merest man and
> nothing more.
> Bid me seem no other !

The quotation is from *Ferishtah's Fancies* : a book, wrote Mrs. Moore on the title-page, " given to me as mine, in more ways than one, by its author. Though not dedicated to me, this is my tribute from Robert Browning, which, with ' Bad Dreams ' in Asolando, no one can understand so well as myself." [1] In the summer of 1884, she had invited the poet and his sister to be her guests at St. Moritz. They occupied the Villa Berry,

---

[1] This copy of *Ferishtah's Fancies*, with Mrs. Moore's comments, is described in W. T. Spencer's catalogue. May, 1900.

which she rented for the season, but they dined, nightly, at Caspar Badrutt's hotel, unaware as they did so that from the table adjoining their own, they were observed all the while by the author of *Erewhon*, who prided himself that, save for Royal Academy catalogue extracts, he had " never read a word of Browning ", and said of *Aurora Leigh*, " I detest it." For ten days or a fortnight, the Brownings enjoyed the beauty of St. Moritz, making daily excursions, in brilliant weather, " to all the most picturesque passes and glaciers " : and then the blow fell : unexpectedly, their hostess was summoned on urgent business to America. Mrs. Moore was distraught at this interruption of what had been, it is evident, a period of exceptionally close and favourable intimacy. She prepared, nevertheless, to depart ; on September 2nd, Browning wrote to George Smith, acknowledging the receipt of the proofs of *Ferishtah's Fancies*, and stating that Mrs. Moore, " on the point of starting for America ", had offered to find there " some publisher for my new Poem who will remunerate its author ". One section of that " Poem ", *Plot-Culture*, lacked, still, its attendant love-lyric : " Leave room for a small poem's insertion here," were Browning's instructions to the printer. " Remember," said Mrs. Moore as she took farewell of him, " I have loved you with the best and most enduring love—Soul-love." Browning's reply to this, the " small poem " afterwards inserted in the proofs, has something of the candour and the passion that, forty-five years ago, had informed the words exchanged between the guilty lovers of *Pippa Passes*.

Not with my Soul, Love !—bid no soul like mine
   Lap thee around nor leave the poor Sense room ! . . .
Take Sense, too—let me love entire and whole—
   Not with my Soul !
Eyes shall meet eyes and find no eyes between,
   Lips feed on lips, no other lips to fear !
No past, no future—so thine arms but screen
   The present from surprise ! not there, 'tis here—
Not then, 'tis now :—back, memories that intrude !
Make, Love, the universe our solitude,
And, over all the rest, oblivion roll—
   Sense quenching Soul !

A year after the publication of *Ferishtah's Fancies*, Robert Browning was invited by Dr. Furnivall to become the President of the Shelley Society. The poet was then in his seventy-fourth year. No longer was it his ambition, as in youth, to render some " signal service " to the " fame and memory " of the Sun-treader ; and firmly declining the offer, he did not hesitate to say so. " For myself," he wrote, " I painfully contrast my notions of Shelley the *man*, and Shelley, well, even the poet, with what they were sixty years ago, when I only had his works, for a certainty, and took his character on trust." Through the intervention of Hookham in 1851 Browning had been offered the necessary grounds on which to base his secession from Shelley. Incongruously, now, it was on the plea of Shelley's inhumanity, his desertion of Harriet, that he chose to condemn one who all his life had been " as a nerve o'er which do creep The else unfelt oppressions of this earth ". Incongruously, indeed : for the man who complained of in-humanity in Shelley was the author of *Ferishtah's Fancies* : a work which, in its complacency, its facile evasion of the prob-lem of evil, its cheerful indifference to human suffering, must have carried dismay into the ranks of the Browning Society itself.

> I know my own appointed patch i' the world,
> What pleasures me or pains there : all outside—
> How he, she, or it, and even thou, Son, live,
> Are pleased or pained, is past conjecture . . .
> > There's the first and last
> Of my philosophy ! Black blurs thy white ?
> Not mine !

No heart, this, that the " stranger's tear might wear " : much less, the utterance of one who, like the " wholly inexcusable " Shelley,

> loved and pitied all things, and could moan
> For woes which others hear not.

In later life, Robert Browning was " brutally scornful of all exquisite morbidness. The vibration of his loud voice, his hard fist upon the table, would make very short work with cobwebs." Shelley, it seems, was to be included amongst the cobwebs. " The longer I know B[rowning]," wrote William Allingham in 1875, " the less do I know how much weight to give to his utterances. . . . I have with pain heard him of later years speak slightingly of Shelley." It was not alone the desertion of Harriet that Browning denounced : Shelley himself, he said contemptuously, was " ' not in his right senses— in the moon ' ". Startled by this table-thumping, confronted with the " loud, sound, normal, hearty presence, all so assertive and so whole, all bristling with prompt responses and expected opinions and usual views ", it is impossible not to wonder, with Henry James, what conceivable " lodgement, on such premises, the rich proud genius one adored could ever have contrived ". It was a question which puzzled Henry James so sorely " that light *had* at last to break under pressure of the whimsical theory of two distinct and alternate presences, the assertion of either of which on any occasion directly involved the entire extinction of the other ". Remarking that " the poet and the ' member of society ' were, in a word, dissociated in him as they can rarely elsewhere have been ", James arrived at the conclusion that Robert Browning " had literally mastered the secret of dividing the personal consciousness into a pair of independent compartments ". But this division (an expedient upon which, at one time, Browning had felt that his own survival depended) placed too severe a tax upon his creative life : and it is to the widening of that schism that we can attribute the rapid suffocation and extinction of genius that took place during the last twenty years of the poet's life. Inspiration extinguished, an excess of energy was released, which expressed itself, jauntily enough, in the garrulous, irascible, highly didactic work of his later years. This was the Robert Browning ," profane and heterogeneous ", who, as he read aloud his own early poetry, gave his hearers the impression that " he was reading the work of another man ". " One man ", wrote Henry James, " is the genius, the other's the bourgeois, and it's only the bourgeois whom we personally know." What James did not suspect (or did not betray, at least, in his story *The Private Life*) was that of these two " members of a firm ", it was the bourgeois alone who now survived. It was the bourgeois—no longer a mere *alter ego* but " the true Robert Browning "—who haunted " gilded salons " ; who, night after night throughout the

London season, "substantially and promiscuously and multi-
tudinously" dining, caused Hallam Tennyson to remark of his
father's friend that he "would never be surprised if Mr.
Browning expired in a white choker at a dinner party".

Was the poet aware of this loss of identity : of all that he
had surrendered when he "flung away" his "youth's chief
aims"? Did the ghost of his dead self ever rise to confront
him? "Browning", wrote William Allingham, "tells me he
has no dreams worth remembering—no beautiful or clever
dreams. 'Except that a few times I have dreamed that I was
among the mountains near Asolo (of *Pippa Passes*) and I said
to myself, "I have often wished to see Asolo a second time,
but now here I am and I'll go and do it." Once I dreamed I
was seeing the elder Kean in *Richard the Third* and he uttered a
line which struck me as immensely finer than anything else in
the play, or than I had ever heard perhaps, and I perceived it
was not Shakespeare's but my own invention. It was in the
scene where the ghosts rise. When I woke I still had hold of
the stupendous line, and it was this—

And when I wake my dreams are madness—Damn me.' "

One of the dreams which Browning had described to Allingham returned, whenever he was ill or out of sorts, to haunt his
sleep. "I am travelling with a friend," he said, "sometimes
with one person, sometimes with another, oftenest with one I
do not recognise. Suddenly I see the town I love sparkling in
the sun on the hillside. I cry to my companion, 'Look!
look! there is Asolo! Oh, do let us go there!' The friend
invariably answers, 'Impossible ; we cannot stop.' 'Pray let
us go there!' I entreat. 'No,' persists the friend, 'we cannot ;
we must go on and leave Asolo for another day,' and so I am
hurried away, and wake to know that I have been dreaming it
all, both the pleasure and the disappointment." It is a pre-
varication we can recognise. "I never look at books I loved
once," Browning confessed : he avoided, no less, scenes associated intimately with his own past life. As he had dreaded,
after her death, to see his mother's roses over the wall, so,
too, he shrank from revisiting Florence : as for Asolo, "my

very own of all Italian towns ", even in his dreams he could not permit himself to return to a place where, before the eyes of a young poet, every tree and flower had once stood " Palpably fire-clothed ".

Forty years went by : and then, on a sudden impulse, a short, abortive visit was made to Asolo in the late summer of 1878. " So can dreams come *false*," wrote Browning sadly. For Asolo, where " things seemed generally more ordinary-life-like ", refused, obstinately, to " light up " for him. Not only had the number of inhabitants greatly increased, but their " roaring, and screaming on high market day ", he complained, " confuses me altogether ". Abortive as it was, the visit had, nevertheless, one specific result. From that time on, " my old dream about Asolo " returned no more to haunt the sleep of Robert Browning.

The poet showed little inclination, thereafter, to return to the hill-city he once loved. That he was prompted to do so, in the last few months of his life, was due to the presence of " a figure there never associated with Asolo before ". In self-imposed exile from her native land for twenty years, at the Casa Alvisi in Venice, Katherine de Kay Bronson had sat " at the wide mouth, as it were, of the Grand Canal " ; where, autumn after autumn in the last decade of his life, she claimed the privilege of entertaining, as the most intimate and closely domesticated of her guests, the white-haired poet and his alert indefatigable sister. An American of Anglo-Dutch extraction, Mrs. Bronson was a soft, indolent woman, blue-eyed, and with chestnut-brown hair drawn back from a round benevolent face. (Spitefully, for " jealousy is cruel as the grave ":— "she has the eyes of a hydrocephalic baby " the Michael Fields observed.) Like Mrs. Bloomfield-Moore, Mrs. Bronson cherished literary ambitions : unlike her compatriot, she was of a discreet and equable disposition. A woman with " a positive genius for easy interest, easy sympathy, easy friendship," she provided for the most eminent of her guests an atmosphere, emollient and yet stimulating, in which, over tiny gilded glasses and polyglot conversation, cigarette smoke blended with the subtler incense of feminine interest and adulation. From the first, Browning seems to have experienced a very real affection both for Katherine Bronson and for the silent suave-

eyed Edith ; an affection which, suspended so felicitously
between the attributes of mother and daughter alike, deepened
at each encounter until it had become the major emotional
preoccupation of the poet's latter years. " My two beloveds,"
he called them. " It is impossible to convey ", he wrote to
the mother, " all I have in my heart, and head, too, of love
for you and ' our Edie '." To the mother again : " I love
you with all my heart," Browning wrote simply. " Bless you
and your Edith."

Early in 1889, in search of upland air and the associations
of *Pippa Passes*, Mrs. Bronson purchased in Asolo " one of the
quaintest possible places of *villeggiatura* ". Barely had her
letter reached London, crowned with " the magical stamp of
Asolo ", before the poet was seized with the desire to return,
once more, to " the beautiful place I used to dream about so
often in the old days, till at last I saw it again, and the dreams
stopped ". The desire to leave London at this juncture was
accentuated, perhaps, by the repercussions, still echoing about
him, of " one of the most odious incidents in my life ". On
July 7, visiting a friend, " I took up on a garden-seat, at hazard,
a new book—opened it where it would open " ; whereupon,
Browning wrote, " I get this direct blow in the face." The
book was the *Life and Letters of Edward Fitzgerald* : the " direct
blow ", the words : " Mrs. Browning's death is rather a relief
to me, I must say. No more Aurora Leighs, thank God ! "
In the poet's reply to this, printed in the *Athenaeum* on July 13th,
the " something very queer and dangerous " whose presence
Chesterton discerned beneath " all the good humour of
Browning ", rose, unmistakably, to the surface.

TO EDWARD FITZGERALD

I chanced upon a new book yesterday :
I opened it, and where my finger lay
   'Twixt page and uncut page, these words I read
   —Some six or seven at most—and learned thereby
That you, Fitzgerald, whom by ear and eye
   She never knew, " thanked God my wife was dead ".
Ay, dead ! and were yourself alive, good Fitz,
How to return your thanks would task my wits :
   Kicking you seems the common lot of curs—

While more appropriate greeting lends you grace :
  Surely to spit there glorifies your face—
  Spitting—from lips once sanctified by Hers.

From the consternation caused by this outburst, Browning was
only too glad to escape : the attraction of Asolo—" immensely
increased by the prospective company of Mrs. Bronson "—
being in other ways, too, perceptibly accentuated. Fewer and
fewer ties, in this last year of his life, bound the poet to London.
At seventy-seven, he had outlived most of the people associated
with his own early life. Eliza and Sarah Flower were dead ;
so were Fanny Haworth, Harriet Martineau, Isa Blagden,
Annie Egerton Smith, and the sharp-tongued Mrs. Procter :
Moxon, publisher of *Bells and Pomegranates*, had died ; and
after him, Leigh Hunt, W. J. Fox, Henry Chorley, Macready,
Barry Cornwall, John Forster, Thomas Carlyle, R. H. Horne,
Alfred Domett and Joseph Milsand. Emphasizing this pro-
gressive rupture with the past, the removal from Warwick
Crescent to De Vere Gardens had forced upon the poet a
reassessment, moral and material, of the circumstances of his
own existence. In literature, this stock-taking was to result
in the backward-glancing *Parleyings* : in life, in the wholesale
destruction of letters and documents whose value to potential
biographers, he was heard to say, added " a new terror to
death." The same year, 1887, had further adjustments to
offer. In the course of it, Browning's long-felt desire to see
his son " advantageously disengaged " from him was unexpectedly fulfilled. Pen announced his engagement to Fannie
Coddington, of New York : " a fine handsome generous
creature ", who had recently inherited upon the death of her
father a substantial private fortune. Browning's relief at this
solution was obvious to all. " You could not do a wiser, better
thing," he told Pen, " than marry the in every way suitable
lady whom you have been fortunate enough to induce to take
such a step, and who, you are bound to feel, behaves with the
utmost generosity." Fannie's generosity endowed her fiancé
with the wholly novel privilege of independence : an emancipation, long-delayed, which Pen did not hesitate to exploit.
Robert Browning, wrote his daughter-in-law, " had already
settled that we should live near him in South Kensington. "

She found herself now, " deputed to break the news " to the poet that his son had no wish to live in England ; that he felt well only when " away from London " ; that it was his fixed intention, which nothing could alter, to settle for the rest of his life in the country which, mutely, throughout the years of exile, he had regarded in every sense as his native land.

" The deposed, the defeated, the disenchanted, the wounded, or even only the bored," wrote Henry James, " have always found in Venice a sort of repository of consolations." Inevitably, under this dispensation, it was to Venice that Pen gravitated : and inevitably, too, the little man who painted pictures so large that they could only adequately be housed in a museum, chose for his future home " one of the grandest and most imposing palaces in Italy ". This was nothing less than " the huge " Palazzo Rezzonico ; in whose " beautiful, cold, pompous interior " poor Fannie sat shivering, while Pen, who had discovered in himself an unsuspected talent for interior decoration, directed a posse of workmen busy on all sides with an ambitious scheme of repairs and renovations. One of his first acts was to restore a desecrated chapel, in honour of his mother : a white and gold alcove, draped with pale green plush, in which he caused to be set up, elaborately inscribed, a copy of the tablet commemorating her death at Casa Guidi. Progressively, thenceforward, in " every piously-kept relic of Casa Guidi and of London years ", Pen was to assemble and piece together the component parts of a long-obliterated pattern. To the Rezzonico, over the years, came not only the books, the chairs, the portraits, the tapestries of Casa Guidi : there too, out of the fabulous past, came a bowed and grey-haired couple : Wilson and Ferdinando, who, after many days and much sorrow were peacefully to end their lives under the protection of one whose childhood, nearly half a century ago, they had helped to guard and to glorify.

In the " rattling, red-velveted carriage of provincial, rural Italy ", Robert Browning arrived, at the beginning of September, 1889 in Asolo. For two hours after leaving Cornuda, he had driven through the beautiful countryside, which, on a June day fifty-one years ago, he had first traversed on foot :

to arrive now in " a dream " at the hill-city, older than Rome, which offered a view of " the Alps on one side, the Asolan mountains all round,—and opposite, the vast Lombard plain, —with indications of Venice, Padua, and other cities, visible to a good eye on a clear day ". Vigorous, voluble and a trifle asthmatic, the traveller alighted. Under crumpled lids, he gazed, bright-eyed, at the flowering walls of Queen Caterina's palace ; at Romano, birthplace of the Eccelini ; at San Zenone, where Alberico was " trailed to death through raunce and bramble-bush " : scenery invested with the patina of legend ; the landscape of *Sordello* and of *Pippa Passes* : cradle of youthful hopes and unbounded ambition. In an awestruck voice : " To think that I should be here again ! " the white-haired poet exclaimed.

In one of the eighteen towers embodied within the " dismantled, dissimulated " wall encircling Asolo, Mrs. Bronson had built her summer residence, La Mura. Almost opposite, in the little house of Signora Tabacchi, were the rooms she had engaged for the poet and his sister : and there, in the modest sitting-room, beneath a shell-adorned frame filled with family photographs and a series of prints representing the history of Venice, on a round pedestal table, Robert Browning wrote his last poetic message to the world. Here the Prologue to *Asolando* was written : and here, too, were added to the manuscript which he had brought out with him from London, the two or three additional poems inspired by this renewal of intimacy with his " two beloveds ". Mrs. Bloomfield-Moore has claimed responsibility for the *Bad Dreams* series, written a few months after the poet had once again spent a holiday under her roof at St. Moritz ; and perhaps the outspoken *Now* is also to be laid to her credit. But in *Humility*, in *Summum Bonum*, in *A Pearl, a Girl*, it is possible to catch a reflection of Edith Bronson : while *Inapprehensiveness* commemorates, circumstantially, a moment on the loggia at La Mura, while, the poet at her side, Katherine Bronson stood gazing out at the ruined castle of Queen Caterina, calmly ignoring in her companion

> The dormant passion needing but a look
> To burst into immense life !

The look, it seems, was not given : a calculated " inapprehensiveness " which preserved the equanimity of the relationship.
Like that " gentle couple ", the mother and son in *Pippa
Passes*, the poet and his hostess remained " Calmer than lovers,
yet more kind than friends ".

> Let me be cared about, kept out of harm,
> And schemed for, safe in love as with a charm ;

the orphaned Pippa exclaims.   At La Mura, this fundamental
need of Robert Browning's was happily realised ; for, " during
the brief days and weeks when his precious life was partly in-
trusted to my care ", it was Mrs. Bronson's whole concern to
interpose herself between him and " Aught sharp in the rough
world's busy thrust " :   a benevolence, sentimental and
domestic, which inspired the placid, reminiscent mood of the
poem *Dubiety*. At ease in " luxury's sofa-lap of leather ",
succumbing to the stillness of noon and of " dreaming's vapour-
wreath ", the poet searches back through the years to discover
the source of his own unwonted sense of felicity.

> What is it like that has happened before ?
> A dream ?   No dream, more real by much.
> A vision ? . . .
> Perhaps but a memory after all !
> —Of what came once when a woman leant
> To feel for my brow where her kiss might fall.
> Truth ever, truth only the excellent !

Dominating the loggia at La Mura, the tower and palace of
Caterina Cornaro seems also to have dominated the imagination of Browning during his last stay in Asolo.   His visit of
1889 coincided with the year, four centuries earlier, in which
the deposed Caterina—Queen of Cyprus, Jerusalem and
Armenia—had taken possession of the castle and the town.
Arriving on a Sunday, October 11th, she brought with her,
in a court of several thousand persons, a dwarf, a German
physician and a singularly handsome young secretary.   This
was Pietro Bembo, afterwards Cardinal : strictest of Cicer-
onians, writer of licentious elegiacs, and the man to whom

Lucrezia Borgia bequeathed the long straw-coloured lock,
" one single hair " of which was later stolen by Byron from
the Ambrosian library at Milan.   Browning was fascinated by
the thought of this " learned and brilliant " little court,
isolated from the stress of contemporary events, and dominated
by the personality of the dark-eyed queen, whose portrait, by
Titian, he had seen in the Uffizi in Florence.   " People always
speak of Caterina with compassion because she lost Cyprus,"
he said ; " but . . . I am sure the happiest years of her life
were those when she was queen of Asolo."   His preoccupation
with Asolo, with the court of Kate the Queen, took an unexpected form.   The man who, half a century ago, recognising
in it the reflection of a long-lost paradise, had invested spiritually in the beauty of " sparkling Asolo ", became filled now
with the desire to implement his sense of ownership.   What he
set his heart on, was the purchase of a disused building, the
Asilo Infantile, and the land on which it stood, once part of the
queen's pleasure-garden : and so great was his eagerness to
acquire this, that he would not rest until negotiations were set
on foot to discover whether or not the municipality would
sanction the purchase.   Meanwhile, he remembered that
Bembo's stay at the court of the widowed queen had been
celebrated by him in *Gli Asolani* : a mannered work, wherein,
to the sound of lute or viol, strolling amongst the laurels and
vine-pergolas of Caterina's garden, the Novitiates of Love
engage in prolonged discussions upon the virtues of Platonic
affection.   Invoking, now, the authority of his predecessor, to
whom is ascribed the invention of the verb *asolare*, Browning
changed the title of his own book from *A New Series of Jocoseria*
—as he had planned to call it—to the Bembo-sanctioned
Asolando.   On October 15th, he composed the dedication to
Mrs. Bronson, and the same day he handed the bulky package
to the postmaster in Asolo.   And now, he wrote to George
Smith, " I shall make the most of the remaining Autumn
days,—walk about and enjoy myself." [1]   The enjoyment
centred, as always, upon La Mura : the court, in exile, of
another widowed Katherine.   Every afternoon, his " beloved
friend " at his side and the carriage piled high with wraps and
rugs, Browning made long excursions into the neighbouring

[1] October 15, 1889.   In the possession of Sir John Murray.

countryside, returning in time to enjoy the hissing of the tea-urn and the sight of the sunset from his favourite chair on the loggia at La Mura. For a fortnight, when the town was visited by a theatrical troupe, he watched " high tragedy and low comedy " from a stage-box in the brightly lit theatre built inside the walls of Caterina's castle. (" Shall I whisper to you my ambition and my hope ? " the seventy-seven year old poet said to Katherine Bronson. " It is to write a tragedy better than anything I have done yet. I think of it constantly.") With Sarianna, very dignified in a " French cap and quaint antique jewels ", he dined every evening at La Mura. Seventy-five years old and disinclined to be idle, after dinner Sarianna sat " busy with her netting in the corner of the little drawing-room ", while Robert Browning read poetry to his " supremely amiable " hostess, or, as he loved to do, played to her on the little sixteenth century spinet whose keys, under his touch, gave forth a tone midway between that of a mandolin and a guitar.

Not until the first unmistakable chill of approaching winter had made itself felt, did Browning consent to take farewell of Asolo and the pleasures offered him at the court of Kate the Queen. He arrived in Venice at the beginning of November, to find, he wrote, that " the whole city is in a tremble about the Small Pox, which rages,—they say—and compulsory vaccination is going on everywhere ".[1] At the Rezzonico, Pen and his wife were waiting to welcome him : and " I wish ", Browning continued, " you were here to see Pen's doing in this huge house : I am really surprised at his developing so much ability without any sort of experience. What I left, last year, as a dingy cavern is now bright and comfortable in all its quantity of rooms. "[2] No longer was Fannie left to shiver between marble floors and painted ceilings, for, by Pen's contrivance, this " stately temple of the rococo " was now heated throughout by " a furnace and pipes ". After two years of marriage, however, Fannie was subjected to other, and less easily remedied sources of distress : a fact which her father-

[1] To George Smith, November 6, 1889. In the possession of Sir John Murray.   [2] Ibid.

in-law, it seems, failed to perceive. Had he not proclaimed her to be, " of all the young persons of my acquaintance ", the one most fitted " to make Pen, with his many peculiarities, the best of wives ? " Believing this, it is not surprising that he should have found it possible to ignore the presence of those tensions which culminated, after his death, in Fannie's separation from her husband and her determination to become an Anglican nun.

" I want to be at home now, though it may not prove easy to get away," Browning confided to George Smith a few days before leaving Asolo. He had no intention of staying more than a couple of weeks at the Rezzonico. On November 30th, he was still in Venice : and, suffering now from a slight chill caught when walking in foggy weather on the Lido, he wrote to Smith to explain the delay. It was the last letter Smith was to receive from the man whose work he had published for more than twenty years. " I had hoped to be back in London long ago," the poet wrote, " but was detained, first at Asolo and then here, by a curious little affair with the Asolan Municipality—about which they have held meetings as many and important as if the question were an international one. I got only an indefinite answer yesterday from what was promised to be the final meeting, and am inclined to wait no longer. . . Before the 12th I trust to be back in good earnest." [1]

> Venice and winter, hand in deadly hand,
> Have slain the lover of her lovely strand,

wrote Swinburne, learning, in London, of the manner of Robert Browning's death. For the chill caught on the Lido developed into bronchitis ; and wholly against his will (" I so much dislike the quality of an invalid ") the poet was persuaded to take to his bed. He had occupied, hitherto, a room on the mezzanine of the first floor at the Rezzonico. Now, his son and daughter-in-law transferred him to their own larger and brighter bedroom, on the second floor, where the devoted Fannie spent her time making hot poultices for the invalid, whose pulse all the while grew steadily weaker. " In the centre of the lofty ceiling of the room in which he lay," wrote William Sharp, " there is a painting by his son. It depicts an eagle

[1] November 30, 1889. Ibid.

struggling with a serpent, and is illustrative of a superb passage in Shelley's *Revolt of Islam.*" Enquiry at the Rezzonico reveals the fact that this picture, painted on canvas and now preserved intact in the vaults of the palace, was removed from " the small room facing the Grand Canal in the mezzanine of the first floor of the Ca' Rezzonico " : information which deprives a conscientious biographer of the opportunity of saying that Browning died, as he had lived, under the symbol of a divided nature. After a few days, the bronchitis began to abate : only to give place, unmistakably, to the symptoms of heart failure. " I feel much worse," Browning said. " I know now that I must die." It was the afternoon of December 12, 1889. On that day, belatedly, a last wish was granted to him : in Asolo, it was agreed to cede to the poet a portion of the soil that for fifty years, self-exiled, he had loved and coveted. Within the same few hours, a telegram was received from London, where *Asolando* had just been published. Pen read it aloud at the bedside. It was from George Smith. " Reviews in all this day's papers most favourable, edition nearly exhausted."

Browning murmured : " How gratifying."

Those, Pen tells us, were his last intelligible words. Soon afterwards, he lapsed into unconsciousness. A few hours later, as San Marco's clock was striking ten, with " a violent heaving of his big chest as he lay otherwise motionless ", the poet died.

On the last day of the year, under a deepening fog and to the solemn tolling of St. Margaret's bell, in the most august social occasion of his career, Robert Browning was committed to an honoured grave amongst his fellow poets in the south transept of Westminster Abbey.

*   *   *   *   *

In May, 1913, by order of the administrators of his estate, the property of the late Robert Wiedeman Barrett Browning, Esq., of Asolo, Veneto, and the Torre all' Antella, near Florence, was sold by auction in London. During a six-day sale, in the course of which the auctioneers' room was " for over two hours inconveniently crowded ", many valuable and important relics of Robert Browning came under the hammer. Amongst these, and included in the sale with the autograph letters, the manuscripts, the tapestries, the carved wood bookcases, the writing-desk, the signet ring, the pickle-forks and gravy-ladles inscribed with the Browning crest, was a small weightless object, carefully wrapped and labelled. It was a flower plucked from Shelley's grave.

BIBLIOGRAPHY

BIBLIOGRAPHY

LETTERS

The Letters of Robert Browning and Elizabeth Barrett Barrett. Smith, Elder. 1899.

Robert Browning and Alfred Domett. Edited by Frederic G. Kenyon. Smith, Elder. 1906.

Letters of Robert Browning, Collected by Thomas J. Wise. Edited with an introduction and notes by Thurman L. Hood. John Murray. 1933.

Robert Browning and Julia Wedgwood. A Broken Friendship as revealed in their Letters. Edited by Richard Curle. John Murray and Jonathan Cape. 1937.

New Letters of Robert Browning. Edited with Introduction and Notes by William Clyde de Vane and Kenneth Leslie Knickerbocker. John Murray. 1951.

Dearest Isa. Robert Browning's Letters to Isabella Blagden. Edited and with an introduction by Edward C. McAleer. University of Texas Press, Austin. 1951.

From Robert and Elizabeth Browning. A Further Selection of the Barrett-Browning Family Correspondence. Introduction and Notes by William Rose Benét. John Murray. 1936.

Letters of Elizabeth Barrett Browning addressed to Richard Hengist Horne. With comments on Contemporaries. Edited by S. R. Townshend Mayer. Richard Bentley. 1877.

The Letters of Elizabeth Barrett Browning. Edited with biographical additions by Frederic G. Kenyon. Smith, Elder. 1898.

Elizabeth Barrett Browning : Letters to her Sister, 1846–1859. Edited by Leonard Huxley. John Murray. 1929.

Letters from Elizabeth Barrett to B. R. Haydon. Edited by Martha Hale Shackford. Oxford University Press. 1939.

BIOGRAPHIES

CHESTERTON, G. K. *Robert Browning.* English Men of Letters Series. Macmillan. 1903.

DOWDEN, EDWARD. *The Life of Robert Browning.* Everyman's Library. J. M. Dent. 1904.

GRIFFIN, W. HALL, AND MINCHIN, H. C. *The Life of Robert Browning. With notices of his writings, his Family, and his Friends.* Methuen. 1910. Revised Edition, 1938.

HOVELAQUE, HENRI LEON. *La Jeuness de Robert Browning.* Paris. 1932.

ORR, MRS. SUTHERLAND. *Life and Letters of Robert Browning.* 1891. New edition, revised and in part rewritten by Frederic G. Kenyon. John Murray. 1908.

SHARP, WILLIAM. *Life of Robert Browning.* Walter Scott. 1890.

WHITING, LILIAN. *The Brownings.* Their Life and Art. Hodder and Stoughton. 1911.

GENERAL

ADAMS, SARAH FLOWER. *Vivia Perpetua.* With a memoir of the author by E. F. Bridell Fox. Privately printed. 1893.

ALLINGHAM, WILLIAM. *A Diary.* Edited by H. Allingham and D. Radford. Macmillan. 1907.

ANGELI, HELEN ROSSETTI. *Dante Gabriel Rossetti. His Friends and Enemies.* Hamish Hamilton. 1949.

ARMSTRONG, A. J. Browning the World Over—a Bibliography of Foreign Browningiana. Baylor University. Waco. Texas. 1933.

BARCLAY, EVELYN. *Diary.* Baylor University. Waco. Texas. Undated.

BENSON, E. F. *As We Were. A Victorian Peep-Show.* Longmans. 1930.

BLISS, TRUDY (Editor). *Jane Welsh Carlyle. A New Selection of her Letters.* Gollancz. 1949.

BROOKFIELD, C. H. E. and F. M. *Mrs. Brookfield and her Circle.* Pitman. 1905.

BRONSON, KATHERINE DE KAY. " Browning in Asolo." *Century Magazine.* 1900.

" Browning in Venice." *Cornhill Magazine.* Vol. 12. 1902.

BROWNING, FANNIE BARRETT. *Some Memories of Robert Browning.* Boston. 1928.

The *Browning Society's Papers.* 1881–1891.

CARLYLE, ALEXANDER (Editor). *New Letters of Thomas Carlyle.* John Lane. 1904.

Letters of Thomas Carlyle to John Stuart Mill, John Sterling and Robert Browning. Fisher Unwin. 1923.

CARR, CORNELIA (Editor). *Harriet Hosmer. Letters and Memories.* John Lane. 1913.

COBBE, FRANCES POWER. *Life.* Richard Bentley. 1894.

Italics. Trubner. 1864.

CONWAY, MONCURE D. *Autobiography, Memories and Experiences.* Cassell. 1904.

Centenary History of the South Place Society. Williams and Norgate. 1894.

CHORLEY, H. F. (Editor). *Letters of Mary Russell Mitford.* 2nd Series. Richard Bentley. 1872.

COLLINGWOOD, W. S. *The Life of John Ruskin.* Methuen. 1900.

CORKRAN, HENRIETTE. *Celebrities and I.* Hutchinson. 1905.

COSS, JOHN JACOB (Editor). *Autobiography of John Stuart Mill.* Published for the first time without alterations or omissions from the original manuscript. Columbia University Press. 1924.

COWDEN CLARKE, CHARLES AND MARY. *Recollections of Writers.* Sampson Low. 1878.

COWDEN CLARKE, MARY VICTORIA. *My Long Life. An autobiographical Sketch.* Fisher Unwin. 1896.

Life and Labours of Vincent Novello. Novello. 1864.

CROSS, J. W. *George Eliot's Life as related in Her Letters and Journals. Arranged and edited by her Husband.* Blackwood. 1885.

CROSSE, CORNELIA. *Red Letter Days of my Life.* Richard Bentley. 1892.

DE VANE, WILLIAM CLYDE. *A Browning Handbook.* John Murray. 1935.

Browning's Parleyings : the Autobiography of a Mind. Yale University Press. 1927.

DOWDEN, EDWARD. *The Life of Percy Bysshe Shelley.* Kegan Paul. Revised edition. 1896.

DUFFY, Sir Charles Gavan. *Conversations with Carlyle.* Low. 1892.

EHRSAM, THEODORE G. *The Incredible Career of Major Byron, Literary Forger.* John Murray. 1951.

ERSKINE, MRS. STEUART (Editor). *Anna Jameson. Letters and Friendships.* 1812–1860. Unwin. 1915.

FOX, MRS. E. BRIDELL. " Robert Browning." *Argosy Magazine.* February 1890.

" Memories." *Girls Own Paper.* July 19. 1890.

FOX, CAROLINE. *Memories of Old Friends.* Smith, Elder. 1882.

FOX, FRANKLIN. *Memoir of Mrs. Eliza Fox. With Journals and Letters.* Trubner. 1869.

FROUDE, J. A. (Editor). *Thomas Carlyle. A story of his Life in London.* Longmans. 1919.

Thomas Carlyle. Reminiscences. Longmans. 1887.

FULLER, HESTER THACKERAY AND VIOLET HAMMERSLEY. *Thackeray's Daughter. Some Reminiscences of Anne Thackeray Ritchie.* Euphorion Books. Dublin. 1951.

GARNETT, RICHARD. *The Life of W. J. Fox.* John Lane. 1910.

GOSSE, EDMUND. *Robert Browning. Personalia.* Fisher Unwin. 1890.

HARLAN, A. B. *Owen Meredith.* Columbia University Press. 1946.

HAWORTH, E. F. *St. Sylvester's Day and Other Poems.* How. 1847.

HAWTHORNE, NATHANIEL. *Passages from his French and Italian Notebooks.* Strahan. 1871.

HAWTHORNE, SOPHIA. *Notes in England and Italy.* Low. 1869.

HAYEK, F. A. *John Stuart Mill and Harriet Taylor. Their Friendship and Subsequent Marriage.* Routledge and Kegan Paul. 1951.

HEWLETT, H. G. (Editor). *Autobiography, Memoirs and Letters of H. F. Chorley.* Richard Bentley. 1873.

HILLEBRAND, HAROLD NEWCOMB. *Edmund Kean.* Columbia University Press. 1933.

HOME, DANIEL DUNGLAS. *Incidents in My Life.* Longmans. 1871.

HORNE, R. H. *A New Spirit of the Age.* Smith, Elder. 1844.

HOWITT, MARGARET (Editor). *Mary Howitt. An Autobiography.* 1889. Isbister.

HUNT, LEIGH. *The Old Court Suburb.* Hurst and Blackett. 1855.

HUNT, THORNTON (Editor). *Correspondance of Leigh Hunt.* Smith, Elder. 1862.

HUXLEY, LEONARD. *The House of Smith, Elder.* Privately printed.

INGPEN, ROGER (Editor). *Letters of Percy Bysshe Shelley.* Pitman. 1912.

JAMES, HENRY. *Portraits of Places.* Macmillan. 1883.
"The Private Life." (From volume *The Private Life*.) Osgood, McIlvaine. 1893.
"Recollections of Katherine de Kay Bronson." *Cornhill Magazine.* Vol. 12. 1902.
William Wetmore Story and his Friends. Blackwood. 1903.

JAY, HARRIETT. *Robert Buchanan.* Fisher Unwin. 1903.

JONES, HENRY FESTING. *Samuel Butler. Author of Erewhon. A Memoir.* Macmillan. 1920.

LEE, ELIZABETH (Editor). *Mary Russell Mitford. Correspondence with Charles Boner and John Ruskin.* Fisher Unwin. 1914.

LEHMANN, RUDOLF. *An Artist's Reminiscences.* Smith, Elder. 1894.

LEHMANN, R. C. *Memories of Half a Century. A Record of Friendships.* Smith, Elder. 1908.

L'ESTRANGE, A. G. (Editor). *The Friendships of Mary Russell Mitford.* Hurst and Blackett. 1882.
The Life of Mary Russell Mitford. Related in a Selection of her Letters to her Friends. Richard Bentley. 1870.

LINTON, W. J. *Memories.* Lawrence. 1895.

LITCHFIELD, H. E. (Editor). *Emma Darwin : A Century of Family Letters.* Cambridge University Press. Privately printed. 1904.

LOUNSBURY, T. R. *The Early Literary Career of Robert Browning.* New York. 1911.

MACPHERSON, GERARDINE. *Memories of Anna Jameson.* Longmans. 1878.

MARKS, JEANETTE. *The Family of the Barrett. A Colonial Romance.* New York. 1938.

MARTIN, SIR THEODORE. *Helena Faucit, Lady Martin.* Blackwood. 1908.

MARTINEAU, HARRIET. *Five Years of Youth or Sense and Sentiment.* Harvey. 1831.

Autobiography. With Memorials by M. W. Chapman. Smith, Elder. 1877.

MINCHIN, H. C. *Walter Savage Landor : Last Days, Letters and Conversations.* Methuen. 1934.

MOORE, MRS. CLARA JESSUP BLOOMFIELD. " Robert Browning." *Lippincott's Magazine.* Philadelphia. May, 1890.

MORLEY, E. J. (Editor). *The Life and Times of Henry Crabb Robinson.* Dent. 1935.

Henry Crabb Robinson on Books and Their Writers. Dent. 1938.

MOSCHELES, FELIX. *Fragments of an Autobiography.* J. Nisbet. 1899.

NORTON, C. E. (Editor). *Letters of Thomas Carlyle.* 1826–36. Macmillan. 1886.

Correspondance of Thomas Carlyle with Ralph Waldo Emerson, 1834–72. Chatto and Windus. 1883.

ORR, MRS. SUTHERLAND. *A Handbook to the Works of Robert Browning.* Bell. 1885.

PALGRAVE, F. G. (Editor). *Francis Turner Palgrave. His Journals and Memories of his Life.* Longmans. 1899.

PAUL, CHARLES KEGAN. *Memories.* Kegan Paul. 1899.

PECK, W. E. *Shelley : His Life and Work.* Houghton Mifflin. 1927.

PHELPS, W. L. *Robert Browning. How to Know Him.* John Murray. 1915.

POPE-HENNESSY, JAMES. *Monckton Milnes : The Years of Promise.* 1809–51. Constable. 1949.

Monckton Milnes : The Flight of Youth. 1851–85. Constable. 1951.

POTTLE, F. A. *Shelley and Browning: A myth and some facts.* Chicago. 1923.

RENTON, RICHARD. *John Forster and his Friendships.* Chapman and Hall. 1912.

BIBLIOGRAPHY

RITCHIE, ANNE THACKERAY. *Records of Tennyson, Ruskin and Browning*. Macmillan. 1896.

ROGERS, FREDERICK. *The Early Environment of Robert Browning*. Privately printed. 1904.

ROSSETTI, W. M. *Ruskin, Rossetti, Pre-raphaelitism*. George Allen. 1898.
The Rossetti Papers. Sands. 1903.

SMALLEY, DONALD. *Browning's Essay on Chatterton*. Cambridge. 1948.

SMITH, CECIL WOODHAM. *Florence Nightingale*. Constable. 1950.

SOTHEBY'S CATALOGUES. *The Browning Collections*. 1913.
The Papers of Lt. Colonel Moulton-Barrett. 1937.

STEPHENSON, H. W. *Sarah Flower Adams. The Author of Nearer My God to Thee*. Lindsay Press. 1922.

STEWART, RANDALL (Editor). *Nathaniel Hawthorne: the English Notebooks*. Language Association of America. General Series. 1941.

STILLMAN, W. J. *Autobiography of a Journalist*. Richards. 1901.

ST. HELIER, LADY. *Memories of Fifty Years*. Richards. 1901.

STUART, JAMES. *Reminiscences and Essays*. Simpkin. 1884.

STURGE MOORE, T. and D. C. (Editors). *Michael Field. Works and Days*. John Murray. 1933.

TOYNBEE, WILLIAM (Editor). *The Diaries of W. C. Macready*. Chapman and Hall. 1912.

TROLLOPE, T. A. *What I Remember*. Richard Bentley. 1887.

WALLAS, GRAHAM, *William Johnson Fox*. Conway Memorial Lecture. 1924. Watts and Co. Allen and Unwin.

WHITE, NEWMAN IVEY. *Shelley*. Secker and Warburg. 1947.

WHITING, LILIAN. *Kate Field. A Record*. Sampson Low. 1889.

WOOLNER, AMY (Editor). *Thomas Woolner. Sculptor and Poet: his Life in his Letters*. Chapman and Hall. 1917.

INDEX

INDEX